PRAISE FOR *A SHORT COURSE IN THE SECRET WAR*

"[The author's] description of Communist tactics and the too often half-hearted countermoves of the Western powers is as revealing as it is saddening. His disclosure of the intricacies of espionage and counterespionage and their demand on the physical, intellectual, and moral resources of agents makes interesting reading."   —*Christian Science Monitor*

"The single finest book on counterintelligence that I have ever read: it is clear, precise, and honest. It is also a lively story." —**Robin W. Winks**, author of *Cloak and Gown*

"This book should be and will be, I feel sure, a revelation to a great number of 'open-faced' Americans who have refused to believe that such things can happen and are happening in the world. . . . Recommended."   —*Best Seller*

"[An] analysis of international espionage, counterespionage, political and paramilitary activities. . . . The author notes the strengths and weaknesses of American and Soviet techniques and illustrates them with incidents of secret operations. He distinguishes between types of secret activities and analyzes the roles of agents, informers, and case officers."

—*Library Journal*

By The Same Author

As Christopher Felix:

Three-Cornered Cover, a novel
(with George Marton)

As James McCargar:

*El Salvador and Nicaragua:
The AFL-CIO Views Of The Controversy*

Lost Victory (with William E. Colby)

A Short Course in
THE SECRET
WAR

Christopher Felix

With a new foreword by
Robin W. Winks

MADISON BOOKS
Lanham • New York • Oxford

To J.G. and T.F.M.—Skillful and generous allies in the secret war of the individual.

This Madison Books paperback of the fourth edition of A Short Course in the Secret War *(originally published in 1963) is an unabridged republication of the third edition published in Lanham, Maryland in 1992, with the addition of a new foreword by Robin Winks and a new afterword by the author. It is reprinted by arrangement with the author.*

Copyright © 1963, 1991, 1992, 2001 by Christopher Felix

New foreword © 2001 by Robin W. Winks

Published by Madison Books
An imprint of The Rowman & Littlefield Publishing Group, Inc.
4501 Forbes Boulevard, Suite 200
Lanham, Maryland 20706

PO Box 317
Oxford
OX2 9RU, UK

Distributed by National Book Network

Library of Congress Cataloging-in-Publication Data

Felix, Christopher.
   A short course in the secret war / Christopher Felix ; annotated with a new introduction by the true author, James McCargar.—[4th ed.]
      p. cm.
   ISBN 1-56833-179-7 (pbk. : alk. paper)
      1. Felix, Christopher. 2. McCargar, James. 3. Spies—United States—Biography. 4. Espionage, American—Hungary—History—20th century.
5. Espionage, American—History—20th century. 6. United States—Relations—Hungary. 7. Hungary—Relations—United States. I. Title.

F743.5.F36 A3 2001
327.1273'0439'092—dc21

                                                                      2001044582

CONTENTS

FOREWORD TO THE
FOURTH EDITION
A QUESTION ANSWERED

Since I first came across this book and, happily, its author—as I worked on *Cloak & Gown*, my study of Yale men in the OSS and CIA—I have praised it. "Widely regarded as the best general book on the methods used in 'the secret war'" and "still regarded as the best book on counterintelligence," were what I said in that study alone. (I also praised his *Three-Cornered Cover*, written with George Marton, as "an excellent novel rich in detail on deception.") That praise extends to this new edition. It is especially gratifying that in his new afterword the author delves more openly into his past experiences—notably his account of H.A.R. "Kim" Philby, the Soviet mole in the British MI-6, with whom he worked for a period.

Still, questions remain unanswered. One concerns the revelation of the true identity of "Christopher Felix." The first edition of this book, a Dutton hardcover, appeared in 1963 (as the author remembers unhappily, during the New York newspaper strike of that year). The listed author was "Christopher Felix." Dell brought out a second paperback edition in 1988, still by "Christopher Felix." Then, in 1992, Madison Books published the third edition. While copyright law required that the cover of the book still identify the author as "Christopher Felix," that cover announced annotation and a "new introduction by the true author." Indeed, on the title page, the "true author" was identified as James McCargar.

The spring 2001 issue of *The Hungarian Quarterly* carries the transcript of an interview with McCargar filmed by Hungarian television in May 2000. The interviewer asked him, "What was the point of using a pseudonym, Christopher Felix?" McCargar answered, "At the time I was still concerned not to cause embarrassment to the State Department. Mind you, this was sixteen years after I had been in Budapest." He added, "When I first wrote that book, I falsified a number of things to avoid anyone putting two and two together. One of the things I said was that I represented an organization which did not exist anymore, which was true. But I intimated I was not employed in the Legation. I was doing that to avoid embarrassment to the State Department. In the latest, 1992 edition, on which the Hungarian edition is based, I corrected all those falsifications in various footnotes, revealing that I was Second Secretary and headed the Political Section . . ."

The question is what—other than the simple passage of time— transpired between 1963 and 1992 to change the author's mind about revealing his identity?

In 1995 McCargar was interviewed at length for an "oral history." This was a project of the Association for Diplomatic Studies and Training (ADST), done at that time at Georgetown University in Washington, D. C. Transcripts of the oral histories done are unclassified and, unless so marked, are open for use by researchers at the Foreign Service Institute in Arlington, Virginia, and in the Special Collection Department at the Lauinger Library of Georgetown University. In addition, in 2000 the ADST published a CD containing transcripts of 893 of the oral histories, including McCargar's.

His oral history reveals that, as usual in such matters, there are complications. While in the Foreign Service, McCargar on at least two occasions served two masters. On both occasions one was the Department of State. In Budapest the other master was known in the State Department as the Pond, but was labeled by its chief, the Secret Intelligence Branch of the War Department General Staff. At another time the second master was the Office of Policy Coordination of the Central Intelligence Agency.

In 1977, twenty-four years after McCargar's last Foreign Service assignment, just as the new Administration was economizing, the question arose of his Government reemployment. The reaction at the CIA was a shrug, at State a negative. The Associated Press correspondent at the State Department, who had known McCargar for thirty years, complained to a senior State Department official. "The CIA says it is State's responsibility," he said. "State says it is the CIA's. Aren't you just whipsawing this man?" The answer was succinct: "That may be," said the official. "But that's the way it is."

Ten years later, in 1987, a question of some recognition by the State Department for McCargar's special services arose. First the file was lost in the Legal Adviser's office for a year. Finally, the Director General sent the question to the Honor Awards Committee. As he told McCargar, "They said they have neither the resources nor the time to go back 40 years on any subject." That same week the Army delivered an overdue medal to a surviving veteran of World War I out in Wisconsin.

In 1991 the prospect of the third edition of this book came over the horizon. It was then that McCargar did his annotating and editing, revealing in the course of it the State Department's involvement in his Budapest operations. I asked him if he had made those revelations out of pique at the State Department's responses in 1977 and 1987. He appeared shocked at the idea. "Of course not," he answered. "In its heyday the Pond had one man—no more—in each embassy where they operated. Now, for that one man CIA and State have substituted 'stations' with multiple personnel in every embassy everywhere. And the publicity! Why, I've seen obituaries of 'John Doe, former Station Chief in Ruritania.'" He frowned. "It's common knowledge."

Again he frowned. "It is, isn't it?"

Robin W. Winks

YOU CAN'T GO HOME AGAIN
INTRODUCTION
TO THE THIRD EDITION

WHAT HAPPENED?

A previous edition of this book appeared in 1988. In the ensuing four years the world turned upside down.

First came the Soviet retreat from the East European satrapies seized at the end of the Second World War. East Germany evaporated; Poland, Hungary, Czechoslovakia, Bulgaria, and Romania regained their independence. In varying degrees their Communist regimes disappeared—though not the consequences of their rule. The strategic and political map of Europe was completely altered.

While this enormous change was being absorbed, disintegration became evident within the Soviet Empire itself. Bit by bit, then ever more rapidly, Communist orthodoxy, long mostly ritual without substance, fell into disrepute. Then, overnight, it was banished from political life. The Soviet Empire was no more.

Consequences were felt everywhere. The mini-empire of the Balkans, the union of the South Slavs, fell apart. Even if a long romantic tradition—and traditional anti-Yanquiism—kept the Leninist flame burning in some hearts in Latin America, throughout Africa and Asia former Soviet clients turned to new answers. The strategic and political map of the world was profoundly altered.

This was totally unexpected.

In the early 1970s I dined one night with Walter Stoessel, a university and Foreign Service classmate. He had by then completed a term as American Ambassador to Poland, was at that moment Assistant Secretary of State for European Affairs, and was about to be named Ambassador to the Soviet Union (following which he would become Ambassador to the Federal Republic of Germany, then Under Secretary of State, and then the first career Foreign Service Officer to become Deputy Secretary of State—all of which I mention to indicate that at least one person at table was fully qualified in foreign affairs). As we always did, we spoke of the future of the Eastern European states—of the possibility of an end to Soviet domination of that important part of Europe. We summed it up with the formula that one day those nations would be free again, but, as I added (not knowing how sadly true it would be in the case of Walter, who died in 1986), "not in our lifetimes." Well, it did happen in mine. As did the collapse of the Communist structures of the Soviet Union itself. But we had not then even considered that possibility.

In Chapter III of Part 2 of this book, I wrote that in the summer of 1947, on a visit to Washington from Budapest, "I was . . . permitted to state my case to a high official, a Presidential adviser." This was Charles E. Bohlen, later Ambassador to Moscow, then Counselor of the Department of State, and acknowledgedly one of the United States' foremost experts on the Soviet Union. I repeat here what Chip Bohlen said to me then about Soviet domination of Hungary and the Soviet Union itself: " 'You are too pessimistic,' he told me about my views on the results of Soviet control of Hungary. 'You should read the reports on the popular initial reaction of the Russian people to the German invasion. After almost a quarter century of terror, they still rose up to welcome the Germans in the naïve belief that they were being liberated. Even the Jews of Moscow, kept in the dark by Stalin as to Hitler's anti-Semitism, rioted in the streets as the Germans approached—convinced that they were to be liberated. These Russian reactions were pathetic, and when they found out the truth, the people fought for Russia. But their initial reaction is proof that people do not forget freedom as easily as you fear.' "

This was a forecast of the Hungarian Revolution of 1956, perhaps. But for the events of 1989 and 1991 it was a statement of faith, not a forecast.

Still, Bohlen came closer than most. In his 1973 memoirs, *Witness to History,* he quoted a 1968 memorandum to Secretary of State Rusk: "I am certainly not predicting that there will be any upset in the Soviet Union. The weight of the established bureaucracy is far too great at this stage for anything of that kind, *but I do feel that in the long run changes will be inevitable—particularly when the present generation of youth grows up—which will be of profound importance for the future of Russia and indeed of the whole world . . ."* [Emphasis added].Bohlen concluded his memoirs with a hope. "The only hope . . . is that at some point the Soviet Union will begin to act like a country instead of a cause."

We may have arrived at that point.

If we have, it means the relegation of ideology to its appropriate place in human affairs. That place is not as a determinant of relations with other states and peoples. Is this not a lesson to be taken from history? From the Thirty Years' War? From the Holocaust? From *jihads*?

There are those who view this world turned upside down, so quickly, as an ideological triumph: the victory of capitalism over Communism. This is, as professors of logic and mathematics are wont to say, a comparison of apples and oranges.

Capitalism? Which capitalism? Whose capitalism? In most of Western Europe managers and entrepreneurs cannot treat their workers as managers and entrepreneurs in the United States do theirs. In the United States financial operators cannot act as unrestrictedly as do their opposite numbers in Europe or Latin America. Capitalism versus socialism? I once aroused the ire of the late C. D. Jackson, Time-Life executive, President of the Free Europe Committee, aide to President Eisenhower, when I argued for the incorporation into an officially blessed activity of a leading East European Socialist. "Don't you understand?" he shouted at me. "Socialism is a dirty word in this country!"

No doubt it was, perhaps still is, the word having been stolen by the Russians, who know the importance of names and words, from their chief enemies, the European Social Democrats—the same Social Democrats who labored mightily with the United States to create and maintain NATO, and who have today put their stamp on European capitalisms (without, for the most part, nationalizing the means of production).

If capitalism is taken as an economic system, or, more accurately, as a system, or systems, of organizing the economy (with as many variations as there are economies), Communism cannot be compared to it. For Communism is a political instrument. It is an instrument for the seizure and retention of all

power in the hands of a self-perpetuating elite. The economic
arrangements which accompany Communism were not adopted
for economic reasons. They were not intended to provide either
less costly or more efficient means of production or distribution. They were intended to reinforce and maintain the power
of the Party—to the exclusion of any possible rivals. Those
arrangements—all, the countless central Ministries, the rigid
chain of command, the classifications of workers, the phony
unions, the imposed hierarchies, the vast apparatus of secret
oversight—were not economic instruments. They were instruments of political control.

This is not to say that economic power does not translate into
political power. Of course it does. But in democratic systems
the possibilities of achieving economic power, or political
power, are open—if not easy. But in the Communist world,
once the Party has achieved power all roads thereto are closed
to all except the chosen.

If the upheavals of 1989 and 1991 were not the defeat of
Communism by capitalism, what then were they?

There are those who claim that Ronald Reagan simply out-
spent the Soviet Union. It is suggested that in a deliberate feat
of derring-do the American President, by embarking in 1981 on
unprecedented expenditures for arms, a field in which the
Soviet Union had to keep pace or admit defeat, quite simply
bankrupted his adversaries.

Certainly the arms race was a heavy burden for the Soviet
economy. But to attribute the changes of 1989 and 1991 to this
single factor is an exercise in tunnel vision brought on by
addiction to economic determinism. It ignores the time gap
between the adoption of arms control by both the Soviets and
the Americans and the Soviet decision to let go of East Germany. It ignores a panoply of historical and cultural factors. It
ignores the differences between the 1989 Soviet withdrawal
from their East European glacis and the 1991 collapse of Communism itself inside the Soviet Union. It also ignores the virtual
bankruptcy of the United States itself following Ronald Reagan's two terms. A victory?

For developments in the years 1989 and 1991, Ronald Reagan
merits regard, even plaudits, for his earlier public change of
tone and outlook which brought him, in the larger interest, to

recognize his adversaries as human beings (ditto for Gorbachev), but not for "a battlefield victory."

What, then, did happen? I am not impressed by the reported yearnings of vast Eurasian masses for the "free market." Yes, as a matter of simple justice they want to reap the rewards of their labor, certainly to live much better than they have all these long years. But as Lane Kirkland of the AFL-CIO has put it, pithily, "The market is a mechanism, not a religion. It performs many useful functions, but justice is not among them."

Nor am I impressed by the current mass enthusiasm for "democracy." Yes, the men and women of the former Soviet Bloc, the peoples of the Soviet Union itself included, want to be able to carve out for themselves spaces wherein their own decisions carry weight. But do their desires include the essential ability to fashion viable compromise, to hear the other, to recognize the primacy of the common weal? Do the Azeris desire democracy for the Armenians of Nagorno-Karabakh? The Georgians for the Ossetians? The Volga Tatars for the Russians among them? The Serbs for the Croats? For the Albanians of Kosovo?

The late Arnold Toynbee's twelve-volume *A Study of History* is no longer in fashion (if, indeed, it ever really was). I find myself quite out of step with his philosophy of history, as he expounds it in lengthy passages throughout. I do find the monumental work valuable from time to time, though, as a sort of encyclopedia of history. Not as well organized as Langer's, but more detailed. It is a treasure house of factual material. And some of Toynbee's judgments do catch the eye. (Example: Why did the Industrial Revolution begin in Great Britain? Because, Toynbee asserts, it was the largest unified, common market at the time.) And what does he have to say about the world in the twentieth century? That the two prime movers of human affairs in our century are Nationalism and Technology.

It seems to me that Communism, as doctrine and in practice, stumbled on both of these prime movers. Out of power, Communists *did* live in the real world of today—one of the reasons they were effective (when directed to be) in the Second World War, and sometimes in opposition afterwards. But in power they cut their own throats. Since the essence of Communism is control, the monopoly of power by the Party, Communists in power had to present *their* concept of the world as reality. Increasingly, as a matter of survival, they were obliged in doing so to misconstrue, to misrepresent, and to suppress reality.

Technology can be a liberating influence. Everyman with his own writing or copying machine is freer than the peasant who must turn to a scribe or a priest to express himself beyond the family table. Certainly air travel today verges on torture—but its advantages to the world population at this stage need no exposition. Innovations in communications open up new intellectual horizons. *If* they are available. As they were not when under Communist control. Of what use computers or copying machines if they are allowed only for Party members? Of what use the airplane if travel is restricted to the Party-approved? Of what use tools of communication if they are withheld from all but a few privileged?

Communist authority undermined itself not only by restricting technology, in keeping with the imperative to control. It also made the arrogant error of not realizing that, as technology spread, people—those controlled masses—would bit by bit find out about it all anyway. And would want it. And would find ways of getting it, realizing as they did that the only way they could do so was by circumventing that same authority that pretended to be their benefactor. In this way mutual trust, the necessary confidence, was undermined. Doctrine became empty ritual. Ideology was shown to be hypocrisy and lies.

Nationalism, the Communists boasted, was a bourgeois relic; Communism had solved all the problems of the nationalities. Stalin was depicted as the expert of experts on the "Nationalities Question." All the nationalities of the Soviet Union lived in exemplary harmony—a false picture of reality that was revealed to be exactly that in the ethnic troubles that beset the Red Army as time wore on. The "allies" of the Warsaw Pact were "brothers." If so, why East Germany 1953? Hungary 1956? Poznan and Warsaw 1956? Czechoslovakia 1968? Gdansk 1970? 1980?

Not that the rulers didn't know the truth. When the American Ambassador to Moscow protested the Soviet 1968 invasion of Czechoslovakia, Gromyko retorted, "We have saved the peace of the world." Very probably he believed it. The real meaning of his statement was that without the *Pax Sovietica* that controlled Eastern Europe, the nationalities, the subject peoples of

Eastern Europe, would begin again their ancient quarrels, with their potential for larger conflagrations. And so the ancient quarrels resume. Now not only in Eastern Europe, but in the Soviet Union itself. The *Pax Sovietica* was the peace of a prison, or of a Potemkin village. Reality was bound to break out of the walls or from behind the false façades.

But of course we didn't know when. Nor did the historians of our time. I once referred to History, in a message for delivery to a U.S. Senate committee (by a more august personage), as "the Queen of the Humanities." And so it is, but it is not a ouija board. I have seen some excellent reportage of *what* happened in these four years, but nothing on why, on what was at the root of these upheavals. Current historians, I think, are most likely too close to it all, and for now are being swept downstream in the flood of change along with the rest of us.

THE ROLE OF "DIRTY TRICKS"

The question arises as to what the techniques described in this book may have had to do with the changes of the past four years.

It is now customary to divide the practice of intelligence into four main parts: collection, analysis, counterintelligence, and covert action. Of these four only covert action (the press's "dirty tricks") was specifically aimed at, primarily, preserving national identities in Eastern Europe as the basis for the ultimate liberation of the Soviet satellites (at an unspecified time generally expected to be far in the future), and, secondarily, at undermining Communist orthodoxy, in both the satellites and the Soviet Union itself. Experiments were made with a number of techniques, some of which were adopted, others discarded either as ineffective or inappropriate, or, as time went on, as obsolete. What it finally came down to was the conveyance of information. And in this the role of the American-supported radios—Free Europe, broadcasting to Eastern Europe, and Liberty to the Soviet Union—was paramount.

These institutions had their origins as covert operations. That is, the operations themselves were neither covert nor clandestine. On the contrary, they were visible and open. What *was* covert was the funding of the Radios by the Central Intelligence Agency. In time, even this ended. After Senator Case (R., N.J.)

rose on the floor of the U.S. Senate at the beginning of 1971 to announce (to no one's great astonishment, but to much fanfare in the press) that the Radios were in fact funded by the CIA, the funding was provided by the Congress initially through the Department of State, and from 1975 on through the U.S. Board for International Broadcasting.

This was the moment for a lively public debate in the U.S. Congress. The Chairman of the Foreign Relations Committee of the Senate, J. William Fulbright (D., Ark.), who had done so much for the growth of constructive international exchange, turned resolutely against the Radios. (Fulbright's opposition occasionally, and uncharacteristically, became vicious: he so publicly insulted Dirk Stikker, former Dutch Foreign Minister, one of the founders of NATO, NATO's third Secretary-General, and a mainstay of European-American relations, in an open Senate hearing that Stikker, who had his "Dutch uncle" side, told Fulbright forthrightly that he would never again set foot in the United States.) Curiously, Fulbright's chief supporting witness in the battle was, in a twist that is difficult to explain, George F. Kennan (who had played a large role in the founding of the National Committee for A Free Europe, RFE's parent institution). But the Congress did not follow Fulbright's lead. Large majorities in both houses, with overwhelming support from the American press, voted for continuation of Radio Free Europe and Radio Liberty.

But success in the U.S. Congress, however essential to funding operations, is not the same as success in those operations where it counts, i.e., abroad. For that, with respect to the Radios, we turn to these four years of change, when at last people in Eastern Europe could speak out freely. What did they say?

Vaclav Havel, the playwright elected President of Czechoslovakia, at the opening of an RFE Bureau in Prague in 1990: "I want to use this opportunity, on behalf of our [Czech and Slovak] nations to thank Radio Free Europe for decades of broadcasting truthful information on developments at home and abroad. I remember the time when Radio Free Europe was, for me, too, the main source of information about the situation at home and abroad. . . ."

At the opening of an RFE Bureau in Warsaw in 1990, the Prime Minister of Poland, Solidarity's Tadeusz Mazowiecki:

". . . Today's event bears witness to the Polish process of change. In this case we are concerned with the free flow of information—an area of great social significance. RFE has made a major contribution to providing the Poles with objective information about events both inside and outside of Poland at a time when information in Poland was restricted and subjected to political ends. . . ." At the same function, Professor Bronislaw Geremek, Chairman of the Solidarity group of the Polish Parliament: ". . . I would like to say, first of all, that for decades the voice of Radio Free Europe has been the voice of freedom, the voice of Europe and the voice of Poland. . . . As Chairman of Solidarity's Parliamentary Club, I also wish to say that credit for what the people of Solidarity—and for what the Solidarity Citizens' Committees managed to accomplish in 1989—goes to Radio Free Europe. Not only to Radio Free Europe as it was in 1989, but also as it has been through all the years. We are all the outgrowth of those seeds. . . ."

The freely elected Prime Minister of Hungary, Jozsef Antall: "As the new Prime Minister of Hungary, I take this opportunity to express the heartfelt gratitude of the nation to Radio Free Europe for its almost forty years of activity. Radio Free Europe has rendered a great service to us: It has given us the gift of truth about our own country and the world at large, and has done so when telling the truth was counted as a crime against the state. . . ."

The Romanian Foreign Minister to RFE's Romanian Correspondent: "Thank you for what you have done over these past years. When you led the Political Program [of RFE's Romanian Service] it was one of the best programs I ever heard. And it was a sign of hope for many, many millions of us in Romania."

The Chairman of the Council of Estonia, at Tallinn: "It gives us pleasure to extend our greetings and thanks to all the men and women at Radio Free Europe–Radio Liberty who have kept the faith with us throughout the years, even during those times when the night was the darkest. As the people of Estonia prepare to reassume their rightful place in the European family of free nations, along with their Latvian and Lithuanian brethren, we feel a strong need to commend all of you, but in particular the Estonian Service of Radio Free Europe, for a job well done. Not that your task is completed. To the contrary— even though you have been indispensable to us in the past, we need you even more in these turbulent times. As long as our media do not enjoy the absolute trust of our people, you have a role to play as a substitute for the free press which we have not known for a half a century. . . ."

In 1991, as the Americans contemplated eliminating, or sharply cutting the Radios in the "new world order," both President Havel and Prime Minister Antall wrote asking that Radio Free Europe's broadcasts be continued indefinitely.

Clearly, something was done right.

Leaving aside the political strategies (never really thought out), we seemed to move, even if unknowingly, so far as technology was concerned, in keeping with the deepest under-currents of our times. The Communists sought to buy off their own people with false substitutes. As though hypnotized, they swam against the current without sensing it; victims of their own "doublespeak," they thought they were headed down-stream.

None of which guarantees smooth sailing to an inevitable, bright future of democracy and the riches of the "free market" for survivors and successors. As William Faulkner put it, "The past is never dead. It is not even past."

WHAT IS NEW?

So something worked. But there is still the question of the validity, in today's world, of what follows in these pages. Much of the technique described, for all four branches of intelligence (collection, analysis, counterintelligence, covert action), is still of use. There are, however, as a result of the passage of time, two omissions.

The first is the scholarship that has grown up around intelli-gence and secret operations. This is so chiefly—though not exclusively—in the United States and Great Britain. Where in 1985 there were some eighty-five courses being given in Ameri-can universities in intelligence or related subjects, I am told that today the number is well into the second hundred. (One minor result of this academic interest has been to relegate my preferred usage, counterespionage, or CE, "to the dustbin of history," so that one now speaks of counterintelligence, or CI.)

The other is the much greater importance of technology in the collection and analysis of intelligence, as it has developed over the past thirty or more years. Yes, cryptography was vital in both World Wars in this century, but cryptography is something that can be viewed as both collection and analysis: deciphering is, one might say, the last stage of collection and the first stage of analysis. It is in the first stages of collection, the actual capture of signals and communications ("Sigint" and "Elint"), that tremendous advances have been made. The same is true of visual observation—i.e., imagery, the transformation of light and heat emissions into visual representations. Technological advances have also had striking effects on analysis. Advances in computer technology have made possible useful analysis of masses of information hitherto inaccessible as a practical matter because of their enormity. To the extent that counterintelligence also relies on collection and analysis within its own specialized field, this is true of CI as well. The impact of these technological advances is not sufficiently noted herein.

Nevertheless, what I still regard as the chief aim of the collection and analysis of intelligence, those matters which have to do with the necessity to know the adversary's intentions are, I believe, not only still valid, but will become more so as time goes on. As for covert action (a broader and more serious concept than the media's sobriquet of "dirty tricks") it is engrossing to observe how not only so many of the techniques discussed herein are still in use, but how many have now entered, in overt versions, into legitimate, public life. Organize! Demonstrate! Get public attention! We are all children of Willi Muenzenberg (1887–1940), the German Communist who in the 1930s, with bewildering rapidity and variety, tied organizations, issues, and publicity into effective packages, and who was described by one of his biographers as "the patron saint of the fellow-traveller."

"YOU CAN'T GO HOME AGAIN"

As the reader who reaches Part 2 of this book will understand, Hungary, and the city of Budapest in particular, played an important part in my life, and in my experiences of "the secret war." For many years it did not seem prudent to attempt to return. Hungarian Communist governments, although they never outrightly accused me of espionage, for a number of years listed me as an undesirable, or at least suspicious, char-

acter in various "White Books" they published from time to
time. Even in years of detente, or that long period beginning in
the 1970s when the Hungarians managed to get out in front of
the rest of the Soviet Bloc in economic change and in links to
the West, it still did not seem prudent to attempt a visit to
Hungary. Detente there might be, and then, in some far-off
land on the other side of the globe, an offense would be done
to the Soviets, and they would look about for a convenient
hostage.

By 1991 those days had passed. In May of that year, forty-
four years after I had left Hungary somewhat hurriedly, my
wife and I boarded the Hungarian hydrofoil at Vienna, and
sailed—rapidly (72 kilometers an hour downstream)—and comfortably down the Danube to Budapest. It is a superb way to
approach the city. Vienna, of course, is not actually on the
great river, whereas the two cities of Buda and Pest are divided
by the Danube, and joined by a succession of impressive
bridges. Change, of course, was inevitable. I had hoped to get
a glimpse of a small peasant cottage on the Danube that I had
rented those many years before for weekends. It had disappeared in the beginnings of a great hydroelectric project envi-
sioned, found to be impracticable when the damage had been
done, and abandoned. Still, there was much that was beautiful
still to be seen, and we sailed into the middle of the great city,
Pest and the Parliament on the left, and on the right, Castle Hill
(Var) with the Royal Palace, residential Buda, and its hillsides
stretching to the north and west.

I was curious as to the reception we would receive. My wife
was passed through quickly by the young security officer at the
quay. But he took a very long time indeed to stamp my
passport. A very long time. It seemed to me he almost blushed
with embarrassment when he finally handed me back my passport. Since the people from the past are still in those positions,
I can imagine what his little book (or screen) said. But in 1991
they bother no one, at least not for the time being.

The Var has been beautifully maintained. The Royal Palace,
rusted steel framework and a pile of rubble when I was last
there, is a superb piece of reconstruction—now a museum and
the Szechenyi Library (and not the seat of the Danubian Federation, as I had been told it would be after Tito's 1947 visit to
Budapest). True enough, if you look closely here and there

throughout the city, some things need attention. But the public spaces are well done and well kept—Heroes' Square, for example. Some of the buildings still need work: they were preparing St. Stephen's Basilica for the Pope's August 1991 visit when we were there, and some of the museums and university buildings are not yet in good shape. On the other hand, it was a pleasure to see the streets with their proper names restored (even though a mania for changing all the house numbers has made finding landmarks—and former homes—difficult).

Like Vienna, Paris, and London—and much more so than Berlin—the city retains a sense of empire. The buildings and monuments are majestic. History is everywhere, and everywhere recognized. The stewardess's lectures on points of interest as we came down the Danube were models of vigorous Magyar patriotism, as were those of the young man who on our first day drove us about the city. (At the Gellert Hotel he announced with some pride, "This is where Otto Habsburg stays when in Budapest.") But you can also hear the sounds of the more recent past. At St. Stephen's, in the chapel where the Saint's right hand is preserved in a golden reliquary, the driver took me into the pews to point out one bearing the name of Count Paul Teleki, with his dates. "This," said the young man, "is where he spent his last day." To which I added, softly, even reverently, "Before his suicide." My reference was to Prime Minister Teleki's well-known fatal protest in 1941 against the German invasion of Yugoslavia. "Oh, no," the young man said. "The Germans killed him." As a friend of the Teleki family, I could have argued the point, but refrained. A whispered argument in a chapel would not have overcome years of a deliberate concoction that served a double purpose for the former masters of Hungary: it fed the orthodox hostility to West Germany, and it sought to deprive a nobleman of the nobility that accrued to his sacrifice.

Restaurants were crowded and booming, the food plentiful and all very good (except the *fogas,* the fish unique to Lake Balaton, not as good as I remembered). The goods in the stores available only for hard currency were, of course, the same that one sees all over the world now in the fashionable shopping streets, and those in the stores available for forints were a bit tacky. Just off the Vaci utca one day a long line turned out to be for waffles! But turning into the Vaci utca itself, the long line there was for shoes.

The most striking thing about the city was, regrettably, the number of automobiles. Worse than Paris. And the driving absolutely insane. The 34-year-old Mayor, a very competent young leader, but obviously carrying a heavy burden of administrative decisions, agreed that there is a serious traffic problem. "They all drive like Italians," he commented. I wanted to remark that at least the Italians know perfectly what their machines can and cannot do, but, again, I refrained. But I did tell the Mayor that I had noted large groups of the kind of young people one sees loitering about the cities of Europe (and the United States, of course), and inquired about drugs and crime in Budapest. He said they have a serious crime problem—robbery and burglary—but that they did not yet have a serious drug problem. They sniff things, he said, but the real drugs are too expensive for them—for the moment. But he did not close his eyes or ears to the possibility that the problem might arise some day.

At a meeting with the President of the Parliament we were given honors: guards presenting arms, an officer leading us up the ceremonial staircase of the Parliament—for Hungarians the *Orszaghaz,* the House of State (the cost of which, when built in the late nineteenth century, would have completely constructed a city for 32,000 people). We were served apple juice and coffee. We had a fairly long and, I thought, very productive talk. As my questions and comments reached their obvious end, the President of the Parliament went to his desk, returning with a small box. He then made a very kind speech indeed, and handed me the box with, as he said, "thanks for all you have done for members of the Hungarian Parliament." In the box was a stunning sterling silver medallion of the Parliament, the lettering "Budapest Parlament" on the obverse, with the new (restored) arms of Hungary and lettering, including "Magyar Köztarsasag" ("Hungarian Republic," not "Hungarian People's Republic"), on the reverse. It was an emotional moment.

It has been a truism for some time that the political distinctions expressed in the terms "right" and "left," based originally on the seating in the French Revolutionary National Convention, no longer reflect political and social reality. This is especially true in the Eastern Europe now finding its way to new forms and solutions. The distinction in Hungary at the moment between "right" and "left" applies to views concerning the speed with which the leftover Communist structures (and leading personnel) should be transformed. The "right," the present governing group, believes structural and personnel reform should be approached gradually, while the "left" urges rapid, radical, and full reform *à la Polonaise* (at least as it was being done in Poland prior to the autumn 1991 elections). In short, the conservatives, the "right," are more ready to compromise with the Communist legacy, while the liberals, or "left," want to do away as quickly as possible with every vestige of Communism (formerly regarded as *the* "left.")

I found the city in better shape than I expected. I felt again the vitality of the Hungarians, which had so struck me on my first arrival in 1946. Which is not to say that the country does not face very serious problems. The combination of foreign debt and trade deficit is menacing. But the Hungarians, astutely, have been sneaking up on the West, so to speak, for some years. They were the first former Soviet Bloc nation to join the Council of Europe. And of the total of Western aid to and investment in the former Bloc countries in 1990, the first full year of such aid and investment, Hungary received more than half.

But . . . but . . . there are differences.

For one, the truth of the title of Thomas Wolfe's great novel, *You Can't Go Home Again,* came "home again" (if the pun may be forgiven) to me in Budapest. Certainly the city was familiar. But there was a certain distance to it all. Somehow, I had the feeling that I could not—at least not in the short time available—really touch, or enter into, this city in whose life, geography, and spirit I had once been so deeply immersed. Perfectly normal, of course, and no cause for disappointment.

For another, I had identical reactions from two Hungarians who know the past. One is of the "right," the other of the "left." But both say the same thing. They are deeply distressed, not by the economic situation, nor by the political situation, but by what they have observed of the effect of all those years under Communist (Russian) domination on the people themselves: the way they think; the way they react to their circumstances; the breadth of the expectation that all will be taken care of by some all-powerful authority—or, more significant, *should* be so taken care of. As one who fought in 1956 said to me, "The tragedy of the country today is that 1956 failed. It gave them thirty-three years more, and those years changed them—not for the better."

The tragic legacy. My guess is that in time it will become a part of that past of which Faulkner spoke.

James McCargar
Washington, D.C.
November 1991

INTRODUCTION
TO THE SECOND EDITION
WASHINGTON 1987

WHAT'S IN A NAME?

I have been asked, more times than I would care to tally, the meaning of "Christopher Felix," or how I chose that name for the original 1963 edition of this book. I would be unhappy with the tally because it shows how penetrable, at least after time, is the armor of a pseudonym. (Already in the late 1960's I received a letter from the President of the British Crime Writers' Association —until then I had not considered myself a *crime* writer—the envelope properly addressed to me, and the enclosed letter opening, "Dear Christopher Felix." In replying I asked how the writer had obtained my identity and address, to which he answered, "Simply by two London telephone calls." The man left me suspended in midair: I still don't know what those two calls were.)

When in a flippant mood—a dangerous springboard—I have sometimes answered, "It means 'Christ! Am I happy to be out of that work!' " Good for a laugh by some, offensive to others, and hardly faithful to the original Greek and Latin. The truth of the matter is that the name came to me—as many fictional names do—in my sleep, or rather, I awoke with it one morning in my mind. I promptly adopted it. One New York friend thought it was "chic" (not my intent). Another congratulated me on the choice: "I rather like it," she wrote. "It would do just as well for an Irish ferryboat."

The suggestion has been made to me—not by editors or publishers, but by a distinguished scholar—that the historical value of this second edition might be increased by revealing various true identities in the book. Apart from my own, already abundantly done by others elsewhere, I have not done this.[1] A sad proportion of those named herein, particularly in Part II of the book, are no longer with us. Even so, to name most of them, at any point, would expose them to the vagaries of later judgments by those with their own biases and purposes. The right to reveal identity should belong to the rightful owner.

The introduction to the original edition pointed out that I had used true names and places wherever possible, but that where this was not possible, I tried to maintain the pertinent point or principle while altering the names, personalities, and circumstances involved. I concluded, "The reader will appreciate that it is one of the rules of the game that I cannot say which is true and which is false." While this is still, in general, the case, I have added endnotes in this edition that reveal some original falsifications, update some of the original observations, and, thanks to a number of attentive and communicative readers, correct some errors in the original. I hope not too many remain.

WHAT HAS HAPPENED SINCE?

In the original introduction to this book I commented that American critics of the failures of the U-2 and Bay of Pigs operations in 1960 and 1961 displayed not "even an elementary knowledge of the conduct of such operations." I observed, "It is of no benefit to those responsible for American secret operations that partial ignorance or lack of understanding of the principles of these operations should be characteristic of the public." And I added that "a general awareness" by the public "that these operations are being conducted" on their behalf, "accompanied by a basic understanding of the principles governing secret operations, produces further understanding of precisely why such operations must remain secret," which is a "prerequisite to a tacit but still essential public support for these vital operations." I concluded that it was "the purpose of this book to contribute to such an understanding."

What then happened, beginning in the middle 1960's and continuing to the present day, was an outpouring, a deluge, of literature on the subject throughout the Western world (that ultimately even had a slight echo in the Soviet Empire). Serious studies, some only ostensibly so, in these twenty or more years, were in the high hundreds. If fiction is included, the output is in the high thousands. (And fiction, to my mind, should be included: a CIA friend once gave it as his opinion that the true substance of secret operations

can only be captured in fiction.) What has been the result? Has
there been a growth in understanding?

I believe there has been. The immediate press comment, at least
in the major dailies and weeklies that might be described as "national," on the faults and defects of the 1985–86 Iranian and Nicaraguan operations run out of the National Security Council
showed a basic understanding of technique, and, best of all, a grasp
of the administrative and constitutional issues involved. Criticism
on moral grounds seemed to have been largely replaced by attention to the more pertinent national and international political consequences of error. Twenty-five years had accomplished something
in the United States.

I exclude from contributions to this understanding much of the
"investigative journalism," principally in book form (which began
well before Watergate). A large part of this output has been errone-
ous in content and intended either to establish the author or authors as experts or to grind particular axes. Talented writers of
fiction, experienced in the field, such as John le Carré or Charles
McCarry, have, in my estimation, made much more valuable contributions—even if that was not their primary aim.

Of course, there has been a vast amount of material to work with
in these years. In the United States there were numerous revelations concerning CIA operations in both the 1960's and 1970's. In
Great Britain the Soviet penetration of the British services surfaced
over two decades. In France in the 1960's the Ben Barka affair and
the refusal of the SDECE's Washington representative to return to
France when ordered brought scandals of the French services into
the open. (It is significant that the only high French official obliged
to resign as a result of the 1985 uncovering of the French operation
in New Zealand against the *Greenpeace,* which resulted in a death,
is frequently mentioned as a potential candidate for the French
Presidency.)

In Germany a succession of revelations of East German and
Soviet penetrations of the *Bundesnachrichtendienst,* of arrests and
flights from East to West and West to East, turned searchlights on
the operations of that service and the West German domestic security services. Even the Russians were not exempt: the Penkovskiy
case and a steady series of defections from both the KGB and the
GRU, eventually widely publicized, brought to public attention the
scope of Soviet secret operations. (And the Russians modified their
own stance in these matters: Soviet agents such as Richard Sorge

and Colonel Abel were publicly honored, and some books published about their exploits and those of the Soviet services.)

When this book was written communications intelligence was already a fully developed field. But the exploitation of space was just beginning. The prospects space offered led to grandiose pronouncements about machines replacing man in the world of secret intelligence, as elsewhere. Notwithstanding the enormous strides that have been made in collection of intelligence by space satellites of various kinds, those predictions have not been fulfilled. The information sought, now vastly multiplied in quantity, still needs to be evaluated by the human brain. And there is always the basic question of intentions. A 1986 interview with Michael R. Beschloss, a rising young historian, whose study of the U-2 affair, *Mayday*, was published that year, made the point: "Richard Bissell, deputy director of plans for the CIA from 1959 to 1962, told Beschloss that in the late 1950's the U-2 provided 90 percent of U.S. hard intelligence about the Soviet Union. Today, its sources are much better, Beschloss says, 'but the problem is that we don't necessarily have a better grasp of Soviet *intentions*. That's something a satellite can't show you.' "

I have not myself worked in intelligence or secret operations for thirty years now. But an occasional glance at the papers is sufficient to show that certain verities continue to reign. While there have been vast technological changes in that time—computerization has accomplished marvels in quantity and speed, but done little if anything for quality—the basic elements of intelligence and secret operations that I sought to outline in this book remain valid. Those changes noted in this edition mostly concern a changing external world. The principles and procedures of the internal world of secret operations are largely constant, as a former Director of the CIA has implied in reference to this book.

One of the great changes of the past quarter century that I discern, though still in its beginnings, does alter some of the emphasis in this book. It is set forth in a note added to this edition:

While the conflict "between the Communist and non-Communist blocs" continues, the world is no longer governed exclusively by this "single conflict." The "two great power centers" are no longer in a position to dictate unilaterally within their own spheres without recourse to force (which increasingly involves greater risks). Neither is even in a position in today's world to solve its own domestic problems with purely domestic solutions. (Note the Soviet Union's difficulties with productivity, and the United States' transformation in three years in the early 1980's from the world's greatest creditor nation to the world's greatest debtor nation.) No "other nations or combination of states" have yet achieved "some parity with them" in terms of power, but the West European GNP now exceeds that of the United States—which has long exceeded that of the Soviet Union. While both superpowers meddle in the Middle Eastern conflicts, they certainly cannot now "divide" that "world between them," and the major shifts in the balance of power now originate in East Asia.

THE SPECIAL AMERICAN PROBLEM

The trend in the United States over the past twenty-five years has been toward increasing Congressional control of initiatives in the field of secret operations. This has resulted in increasing frustration in the Executive Branch. (Open debate in the Congress of so-called "covert" operations in Angola or Nicaragua makes a mockery of the word "covert" and a tragic farce of the operations themselves.) There are solid citizens with experience in these matters who feel that the President is now hamstrung in his conduct of the nation's foreign relations.

The manner in which the "debate" on this issue has progressed over the years has worsened rather than clarified the situation. In response to the performance in the Nixon White House, as well as to revealed illegalities and excesses of the CIA, a new President in effect co-operated with the Congress in limiting the scope of action of the CIA—and, without the President apparently realizing it, his own possibilities of action. A succeeding Administration, frustrated in action by the established restrictions, and in policy by the Congress, took matters into its own hands, and centered secret operations in the White House itself—an alternative decisively rejected by clearer thinkers already in the period 1946–48. The result is "chaos" in the White House, baleful glances from the Congress at the CIA, and the potential for further restrictions on the Executive Branch not only in secret operations but in foreign relations generally.

This is the "special American problem." For both parties to this conflict between the Executive and the Legislative have right on their side. The Executive *is* too restricted by current legislation and practice, and the Legislature *does* have a right to consultation and knowledge, and in specified cases, decision, with respect to foreign policy and the expenditure of funds in furtherance thereof.

I would not venture to prophesy future developments in this conflict—which is not new to the Republic, though exacerbated during the past forty years by the development of secret operations as an authorized arm of Executive action. It is clear, however, that under our system this conflict will not disappear, because it is a part of the balance of powers built into that system. It can there-fore be rendered manageable only by the sole instrument available to reconcile the irreconcilable—compromise. Spineless, ugly word to ideologues and extremists, but to those who understand, com-promise is the daily cement of a democratic system—along with observance of the law and at least occasional and genuine humility (however clandestine). All three are as indispensable to and within the Executive as within and to the Legislature.

BALANCING THE WHEEL

Besides some fields of private endeavor, in which the touchstone has always been international relations, I have had considerable and varied experience in both secret operations and diplomacy. There is no question about it, secret operations is a fascinating field. This book gives only a partial taste of the excitement and the hold on one of the work. So, even though spoken flippantly, was I *really* "happy to be out of that work" when it ended thirty years ago? The answer is, "For a time, no." It takes a while to appreciate the valley after one comes off the mountain.[2]

But my feelings are not the point. What my experience over some forty-five years offers is the much more important opportu-nity for a comparison, in terms of contribution to the national interest, of secret operations and diplomacy.

In both fields I made lasting friendships that continue to grow with the passage of time. The people in both the CIA and the Foreign Service, give or take the customary leaven of knaves, are of high caliber. As organizations, of course, both the State Depart-ment and the CIA are monsters—though the CIA has a slight advantage in greater flexibility. Walter Lippmann used to speculate that the basic problem facing certain powers in this century was the adaptation of social organization to great size, and he considered the American contribution to this problem unique. It was only the United States, he said, that was successfully reconciling size with liberty and democratic processes. Both the State Department and the CIA are examples of institutions seeking to reconcile great size with excellence and efficacy, although for much of the past two or three decades their efforts have not met with great organizational success (as distinct from individual or personal excellence, not always recognized or rewarded). The State Department has fallen into the hands of administrators and managers, and the CIA, as an Inspector General of the agency once said to me, "is now run by lawyers and accountants."

There is no love lost between the two, to the point that Foreign Service people of the generations now retired and retiring find it almost impossible to believe that a Foreign Service Officer could be detailed—as I once was—to the CIA. (These skeptics have a point: my detail was to the Office of Policy Coordination, which was only administratively in the CIA. The OPC operated independently of the Director of Central Intelligence, under the authority of the National Security Council and the guidance of the Policy Planning Staff of the State Department—an arrangement to which General Walter Bedell Smith, when Director of the CIA, put an end, and to which many writers on these matters, and some State Department officials, pay all too little attention.)[3]

As a CIA friend observed, "The Foreign Service's feelings about the CIA were well earned. We destroyed the careers of a whole generation of Foreign Service Officers." And as a Foreign Service friend remarked of the political outcome of covert operations over the years, "I never saw the CIA do anything that we couldn't have done better."[4] As usual in such cases, there is some truth in both statements.

But again, personal feelings, in this case rivalries, are not the point. The point is how the United States is best served. Plainly there is not only room but a role, a need, for both services. Good intelligence is fundamental to diplomacy and the elaboration of foreign policy. Secret political, economic, and, when necessary, paramilitary operations are an adjunct to diplomacy.

All this is, of course, elementary. But if I felt in 1961–62 that wider and greater understanding of intelligence and secret operations was desirable and even necessary in order that the requisite support in public opinion for those activities be forthcoming, twenty-five years later I feel that the wheel is again out of balance.

There is too much attention paid by the public to the fascination of secret operations—perhaps as a result of that deluge of literature on the subject—and too little to the primacy of diplomacy in the conduct of our foreign relations. The Executive is too much absorbed in the possibilities offered by secret operations, and not enough in the elaboration of effective diplomacy. The Congress's suspicions of the CIA have too much to do with observance of the Legislature's prerogatives and not enough with ascertaining an appropriate balance between diplomacy and secret operations. The interview with Michael Beschloss cited above went on: "You can get some help from human espionage, but that's a weak reed. Each side needs a very subtle understanding of the other's decision-making process, its interests, ambitions and anxieties." That is in the province of diplomacy.

It is appalling to compare the penury characteristic of our representation abroad, such as the closing of important American consulates around the world, with the capabilities of our secret establishment. In the 1940's and 1950's the Congress couldn't do enough for the CIA—or little enough for the State Department. Bit by bit functions of the State Department were eroded and transferred to the CIA, communications, cartography, and some foreign management operations among them. The imbalance, conceptual and functional, persists. (Even today, the old "cookie-pusher" image of diplomacy, so dear at one time to the American media, lingers in the halls of Congress, particularly among very conservative Members, and colors votes on the resources to be devoted to it. The saying in those same halls is that foreign affairs have no constituency, a belief shared, to judge from the actions and attitudes of the great majority, even by the millions of Americans who owe their livelihoods to our export industries.)

It is appalling to realize that the total expenditures of our diplomatic establishment amount to two-tenths of one per-cent of the Federal budget. The failures of conception and execution in this domain, of attention and values, that the relevant facts and figures reveal cannot be laid at the door of one or the other of our political parties, or the Congress or Executive alone. The fault, of long date, is bipartisan and shared by the two branches of government—and the public. Who will right the wheel?

—James McCargar

1. For some of the prior revelations of my own identity, see Patrick Seale and Maureen McConville, *Philby: The Long Road to Moscow.* London: Hamish Hamilton, 1973; Nicholas Bethell, *The Great Betrayal.* London: Hodder & Stoughton, 1984; Henry S. A. Becket (Joseph C. Goulden), *The Dictionary of Espionage.* New York, Stein and Day, 1986 (name misspelled and professional affiliation—CIA—wrong); Charles Gati, *Hungary and the Soviet Bloc.* Durham, Duke University Press, 1986; Robin W. Winks, *Cloak & Gown, Scholars in the Secret War 1939–1961.* New York, William Morrow and Company, 1987.

2. And then shadows can last long in the valley. One example: When I had been a mere twenty-five years out of intelligence and secret operations, a tyro in international affairs who, as an academic, had written one good book of domestic history, and then, astride a giant ego, rode into Washington and the bright glow of foreign relations (where his own light ultimately faded), decreed my exclusion from private work of lively interest and promising opportunity with the dictum, "We can't use him. He's an intelligence officer." Neither the first nor the last time.

3. Bill Colby, Director of Central Intelligence 1973–76, in his memoirs gives a slightly different version of the status of OPC: "The matter [of secret political operations] was put to Truman. He agreed. In June 1948 the National Security Council issued Directive 10/2 authorizing the CIA to undertake secret political and paramilitary operations. A special unit, euphemistically entitled the Office of Policy Coordination (OPC), was set up to carry them out, under the direction of the Secretaries of State and Defense with the Director of CIA. . . . Frank Wisner . . . was named to head it. . . ." (William E. Colby and Peter Forbath, *Honorable Men: My Life in the CIA,* New York, Simon and Schuster, 1978, p. 73.) The difference between this and my version (we were informing and consulting the Joint Chiefs of Staff from the earliest days of OPC) lies in the role of the Director of CIA. Colby came to OPC after I had returned to more standard diplomatic functions in the Foreign Service. In the period while I was at OPC, then-Director of CIA Admiral Roscoe Hillenkoetter was not consulted by Frank Wisner. The Director of CIA only assumed what was to be his commanding role with the entrance on scene of General Smith.

4. Those considering a career in either the Foreign Service or the CIA should be aware of dangerous shoals. Navigational skill consists in avoiding the cross fire between two organizational monsters. During one difficult passage in my affairs, long out of the government and without pension rights, I sought relief on the basis of my past services. The Director of Central Intelligence wrote to a senator who had kindly taken an interest in my problem: "Mr. McCargar worked at the CIA . . . but he was actually on detail from the Department of State. Hence, this does not give us any basis for qualifying him for retirement privileges. The closest he came to

working for us was when he was employed by [Free Europe Committee]
. . . but his employment there does not meet the tests of federal employment. He was the employee of what has been decreed by the Civil Service
Commission Board of Appeals and Review as a nongovernmental entity
. . . I wish we could help . . . but I'm afraid it's out of our hands." Two
months later, when the State Department also refused any assistance, a
journalist whom I had known well in Hungary approached a panjandrum
of the Division of Foreign Service Personnel, suggesting something ought to
be done. The official replied, "It is the CIA's responsibility, not ours."
When it was pointed out to him that the CIA has said I should address
myself to the State Department, and that I was thus being whipsawed
between the two organizations, his answer was, "That may be. But that is
our position." And so it has remained to this day.

INTRODUCTION
TO THE FIRST EDITION

The techniques of secret operations are as old as the human race; they are by no means diabolical inventions of the Russians or symptoms of a human spiritual decline. The intensity of their application in the past fifteen years is simply the result of the principal form taken by the historical conflict of that period. But it was only in 1960, with the U-2 case, followed by the failure of the American-directed Cuban invasion in 1961, that the secret war, and the American part in it, came actively to American popular attention. Until then, general American awareness of these operations, at least in comparison to other people's, had been remarkably slight. Understanding was largely limited to surface impressions gained from melodramatic films, spy thrillers, and surcharged memoirs. Secret operations were mostly viewed as an exotic growth, something that went on elsewhere, certainly not a part of the daily atmosphere and facts of American life.

How many Americans have seriously had to consider to whom they would turn in exile or how they would behave under occupation? These questions, closely related to some aspects of secret operations, have been part of the practical, daily thoughts of every resident of at least all of Europe and Asia, more than three-quarters of the human race, at some time—or times—in the last thirty years, and for centuries before that.

It was two defeats that brought, not without shock, some sense of the scale, prevalence, and importance, even gravity, of secret operations to the attention of the American public in 1960 and 1961. Discussion and comment were widespread. Nowhere, however, in the public prints—with the exception of a few analysts who singled out political ineptitude in the Cuban operation—have I seen good, competent, constructive understanding of the reasons for these failures. A man who had some responsibility in the Cuban operation said to me afterward that while there was plenty to criticize, and plenty of criticism, he had yet to read one American critic who displayed even an elementary knowledge of the conduct of such operations, of the type which would produce a valid commentary useful to a public which he admitted had every right to be concerned. This may perhaps be an exaggeration; but it would seem fair to state that naïveté in these matters is far from unusual among Americans.

It is of no benefit to those responsible for American secret operations that partial ignorance or lack of understanding of the principles of these operations should be characteristic of the public. Quite the contrary. An at least elementary public awareness and understanding is a positive asset. A public more sophisticated in these matters is less prone to ill-conceived and purely emotional reactions in the event of error or failure. The Cuban operation warranted vigorous criticism, but a sometimes deliberate, sometimes merely ill-informed confusion of moral, morale, policy, and technical questions could not clarify specific error; it could only complicate the general unease.

It is my impression that every American failure in the secret war which could be qualified as serious—and serious is to a considerable extent synonymous with publicly known—has either been caused or compounded by those responsible ignoring or brushing aside the classic principles of secret operations. So much for those directly responsible. But the citizen has a responsibility too. It is in no way connected with knowledge of the details of any specific operation. It is connected with, at the minimum, a general awareness that these operations are being conducted, in his name and on his behalf. Such an awareness, if accompanied by a basic understanding of the principles governing secret operations, produces further understanding of precisely why such operations must remain secret. Such understanding is the prerequisite to a tacit but still essential public support for these vital operations. It also gives the citizen the possibility of seeing more clearly the world conflict around him; it enables him to recognize more easily the true content of Soviet maneuvers in the field; and it helps to insure that his reaction in the event of failures is a direct response to the facts of the case, not a misguided emotional outburst to be exploited by either demagogues or the enemy.

It is the purpose of this book to contribute to such an understanding.

This is neither a scholarly treatise nor a historical survey nor a textbook. It is simply a record of my own recollections, experiences, impressions, reflections, and conclusions resulting from some sixteen years in secret operations, all in the service of the United States, and in a variety of countries and organizations. It is my hope that from this informal collection there will gradually emerge for the reader that understanding of the principles of secret operations which is the purpose of the book. Beyond that, it is my hope that, from the personal opinions, criticisms, and comments which occur throughout, and for which I take sole responsibility, the reader will gain some idea of the hard realities and problems which face those responsible for these activities. Lastly, it is my hope that the unconventional perspective from which this book is necessarily written will contribute, however indirectly, to that most desirable objective, the American's realistic understanding of himself and of America's place in the world.

Because secret operations deal with the relations between men, they are a subject as complex as man himself. The most important single fact to be borne in mind about them is that everything concerning them is relative. There are no absolutes. There are, however, certain classic principles which reflect centuries of experience in secret operations and which are in turn applications of historical human insights into human nature. But precisely because secret operations involve the application of human insights into human nature in constantly shifting and changing circumstances, these classical principles can never be observed to perfection. They are ideals which the professionals of the secret war forever seek and never find. Compromise, invention, adaptation govern their decisions and actions. But the measure of their competence and skill is the degree of their perseverance and success in bringing their compromises, inventions, and adaptations to a relative approximation of the classic principles.

The explanation of secret operations is complicated by the obvious fact that nothing can be said which will give the enemy some information or advantage he does not already possess. The appearance of this book under a pseudonym is therefore less for my own protection and convenience than to safeguard certain existing operations with which I was associated in the past. Throughout Part I —which discusses the generally recognized categories and aspects of secret operations—and Part II—a detailed account of a particular operation in which I participated, being a concrete illustration of the complexity of the work—I have used true names and places wherever possible. Where that has not been possible, I have tried to maintain the pertinent point or principle, while altering the names, personalities, and circumstances involved. The reader will appreciate that it is one of the rules of the game that I cannot say which is true and which is false.

PART 1

Fundamentals and Forms of Action

VIENNA 1956

At 3 o'clock Sunday morning, November 4, 1956, I returned to the hotel in Vienna where I had been staying for three days. I paused to leave a call and exchange a few idle words with the hall porter. Nostalgic early morning music from the radio behind the telephone switchboard echoed through the empty lobby. I went to my room, and within a few minutes after getting into bed, was asleep. At five minutes past 4 the telephone rang. Switching on the light, I reached sleepily for the receiver, my brain stumbling through possible reasons for a call at such an hour. It deliberately side-stepped the possibility that was all too real.

Knowing but discreet, the hall porter's voice came through to me. "Sir," he said, "there is an emergency broadcast coming from Hungary. Imre Nagy, the Prime Minister, is speaking. I thought you would be interested. Just a moment, I'll put the telephone next to the radio." And so I lay in the Vienna night and listened to the voices of Nagy and interpreters announcing, in terse and stricken but courageous tones, that the Russians had attacked Budapest at 2 o'clock that morning. They were recordings, made less than an hour before, and were repeated continuously in Hungarian, Russian, French, English, and German. I turned cold; I continued to listen, stunned, hoping for a word that it was not true. Over and over, the Magyar accents repeated the brief and terrible announcement in the five languages. I lay there, picturing the columns of Russian tanks advancing through the darkened streets, firing mercilessly into the crowded apartments, into the proud and poignant city only four hours' drive to the east—a city I had known well.

The porter's voice brought me to my senses. I thanked him, put down the receiver, and considered what I had to do. The answer was nothing. As the Russians well knew, if anyone had fomented the

Hungarian Revolution of 1956, that astounding moment of truth shared by a whole people, it was the Russians themselves and their handful of Hungarian servants. We, the Americans, had had nothing to do with it. In the two weeks since its eruption, the United States had substituted baffled wonderment for a policy, and was headless besides: the President was campaigning for re-election; the Secretary of State, who carried foreign policy in his hat, had had to temporarily hang it up while undergoing surgery; the Department of State was being run by a first-rate petroleum engineer. The Russians, it must be said, were equally baffled; they hesitated and vacillated. The night's news meant that they had finally estimated the American reaction—correctly, as it turned out—and had therefore found a policy—now being put into effect with the guns of the Red Army.

My own purposes at Vienna were simple enough. The political operations in which I was engaged concerned Hungarians outside of Hungary, and my principal tasks had to do with the tens of thousands of Hungarian refugees pouring over the border into Austria. So far as events in Hungary were concerned, my mission was purely that of an observer; if a contact should develop with the new Hungarian revolutionary regime, I would maintain it while seeking new instructions. Indeed, only eight days before, an exiled Hungarian, a former very high postwar politician and Cabinet Minister, had told me that he had telephoned Budapest and spoken to members of the new Imre Nagy Cabinet, who had said simply, "Speak for us in the West. Make them understand our neutrality." I had assisted this man then to travel to Vienna, not with the intention of his re-entering Hungary, but only so that he could be in closer contact with his colleagues and compatriots now in the Government. He had, on arrival in Vienna, been immediately deported to Switzerland on, of all things, the representations of the American Ambassador to Austria. I had, therefore, on my own arrival in Vienna, sent word to one of his henchmen who was now somewhere in Hungary carrying a letter from the former Minister to the leading non-Marxist political personality in the new Government.

There was nothing I could or need do about this courier. I telephoned to a post near the Austro-Hungarian border, where I learned only that the border was still open, refugees were still crossing, and that the sounds of heavy gunfire could be heard on the other side, from the direction of Györ, the nearest large town. That done, I think I briefly lost my reason. A boiling rage overcame me; it was as though a fever swept through my brain. I did not curse the Russians —I seemed to feel almost that I knew them too well for that. I did not rant at our own impotence—the American Government seemed to me somehow pitiful and irrelevant at that moment, hardly to blame for its troubles. My anger instead was vented upon the British and French, whose adventure at Suez I wildly blamed for giving the Russians the pretext for their action in Hungary. I swore, in a kind of momentary delirium, that I would never again set foot in France or England, I would devote myself to exposing their monstrous cynicism in sacrificing Hungary for Suez, and so on. (Secret agents are not necessarily coldly unemotional, and the secret agent's objectives are to him, necessarily, of paramount, and highly personal, importance.) None of this had anything to do with the facts, of course. The British and French operation at Suez was conceived and prepared well before the Hungarian Revolution of October, which took the British and French, as I well knew, as much by surprise as it did the Russians and Americans. I realized all this in the morning, after a few hours' sleep—and I also remembered the past, which did much to explain the seizure which had overcome me in the night. But the preface to that story of the past is—a short course in the secret war.

CHAPTER I

The Secret War

At the end of the Second World War the American public generally felt that the fighting was over. Postwar problems were recognized to exist, but they seemed, to most Americans, to involve such things as rehabilitation, economic questions, some political negotiations—but nothing of conflict. Organized mothers' groups in 1946 cornered the Chief of Staff of the United States Army—later to become President—in the halls of the Capitol, preventing him from attending Congressional hearings while they demanded he "bring our boys back home." In the same period, the largest mass-circulation magazine in the country exulted in an editorial entitled "The American Century." The mood was one of a problem definitely solved, and of power. But the secret war had already begun.

The power was real, even if the mood was contradictory and in some respects reckless. But power in human affairs has its own organic characteristics. It both attracts and repels. In either case it inspires an underlying, even subconscious fear. This effect cannot be dissipated by protestations of peaceful intent or even by good works. It can ultimately be truly dissipated only by a relative change in the balance of power. The great American postwar success, the rebuilding of Europe, was not a success simply because it demonstrated that we did not intend to use our power to infringe on the independence of European nations; it was a success precisely because it eventually and genuinely restored to Western Europe a measure of the power, political, economic, and military, which was almost exclusively ours in 1946. The Western European nations feared our power then, but for historical, ideological, and political reasons they feared that of Russia more. They were therefore, on balance, attracted to American power.

For the same reasons, the Russians were repelled by our power. In the light of their particular ideology, it was perfectly clear to them that with the destruction of German and Japanese power, the United States became the principal foe of the Soviet Union and its Communist allies throughout the world. It is of no moment that a man trained in Western logic would distinguish at this point between a potential and an actual foe. The so-called doctrine of ultimate consequences is basic to Communist logic. Under this doctrine it is not merely legitimate, it is politic and necessary to treat an unconverted man (or a nation) in the present as though he already were what he is potentially capable of being in the future—namely, an active enemy. This kind of thinking owes less to Marx than it does to professional, universal military doctrine. The genius of Lenin—even if it was, from the viewpoint of Western civilization, a regressive genius—was to reverse Clausewitz's famous "War is a continuation of politics by other means," and to apply to politics, both national and international, the doctrines of war. Lenin was perfectly well aware that this was a step backward in civilization, but he justified it in terms of the class war. He was also in theory aware that to treat a potential enemy as an actual enemy is ultimately to make him an active enemy, but he was blind to the full relation of this cause and effect in practice since Marx's fulminations, Russian terror, and Western error had steeled him to see his aspirations surrounded by a hostile world in which only the doctrines of war could prevail.

Thus, as the defeat of the Axis became certain, the Soviet leaders adopted—certainly not in sorrow but neither with any particular rancor; one might say almost automatically in response to the dictates of their analyses of history—the view that the power of the United States and its allies, but especially that of the United States, was hostile to them. This "new line" was by no means as hidden or obscure—and certainly not as new—as one might have thought. In June of 1945, immediately after the victory in Europe, and while preparations were just getting under way for some combined Soviet-Allied operations against Japan, I was obliged, as an American intelligence agent, to report to Washington that the Party agitators in Soviet factories had begun a "new line" emphasizing the fundamental hostility of the United States to the Soviet Union. At that moment, to avoid too quick a turn in view of the wartime alliance —never overpopularized in the Soviet Union, but nonetheless an undeniable fact—the story was that with the death of Roosevelt, the great friend and defender of the Soviet Union, the American capitalists had a malleable tool in the person of President Truman, and fears were expressed as to future American policy toward the Soviet Union. Every subsequent irritant in Soviet-American relations could thus be presented to the Soviet masses as an evidence of the predicted American hostility—or be taken by the Party leadership, as with the abrupt termination of Lend-Lease, as confirmation of the correctness of their own policy.

Besides his estimate of America as the enemy, Stalin had in mind his own projection of Soviet and Communist expansionism. In this sphere he could only forecast that U.S. policy would become actively hostile to Soviet expansion at some point; what he did not know was where that point lay. The Russians therefore set themselves two tasks: one, the probing of Western policy to see how far they could expand Communist gains without encountering applied superior power; the other, the whittling down of Western and especially American power. Not only was that power, in their eyes, too great and menacing to be endured, but its reduction coincides absolutely in time and space with the world triumph of Com-

munism, which their ideology teaches is inevitable, however long it
may be delayed.

The probing operation continues. It takes place openly—in diplomatic conferences, in summit meetings, in conflicts such as the
Korean War, in crises such as Berlin and Cuba. It is the overt
confrontation of power.

From the Soviet point of view, their other principal task, the
attrition of American power, takes place in two ways. The first is
overt. It is simply as rapid an increase in their own power as their
energies can produce. They allot the minimum consistent with the
maintenance of internal stability to consumer goods; they insist on
a high rate of capital investment and of economic growth, all in the
interests of greater economic power. Their own absolute increase in
power means a relative decrease of American power. This is obviously also true of their military establishment. Their timing and
publicizing of space exploits is simply a ready means of impressing
the world with their own absolute increase in power, and all the
better if it also demonstrates an increase relative to the United
States. All of this, however, is within the confines of their own state
and economy.

The second method for reducing American power takes place
outside of the Soviet state. Its primary objective is to reduce American power in the rest of the world. Its secondary objective is to
substitute Soviet power for American power whenever possible.
The techniques of this method are many: espionage—to reduce the
advantages of Western technology and military secrecy; political
and psychological warfare, as in the Peace Campaign or in the
struggle for dominance over the international labor movement or
over newly independent states; the fomenting of civil strife—
known as paramilitary operations or unconventional warfare—in
areas buttressed by American power, as in Laos or southern Vietnam. These techniques all have one common denominator: they
are secret operations; they avoid the open confrontation of power.
They are conflict behind a curtain, so to speak, the curtain being
the tacit acknowledgment of both sides that the open confrontation
of war is undesirable. This conflict consists of the secret operations
of the Soviet Union, its allies and partisans, and of the United
States, its allies and partisans. Winston Churchill christened it the
Cold War.

Churchill's phrase has popularly been taken to describe a state
of mind, an attitude of nations toward each other, characterizing

the years since the end of the Second World War. It is clearly more
than that, being also the secret maneuvers and conflicts which are
the real and predominant content of the Cold War. These secret
maneuvers and conflicts—the secret war—are not the products of
some mysterious black art. They are complex, but they are also an
ancient, universal, and continuous part of human behavior. Athens
had countless troubles with Persian- and Spartan-instigated sub-
versive groups in its allied and tributary states, not to mention the
ideologically pro-Spartan oligarchs of Athens itself; Metternich's
chief of intelligence daily pieced together and read the contents of
the wastebaskets provided for foreign delegations at the Congress
of Vienna in 1815; from the French point of view the American
Revolution was originally a secret operation against Great Britain.
And so it goes in our day: Soviet agents arrested in the West,
Western agents uncovered in the Communist empire; move and
countermove in Germany, in Iran, in Guatemala, in Vietnam, in
Laos, in Cuba—and countless other places unmentioned. The
twentieth-century state, eyes on the stars, drags neolithic man on
into a schizophrenic future.

The purposes of secret operations are those of state, but their
substance is the relations between people. This basic fact is obscured primarily by the secrecy of these operations; it is also obscured by the existence of a professional lingo which—like all technical language—is used by professionals for greater precision and
misused popularly to the confusion of the layman. I make free use
herein of the term "secret operations," for example, not only because it is generally understandable, but also because it is a generic
term embracing sharply different forms of secrecy: it covers a mul-
titude of sins. These forms of secrecy which pertain to secret operations have nothing to do with the classifications of secrecy used by
Government departments: Top Secret, Secret, Confidential, Restricted, etc. These latter are merely designations indicating, in
general, what groups of people shall have access to the specific
information so labeled. The forms of secrecy are fundamental to
secret operations and pertain to the techniques by which secrecy
will be established and maintained. Thus something overt can be
secret, and anything covert or clandestine is—or should be—secret, but something secret is not necessarily covert or clandestine,
and anything clandestine is decidedly not covert and vice versa.
Anyone who has managed to work his way through that is entitled
to an explanation.

In secret operations the meaning of "overt" is not only "open and visible"; more importantly, it also signifies that the person or activity is in fact what he or it is stated to be. This does not mean that secrecy is absent. The United States Navy is exactly what it says it is, the marine arm of our military establishment. But its war plans, many of its ship movements, even in peacetime, and countless other aspects of its equipment and operations are secret, that is, knowledge about them is restricted in varying degrees. More to the point, the Central Intelligence Agency, our principal arm in the secret war, has overt personnel and functions, even though virtually all of its activities are secret. The CIA is required by published statute to prepare the national intelligence estimates for the National Security Council. The personnel who do this work are overtly employed by the Agency, but the preparation and the estimates themselves are secret. Similarly, the Director of the Central Intelligence Agency and his two principal deputies are overt officials, although responsible for our secret operations.

The identity of the American CIA Director's British counterpart, on the other hand, is secret, and is withheld from all except those needing to know. The West Germans have come up with an unusual variant on this in the fact that the identity of the head of the German service, General Gehlen, is known, but only a handful of authorized persons, including but a few of the personnel of his own organization, know him by sight as such; he appears in his identity of General Gehlen only to this small group, a practice made easier by the reported fact that there is only one very old photograph of him in existence. This is not to imply that either the British or German arrangement is necessarily superior to our own; it was long ago decided that the British solution was not adaptable to our form of government and public life, and the German case is largely a fluke resulting from the chaos and confusion of the German defeat and the deliberately self-effacing personality of Gehlen himself. The desire for anonymity and the exercise of great power without public recognition are not generally characteristic of the American personality or system.

Interestingly enough, the Soviet arrangement, although differing in important respects, corresponds more closely to the American than to the British or German solutions, at least to the extent that the Committee on State Security is an overt organization and its chairman's identity is known. The French, on the other hand, tend to resolve the problem more in the British fashion. They admit, as the British do not, the existence of an overt organization—the Service de Documentation et Contre-Espionage, which is attached to the office of the Prime Minister—but they neither publish nor publicize the identity of its director. It will be seen from these arrangements that, in secret operations, while the various combinations of overt and secret reflect the different national circumstances, that which is overt is in even lesser proportion to that which is secret than the visible part of an iceberg to its underwater mass.

Of even greater importance to secret operations than the resolution of the problem of what may be overt and what must be secret is the distinction between clandestine and covert. Both are secret, but in different ways.

Let us suppose that the United States is faced with the problem of sending an agent who is a communications expert to join anti-Castro guerrilla forces in the mountains of eastern Cuba. (The illustration could quite as well concern a Soviet effort to send a similar agent to Iran, a similar British problem in Iraq, a Communist Chinese problem in Malaya, and so on around the globe.) If this agent was sent aboard a United States Navy submarine which surfaced in the dead of night off a deserted beach on the northeast coast of Cuba, where, by prearrangement, a small group of guerrillas met our man as he stepped ashore from the submarine's inflatable raft and conducted him to the safety of the mountains—this would be a clandestine operation. That is to say, its secrecy depends upon skill in utilizing natural circumstances to hide the operation, to render it invisible to the enemy. There is no effort to disguise the operation; it is secret only because it is hidden, but it is exactly what it appears to be. There is obviously a very large element of chance in any clandestine operation; a patrol passing the beach at an unforeseen time, a fishing boat coming upon the scene unexpectedly, any of a number of possible circumstances could destroy the operation's secrecy—and the operation.

A covert operation would attempt to minimize precisely this element of chance. If our communications expert posed as a foreign agronomist, complete with false identity papers, entered Cuba with Cuban Government permission, and, while on a tour of the eastern provinces, vanished one day into the mountains—this would be a covert operation. Skill is also a vital element in the secrecy of such an operation, but its most important element, and its distinguishing feature, is the use of a cover—in this case the agent's pose as a foreign agronomist. A covert operation is visible:

no effort is made to hide it from view; the major effort is to disguise it. It is not what it appears to be. In brief, the working distinction between the two forms of secrecy is that a clandestine operation is hidden but not disguised and a covert operation is disguised but not hidden. Covert operations constitute the major part of the secret war, and cover, which is discussed elsewhere at length, is probably the most important single technical element in secret operations.

Obviously neither type of operation is easy, but certainly a clandestine operation is less difficult than a covert one. By the same token, a clandestine operation is considerably more risky than a covert one. Most operations are in fact, however, a combination of clandestine and covert. To pursue our communications expert further, let us assume that, having safely landed on his beach and met the conducting party, the problem is then to reach the safety of the mountains. To travel at night would risk arousing greater suspicion —and thus greater risk of investigation—if a patrol were encountered. Accordingly, the party waits until daylight to set out, and when it does, our agent is dressed to look like a *campesino*, making his way with his companions from one village to another. At this stage he is covert, even if not perfectly so. Our foreign agronomist, on the other hand, has the advantage of his cover right up to the moment when he joins the guerrillas—caught at any point prior to this, even in making contact with the guerrillas, he has a valid cover of merely studying the soil and terrain—but once with them, and a part of their activities, he is clandestine, as are the guerrillas themselves.

The fact is that while covert operations are generally more desirable for their lessening of the risk of discovery, all covert operations invariably have some moments, however brief, when the cover does not logically hold and when they are therefore clandestine. The important point is to recognize these moments with the utmost clarity as being clandestine and to hold them to an absolute minimum, for these are the times of greatest danger. It is for these moments that the enemy is watching.

While both types of secret operations are used in war and in peace, clandestine operations are more numerous in wartime and covert operations are the common form in peacetime. The reason for this is that the consequences of discovery are generally greater in conditions of peace than in war. From the viewpoint of the individual agent, of course, the maximum consequences are the same—usually death or imprisonment, depending on the objectives and particular circumstances of the operation. But the purposes of secret operations are those of state, and for the state the consequences of discovery can be vastly different. When British aircraft during the Second World War dropped agents by parachute in German-occupied France or Poland—clandestinely—their discovery by the Germans did not affect the relations between Germany and Great Britain. An act of war, a hostile act, in wartime is but another item in the openly acknowledged contest to alter the balance of power. A clandestine act, because it involves the state, is considered a hostile act, and a hostile act in peacetime can, and usually does, disrupt in greater or lesser degree the complicated fabric of relations between states. In effect, the Soviets refused to have any further dealings with the American Administration after the U-2 affair—a consequence which was fraught with danger for the entire world.

Accordingly, states have recourse in peacetime to the greater security afforded by covert operations. Their greater security does not lie only in the fact that they minimize the risk of detection or of involvement of the state. They also benefit from a tacit agreement between states, itself the sum of long historical experience, whereby covert operations are recognized as a peacetime avenue of action which, when used, will not upset international apple carts.

The very reasons for which states undertake covert actions reinforce this tacit agreement. The reasons are various. It may be, as in espionage, that the national security requires it, and the mission can only be accomplished covertly. It may be, as in most covert political operations, that effectiveness would be nil if it were generally known that the activity had its origins in or support from a foreign government. It may also be, as in the support given to paramilitary operations, that the activity is considered necessary but is not consistent with existing friendly official relations; or, most importantly, the activity would, if undertaken overtly, risk bringing into play forces which would either defeat the mission or seriously alter the international political balance.

These reasons have, in the past, been traditionally understood between states; the covert operations which stem from them have been tacitly accepted as providing each state with the flexibility they need for self-protection. From the national point of view, at least between states of relatively equal power, the result is a sort of mutual back-scratching arrangement. From the larger point of view, the arrangement has a solid and useful foundation: it permits the pursuit of constructive, progressive policies on the overt level while preserving, on the covert level, the national safety and interest intact until more idealistic overt policies have produced concrete international results. In this light—and it is the light they read by—the Soviets fully comprehend the seeming contradiction between our own support of the UN and our support of the 1961 Cuban invasion. The rude noises Khrushchev made at the time of the Cuban invasion were in fact addressed, not to our support of that operation, but to the fact that our involvement in it was clandestine, not covert.

This politic understanding between states, it might be noted, also has a broadly beneficial effect in wartime. At a time when overt policy is necessarily harsh and publicly inflexible, covert operations provide an avenue for probing for more realistic and less costly accommodations. Thus, American covert operations centered in Switzerland during the Second World War succeeded in bringing about the German surrender in Italy contrary to Hitler's express orders, with a great saving in life and property.

This tacit agreement among governments, reached over thousands of years of experience, to let each other more or less off the hook is based, however, on the strict observance of another tradition. While a clandestine operation must, by definition, be recognized as hostile, a covert operation's patent hostility can be ignored by the victim who uncovers it only if he receives the co-operation of the author of the act. Here is the origin and sanction, even sanctification, of the established custom of silence, or at most of flat disavowal, by the responsible government when a covert operation has been uncovered.

This is one explanation—whatever others there may be—of Khrushchev's rage when, even with the talkative U-2 pilot Powers in his hands, he stated publicly his certainty that President Eisenhower was not personally responsible, only to have the President publicly avow his responsibility. For, in the professional context of the secret war and covert operations—and if nothing else Khrushchev is a professional—avowal of responsibility has a specific meaning. It is interpreted by the enemy as a threat, since it means, in the context, that the avower not only ignores established custom, but also the basis of that custom, which is the maintenance of the international political balance. The avower therefore puts himself in the position of demonstrating indifference to the international political balance; his avowal may even be taken to imply that he intends to change it by any and all means.

Even the manner of avowal also has a specific international meaning. It is not necessary to make a public statement. The use of airplanes in the American operation against the Arbenz Government in Guatemala—surely one of the most flamboyant in history—was a clear revelation of United States backing and participation. It was my understanding at the time that several CIA officials had argued vigorously against the use of airplanes—even to the point of tendering their resignations—on just these grounds, but that their arguments were overruled at Cabinet level since it was desired to make clear to the Soviets that we would not hesitate to use any means to destroy Communist bridgeheads in this hemisphere. It would seem in this latter case that the warning conveyed in this implicit avowal didn't take.

But then, covert operations are not a way to convey international warnings. Avowal of a covert operation, however implicit, is a hostile act, and it is wise never to indulge in hostile acts unless one is able and prepared to back them up. Or, as the Russians say, "If you say A, you must be prepared to say B." And, as we might say at this point, if you are going to meddle with the classic principles which govern the secret war, don't be muddled.

I have no doubt that some American muddling in these matters stems from a certain defensiveness in the face of Soviet aggression in the secret war, a kind of "We don't care if we are hostile, you were hostile first" attitude. Such an attitude can lead to a certain irresponsibility in the conduct of secret operations, and, more importantly, by alienating important foreign opinion, reduce the effectiveness of many of our operations addressed to that opinion. This plays into the hands of the Soviets and their propaganda allegations. It is true that the tacit convention which eliminates covert operations as a valid cause for war is largely based on historical practice with respect to intelligence and counterespionage operations. But the secret war today includes a great deal more than just espionage. It includes a vast range of political operations, running a gamut from simple propaganda operations, through enormous world-wide movements designed to capture the loyalties and support of peoples everywhere, to paramilitary—sometimes called unconventional or guerrilla warfare—operations in critical areas.

It is likewise true that the blame for this situation today, the spread and intensity of the secret war, rests squarely on the Soviets.

Although other Western nations were more realistic than ourselves, the United States had no permanent, peacetime, unified intelligence organization until 1946, when the Central Intelligence
Group was created as a bridge between the wartime OSS and the
Central Intelligence Agency which was established the following
year. Even the Central Intelligence Agency was limited initially to
intelligence functions. As General Marshall reportedly said when
Secretary of Defense, "I don't care what the CIA does. All I want
from them is twenty-four hours' notice of a Soviet attack." (The
twenty-four hours is now down to fifteen minutes—or less.) The
United States had no organization of any kind for the conduct of
political or paramilitary operations until one was hastily assembled, within the CIA in late 1948, after the Communist *coup d'état*
in Czechoslovakia. Nevertheless, it is precisely in this area of secret
political and paramilitary operations that the Soviets have decided
that their greatest opportunities lie. While much of American overt
policy—the rebuilding of Europe, support of the United Nations,
the Alliance for Progress, a world-wide chain of military alliances
—is aimed at lessening the secret war, this is not enough. The
Soviets have long since chosen—and give no evidence of having
altered their choice—to challenge us by means of the secret war.
To ignore it would be folly; to lose it could be fatal.

The secret war has, of course, both offensive and defensive aspects. The two are naturally inseparable, but all governments, as a
practical matter, distinguish organizationally between the two. The
offensive aspect is embraced by the term "secret operations"; the
term "security" covers the defensive aspect. The principles governing the conduct of the two are identical. Nevertheless, an administrative separation between the two is universally employed:
activity inside one's own country—largely, of course, defense
against the enemy's operations—is defined as security, and the responsibility therefor given to security agencies; one's own operations abroad, however, are by definition offensive, and the responsibility for them is entrusted to a separate secret operations agency.
In the United States the division is between the FBI—domestic
security—and the CIA—foreign intelligence and operations; in
Great Britain between MI-5—sometimes operating behind the
cover of, but not to be confused with, Scotland Yard—and MI-6; in
West Germany between the Office for the Protection of the Constitution and the Gehlen Organization; in France between the Ministry of the Interior and the SDECE. In Communist countries the

administrative separation is not so rigid, but generally speaking the domestic functions are performed by the Ministry of the Interior—in the Soviet Union by the Committee on State Security, since the reorganization of the secret police following Beria's downfall—and the foreign functions by Military Intelligence.

Whatever the administrative separation may be, it is generally difficult to observe, and is in many countries a source of intense internal friction. Many offensive operations abroad, particularly political operations, must be based at home. Furthermore, both domestic and foreign intelligence services have overlapping interests in foreigners on the national territory. In the case of foreign intelligence or political operations uncovered on the home territory, there are frequently even sharply conflicting interests.

The defection some years ago of Otto John, head of West Germany's Office for the Protection of the Constitution, to East Germany was felt by many observers to have been largely a result of his defeat in a power struggle with General Gehlen over conflicting interpretations of responsibility within West Germany. During the Second World War the American FBI was even granted certain responsibilities abroad—notably in Latin America—while the OSS was to operate in active theaters of war. (While it antedated the creation of the OSS, it is a fact that the first foreign intelligence report I ever read was an FBI document reporting on a prewar high-level Nazi dinner in Berlin.) Such frictions are by no means absent from American operations. In 1949 there was a noteworthy performance in the city of Washington itself in which a continuing difference of opinion between the FBI and the CIA over the disposition to be made of a Soviet defector resulted in an open brawl between the two in a public restaurant where the Russian was dining.

Since the principles and techniques of the secret war as waged abroad and at home, offensively and defensively, are the same, however, and since my own experience has been in the offensive aspect of that conflict, this book centers almost exclusively on the secret operations conducted by nations outside their own borders. It is, indeed, the present high level of activity in this sphere, rather than the automatic reaction of increased defensive activity by domestic security agencies, which is the distinctive mark of today's secret war.

But there is nothing historically new in today's situation of aggression in secret. History is dotted with similar periods of intense secret conflict in preparation for, in conjunction with, or separate from open and conventional warfare. The only novel factor today is mutual recognition of the prohibitive cost of open, nuclear war. But this merely reinforces, granted the expansionist aims of the Soviets, their decision to proceed by means of the secret war, to apply Leninist doctrine to international relations. In brief, they accept the tacit convention concerning covert operations as applying far beyond mere espionage, and they have studied, expounded, expanded, and refined the techniques of secret operations in order to apply them to international political and social conflict. In this they have proved, so far, peculiarly adept. There is no reason, however, why the distinction should remain permanently theirs.

CHAPTER II

The Power of Secret Knowing

A distinguished Englishman, then the chief of His Britannic Majesty's secret services, once showed me, with justifiable pride, his extensive library on secret intelligence and operations. With wry amusement he chose an ancient volume, which turned out to be the journal of one of his predecessors, the secretary to Sir Francis Walsingham, who was, besides his many other duties, in charge of intelligence for Her Majesty, Queen Elizabeth the First. Opening the book at random we glanced at an entry in which this gentleman, almost four centuries before, noted: "I today went out and hired me a base fellow." He then went on to record the "base fellow's" duties, which were quite simply to inform on a particular group of his fellow subjects.

Although the officer's terminology is today archaic, something of his attitude remains with us. Those who inform in secret, those who are not what they appear to be, those who accept hospitality

in order to probe the weaknesses by which the host can be brought
to his knees, those whose true purposes are masked behind a tissue
of lies and stealth—all such people generally inspire what we take
to be a certain repugnance. In America it is usual to identify this
repugnance with morality: to feel thus is to be a moral person. The
story of the parent punishing the child who tattles instead of the
culprit is almost—but unfortunately not completely—a relished
part of American folklore. The story has often been recounted of
Henry Stimson's cold reply when, as Secretary of State, the American codebreaking operation was explained to him. "Gentlemen
don't read each other's mail," he said, pushing aside the pile of
proffered telegrams.[1]

Regretfully, I must demur from the viewpoint that this repugnance is an evidence of moral quality in the person experiencing it.
It is, in modern man, no more a sign of a moral attitude than the
apparent contempt for his hireling reflected in the phraseology of
Good Queen Bess's police chief. Resentment and dislike in both
cases, yes, but in neither case caused by anything so reassuring as
moral or social superiority. On the contrary, it is the very need for
reassurance which provokes the assumed superiority. For what the
informer or secret agent really inspires in us is fear.

Historically, in every age, in every kingdom, in every state, informers have played a key role as one of the means by which rulers
have maintained their power over the ruled. In ancient Athens
there existed an entire class of people who made their living and
were entitled to some important privileges by virtue of being informers; their existence and their privileges were a principal bone
of contention between the democratic and oligarchic factions, but
they were still used even in the periods of democratic rule. Byzan-
tium, Renaissance Italy, Stuart and Puritan England, the Japanese
Shogunate—all contained a similar class. Great as was Napoleon's
power over France at the height of his career, it was thoroughly
consolidated by an enormous network of informers established by
his redoubtable minister of police, Fouché, often described as the
founder of the modern police state but, historically speaking, far
from an innovator. As an English journal described the situation in
1887, "In the absence of 'informer' evidence, the great majority of
cases would fail for want of legal proof." Today, in the United
States of America, if you denounce your neighbor to the Treasury
for income tax evasion, you will receive a negotiable percentage of
what the Treasury collects. Every American municipal police force

in any town or city of size is dependent in large measure on informers. The FBI assiduously adds to its files, both criminal and political, by means of informers. Whether used to reinforce the police
power or political power, informers are a universal prop to authority.

Culturally, the memory of the days when political power was
greatly dependent upon informers lingers in our civilization. Even
without the living example of the technique offered by modern
Communist states, we are all instinctively fearful of the informer,
the secret agent. Whether we know our history or not, our particular civilization remembers, with unspoken fear, that the informer,
the man operating in secrecy, is a threat to every man's life and
physical freedom. To be denounced is to run afoul of authority; to
run afoul of authority is to be exposed to the cost and the caprice
of justice—and justice, at its best human and imperfect, is always,
to greater or lesser degree, but one aspect of the established political power.

Resentment against the informer and secret agent is not only a
matter of historical memory. Any organized society is intolerant of
those who set themselves apart from the prevailing norms. Any
group's major rewards are reserved for those who most wholeheartedly accept and most vigorously personify the group's ideals.
Psychologists, sociologists, and philosophers have abundantly remarked the similarity between the position of the artist and that of
the criminal in any society. What the two have in common is the
fact that they set themselves apart from society; they are by nature
skeptical of its ideals, of its morals and interests; they arrogate to
themselves the right to reject the established code and to live by
their own. It is human nature to resent such independence, even
arrogance. This resentment is the price the artist pays for the independent point of view which nourishes his art; punishment, the
active expression of this resentment, is the price the criminal pays
for his attempt to achieve the society's aims by asocial means.[2]

The secret agent is akin to both the artist and the criminal. His
techniques are similar to those of the criminal: they are illegal or
antisocial. His point of view is similar to that of the artist in that he
does not accept—at least after sufficient experience he should not
—the society's myths about itself. He is prone to see the society
from a distance, to exploit its customs and relationships for ends
which are not part of its publicly avowed ideals. While the secret
agent's work gives him a valuable opportunity to see from a

broader, more realistic, even if harsher perspective, he is nonetheless a man apart. We sense this, and we are disturbed by it. The fact that the secret agent in effect abuses the habits and relations of our society with the sanction, however secret, of established authority, only adds resentment to the disturbance. He is a species of legal criminal; his connection to sources of power only reinforces the underlying human reaction that he is not only a man apart, but a privileged one at that. He adopts the stance of the artist or criminal, but by a special dispensation of the powers-that-be, he is exempted from the normal risks of such behavior. This cannot help but strike us as unfair and abnormal.

The secret possessor of information produces a feeling of unease in us for an even more fundamental reason than the political history or social organization of the human race. It is simply that in any situation of human conflict information is power. Blackmail, that is, the exercise for personal advantage of the power conferred by information about another's wrongdoing, is only a crude and specialized expression of this power. The power of one man over another by virtue of superior information extends far beyond the special situation of the wrongdoer. This power is an element in every situation of human competition or conflict.

The businessman's assets are not limited to his inventory and his holdings of cash and securities; they include notably what he knows about his competitors. The responsible lawyer before entering into negotiations studies every available source for information on those whom he will be confronting. Indeed, the American business community alone generously supports a number of enterprises whose sole function is purveying information about persons and corporations. The employer telephones concerning a prospective employee: "What do you know about him?" The suitor who knows his rival's plans is thereby enabled to forestall them. The general preparing an attack must know the relative strength of the forces opposing him. It is worthy of note here that the student who steals the questions for his examination is not in fact making use of the axiom that information is power. The axiom is true of situations of competition and conflict; the student by his action shows that he has misinterpreted a situation of long-term competition with his fellow students as being a temporary one of conflict with his professor. His secret and misdirected action to uncover what is in his professor's mind is of no avail against the long-run competition of his fellow students. The principle, "Know your enemy," has a double meaning.

By and large, for information to be power it must be secret. (The qualifying "by and large" covers the instances where the opponent has not, so to speak, done his homework: he has not prepared himself for the encounter or marshaled his resources in the most efficient manner. In this case, he is by definition in an inferior position and has, in effect, abandoned the contest.) Our business-man whose assets include what he knows about his competitors also has liabilities which consist of what his competitors know about him. But what he knows they know about him is not a liability; that much he can take into account in estimating and meeting competition. What he does not know that they know about him, his resources, and his plans is precisely what they can use against him, to outwit and outmaneuver him. The rival of our suitor, knowing that his next maneuver has been given away, can alter it. If the defending general does not know that the size and state of his forces are known accurately by the enemy, and he sees no reason to reinforce or regroup them, he thereby confers value on the attacker's possession of that information. This is basic to all human competitive activity or conflict. Therefore, for a fundamental human reason also, the secret agent, the informer, provokes in us a feeling of unease. We do not know what or how much he knows.

Fundamental as these reactions may be, they are not, of course, the entire story. Other pressures tend to produce quite opposite reactions, particularly in our own times. A trace of envy of the supposed ability of the secret agent to cast aside established conventions and relationships is apparent in the fiction about private detectives and in spy thrillers. Romanticized, melodramatic, they are first cousins of the Anglo-Saxon legend of Robin Hood, the Teutonic Til Eulenspiegel, and Islam's Nasreddin.

The ideological content of the secret war today—which resembles nothing so much as the European religious wars of the Reformation and Counter Reformation—plus the enormous growth in population have brought the prestige of the state to bear on the question of informing. The theory is advanced, and supported by all the power of the state, that it is the duty of every citizen to inform. This is official doctrine even in the United States, although it is by no means clear that every American citizen has wholeheartedly accepted it. I have been, of necessity, many times approached

by the FBI, or by other security agencies, about various of my
fellow citizens. I have each time accepted the official view that it
was my duty to speak fully; but the only times that I was ever able
to do so without an underlying feeling of discomfort were when I
realized that I was in a position to help someone unjustly under
suspicion—a far from infrequent occurrence. Informing to the FBI
is still in America a matter of individual conscience. It is not clear
whether this is still so when the investigating body is a Congressional committee and the issue is the denunciation of other citizens. But the pressure of official morality is on the side of informing, and it is probably accepted by the majority of Americans at
this stage.

More important, however, than either escape fiction or official
morality as counterweight to an instinctive negative reaction to the
secret agent is the age-old principle, "It depends whose ox is
gored." This principle succeeds in polarizing and simplifying the
matter, so that my agent is a hero and yours is a villain. Attitudes
within the nation toward the "base fellow," the police informer,
the FBI informant, the Senator's secret source in a Government
department, the bank's confidential investigator, the private detective for hire, depend on to whom you talk. Discussing this subject,
a former vice-chairman of the Democratic National Committee
told me that his ouster from that post had come about because
another faction in the party had subverted his secretary—with
money—so that all his confidential correspondence was betrayed.
He had finally become philosophical about it, but it took years for
his rage to subside. On the other hand, one of the most imperturb-
ably jolly men I ever knew was a man who commanded a six-figure
annual income because his confidential connections in the U.S.
Government were such that he could inform his clients in private
industry of the details of their competitors' plans and contracts.

Among nations, in the international secret war of our time, the
problem is even more simplified. Here, it is the sacred cow of
nationalism that decides whose ox is gored. This standard of judgment is inculcated early. Every American child exposed to American history knows the story of Nathan Hale, the Connecticut mili-
tia officer who volunteered to go behind the British lines disguised
as a schoolmaster in order to provide General Washington with
information about British forces on Long Island, and who was
caught and hanged by the British. American children also know
about John André, the British officer who, on behalf of General

Clinton in New York, secretly negotiated the agreement with Bene-
dict Arnold to deliver West Point into British hands, and who was
caught and hanged by the Americans. Concerning these two secret
agents, a leading American encyclopedia phrases the opening sen-
tences of the entries under their names as follows: "Hale, Nathan;
1755–76; American patriot in the American Revolution," and
"André, John; 1751–80: British spy in the American Revolution."
At the same time, few British children have ever heard of Nathan
Hale, and Major André is commemorated in Westminster Abbey.

The arrangement is emotionally very practical, since it allows us
to separate the conflicting elements in our ambivalent attitude toward the secret agent into "good" men and "bad" men. It is also
useful in guiding popular feeling into support for the state. Thus,
many Western observers commented unfavorably on the virulence
of the prosecutor and of the Soviet press during the Moscow trial
of Francis Gary Powers, pilot of the U-2. On the other hand, a
judge trying an accused Soviet secret agent in New York in the
summer of 1961 stated in court that "conspiracy to commit espionage is analogous to mass murder," a remark the press reported
entirely without comment.

This simplification into melodrama is avoided by the professionals of the secret war. It is neither a lack of patriotism nor of determination to win, but a simple recognition of the facts of international life, an unwillingness to underestimate their tasks, and a
desire for precision which lead them to use a different terminology
from that employed by public orators, prosecuting attorneys, and
mystery writers. Thus the words "spy" and "enemy" are not used
among professionals; they become, respectively, "agent" and "the
opposition." And there is in this certainly a tacit, even if precarious, mutual respect which is the universal mark of competing professionals. This mutual respect should not, of course, be confused
with any code of chivalry; the basic theory of this kind of conflict
begins with the premise that no holds are barred.

The possibility of isolating and identifying a class of professionals in this type of conflict is a unique feature of modern times. The
conflict itself, its techniques and maneuvers, are as old as mankind
because they are an intrinsic aspect of human relations. Before the
end of the eighteenth century, these skills were part of the attributes of every man concerned with public affairs. The famous description of Jefferson— "a gentleman . . . who can plot an
eclipse, survey a field, plan an edifice, break a horse, play the vio-

lin, dance the minuet"—could, if applied to almost all of his peers and contemporaries, have included "and conceive and execute a secret political intrigue." Benjamin Franklin and Silas Deane, among Jefferson's American contemporaries, distinguished themselves in this field. And to this day, the bribes and clandestine intrigues of Don Bernardino de Mendoza, Ambassador of Philip II of Spain to the court of Henry III of France, who—by playing on the ambitions and avarice of the Duc de Guise, the selfishness of Catherine de Médicis, and the Parisian Catholic mobs' suspicion of the Huguenots—insured that France would be so embroiled in internal strife that she could make no move either to aid the English against the assault of the Spanish Armada or to endanger the exposed Spanish flank in Flanders, remain a model of a successful combined secret intelligence and political operation. In effect, an important military victory, however temporary, was won for Spain without a single Spanish soldier ever being involved.

Ambassadors today are often expected to obtain similar results; they are enjoined, however, from using Mendoza's techniques. A division of labor in this, as in all other fields, has developed whereby only a particular group of people work with these tools. These are the professionals of the secret war. These professionals are not limited to officials and agents of the Central Intelligence Agency in the United States, of MI-6 in Great Britain, of the Service de Documentation et Contre-Espionage in France, of the Gehlen Organization in West Germany, of the State Security agencies in the Communist countries, or of their numerous counterparts in other governments around the world. The circle is larger and more flexible than that. To be sure, these official employees constitute a core—and, in our day, a bureaucratic growth—among those who may be termed professional. But beyond them anyone who at any time has had to master in action the techniques of secret operations against a stake involving his life, his freedom, or his livelihood must also be counted a professional.

Such mastery is not necessarily a matter of formal training. All governmental secret services maintain training divisions and schools, but mere exposure to their courses does not make a professional. The man must be tried. The fact that I was myself some eight years actively engaged in secret operations before I was finally dragooned into a training course does not of itself prove the point. However, the successes of the American Abolitionist underground in the mid-nineteenth century are a persuasive example, as

were the various European undergrounds organized during World
War II. In these resistance movements there were neither time nor
facilities to train the thousands of men and women who entered
into clandestine life. Some died learning, some had a natural talent,
some learned and lived—all were professionals and remain such,
whatever their later work. The experience, if genuine, and however
gained, makes a professional and marks a man. The Director-Gen-
eral of the French Sûreté once remarked to me apropos of some of
his own more lurid Resistance experiences that he did not believe a
man could fully understand our age unless he had spent some time
in prison. The remark is not inapplicable to secret operations.

The individuals who work inside the circle of secret operations
share one thing in common: a conscious awareness of their purpose
and function. Beyond this, however, there are great differences,
individually speaking, in degree of knowledge and in function. So
far as degree of knowledge is concerned, the scale is hierarchic:
that is, the man at the bottom of the hierarchy—in theory—knows
the least; the man at the top—again in theory—knows the most.
Information is power in this context too. The reason that this hierarchic arrangement does not work perfectly in practice is because
secret operations, while secret in their conduct and techniques,
deal with the relations among human beings and are therefore ac-
cessible or visible to the correct perception. After a certain amount
of experience has been gained, a competent agent develops this
perception; he knows in principle what secret operations are being
conducted, and he can often recognize them in fact and detail
when he himself is unconnected with them. To compensate for this,
as well as to protect information from too wide a dispersion, compartmentalization—only a bureaucracy could have invented such a
word—is standard practice in all secret services. This is simply the
organized application of the principle that an individual may know
only that which he needs to know for the performance of his own
tasks. In a secret intelligence operation, for example, the ideal—
not often achieved—is to limit any individual agent's knowledge of
the identities of other agents to one only, or, at a maximum, two.
This minimizes risk, safeguards the secrecy which makes information power, and confines broad knowledge to a relatively small
concentration of persons at the very top of the hierarchy. In this
sense, the oft-used simile which likens secret operations to an octopus is especially apt.

The tentacle of an octopus has no organ enabling it to know

what the other tentacles are doing, and yet it does not act independently. A single brain guides the movements of all the tentacles, co-ordinating them by means of nerves and muscles. The muscles of the octopus of secret operations are the ingredient of discipline in the human relations of the personnel of the operations. If this discipline—the muscle—is ineffective, obviously the operation—the tentacle—is defective. However, what constitutes effective discipline in secret operations is not the same as the military version of this quality; it is described in detail in the next chapter.

The nerves, however, must be visualized as a chain of knowing, in which the sensitivity or electric impulse which determines the function of the nerve is represented by the control of knowing. By control is not necessarily meant the limitation of knowledge; this is the function of compartmentalization. Control means simply knowing who knows what. It is important in secret operations for the reason that a man possessing certain knowledge will behave differently than if he did not possess that same knowledge; he will also have a different understanding or conception of himself and of the circumstances surrounding him.

This is obviously not true to the same extent of all kinds of knowledge, or even of the same item of knowledge in all circumstances. The knowledge of Hopi Indian lore would not particularly affect an American agent working in Poland, but his knowledge of the identity of every other American agent in Poland would be a dangerous risk for all the other agents, besides endowing him with undesirable power and possibilities of action. A more concrete example was the Allied invasion of Normandy. Everyone in the British Isles in 1944 knew there was going to be an invasion; only a specifically authorized few—the "bigoted"—knew the date or place; and even fewer knew both. And no one knew either or both without having that fact recorded in a central register—which is a more than usually formal version of control. When Hitler contemplated the invasion of the Soviet Union, the German Ambassador to Moscow was kept totally in the dark until the attack had already been launched. Knowing the Ambassador's sentiments against such an attack, Hitler and Ribbentrop well knew that he could not perform his task of allaying Soviet suspicions if he possessed the knowledge. Again control.[3]

To some extent this matter of control is one of the functions of counterespionage. However, it is also a daily ingredient in the work of anyone engaged in secret operations. It can become a passion.

One of my colleagues, directing an operation in which control was one of his principal preoccupations, gave a vivid example of how far this passion can go. An associate, coming into his office one night to work, strolled across to his window before switching on his light. Looking across the courtyard, he saw my colleague, in his office, locked in passionate embrace with his secretary. Reflecting but a moment, the observer went to his telephone and dialed the appropriate number. Regretfully relinquishing his secretary, my colleague answered his telephone, only to have the voice of the unseen observer say, "This is God speaking. Aren't you ashamed?" As my colleague later confided to a friend, he finally broke off the relationship with the girl, since all he could do when with her was worry about the fact that he didn't know who knew.

Neither discipline nor control, of course, are the object of secret operations, any more than mere motion is the object of the octopus's movements. The octopus seeks food; secret intelligence operations seek information. The information sought is by no means limited to that concerning actual or potential enemies, although that is of primary importance. Relations between states, even in an organized bloc such as the Soviet Union and its satellites, always have sufficient elements of conflict and competition so that information about each other always has value. One measure of the degree of friendliness in relations between states is the quantity and type of information they make readily available to each other. Even among the closest allies, however, there is information which is withheld—and therefore sought. If it is withheld because it would adversely affect relations, then it is of value as revealing negative elements in those relations. If it is withheld as a prerogative of sovereignty, an exercise of independence, the very reason suggests that the information is power. And in the case of a friendly but not allied state, there is always the added attraction that a mutual friend can often tell you much about your enemy— even if he is also performing the same service for your enemy with respect to you. Nevertheless, secret operations between allied friendly states are usually held to a minimum, and the greatly preponderant effort is to find out about the enemy—actual or potential.

The information sought about the enemy concerns his capabilities and his intentions. It is much easier to find out about capabilities than it is about intentions. The difference is that between poker and chess. In poker that which is hidden is the strength of the opponent. His intentions play no part in the game, which revolves around guessing or deducing his strength—his capabilities. Thus the characteristic play in poker is the bluff—the masking of capabilities. In chess on the other hand, the opponent's strength is on the board, readily visible. The game centers entirely on the opponent's intentions, and the characteristic play is the feint—the masking of intentions. In poker the player wants to know what cards his opponent holds; in chess he wants to know what moves his opponent intends to make with his visible resources. Obviously, of the two, intentions are of much greater importance, since from them flows action.

Intentions, however, are so difficult of access that a major role of diplomacy is simply to analyze intentions. Secret operations seek to reinforce the analyses of diplomacy with concrete information.

One of the constant dangers to national destiny—and to international peace—is the fact that military doctrine resorts to an extrapolation of intentions from capabilities, based on an underlying assumption that intent is always hostile. In its simplest form, this means that if a man has a gun, he intends to shoot you; *ergo,* if you find out that your neighbor has a gun, either you get a bigger gun or you move out of the neighborhood or you force him out of the neighborhood or you shoot him first. This is indeed the proper way to run an army, but far from a responsible way to guide the destinies of a whole people.[4]

Accordingly, a greater value attaches to the information concerning enemy intentions which is produced by secret operations than that concerning enemy capabilities, provided, of course, that information on capabilities is at a reasonably satisfactory level. Before and during the Second World War, one of the favorite problems of all secret operations travelers on the Trans-Siberian Railroad was whether the Soviets had built a tunnel under the Amur River at Khabarovsk, where the railroad crosses the river on a highly vulnerable bridge. The interest stemmed from the fact that if there was no tunnel, and the Japanese destroyed the bridge in the event of hostilities, then the Soviet Maritime Provinces to the south, including the port of Vladivostok, would be cut off from Soviet supplies. If there were several foreigners on the train, you could usually tell who of your fellow travelers were connected with secret operations: even if the train crossed the river at 4 in the morning, there would always be a few strollers about in the corridors, peering with bland bafflement into the murk, trying to distinguish a likely-looking spur track. (I reported the tunnel was built, but I don't know to this day whether I may not have been looking at a false entrance. The Soviets knew about all those early morning risers too.) Nevertheless, this information, interesting as it might potentially be, could not compare with the immediate and more important value which attached to my report in 1945 on the changed line taken by Communist Party agitators in the Soviet factories, as but one indication of inimical Soviet intentions toward the United States.

When all this information has been gathered, however, the job of secret operations is by no means finished. Secret information is indeed power, but it is only power in a situation of conflict or competition. And in such a situation, power is meaningless unless it is used, either implicitly or directly, to achieve desired goals. In the secret war those goals are the fulfillment of national policies; they require the adaptation of secret intelligence operations techniques to political conflict.

This adaptation encounters serious obstacles, however. Every secret operation produces information; a purely political operation —a youth festival, for example—also produces information and depends for its execution upon information. On the other hand, it is almost never that an intelligence operation is without political effect or implication. This interrelation of information and politics, of information as power, and the use of that power, is one of the major problems of secret operations. Ideally, the two should be divorced—but they cannot be. The great majority of secret intelligence operations at some point utilize an agent, or numbers of agents, whose purpose in the operation is political: they are against somebody or they are for something. At the same time, the purely political agent is to information as flypaper to a fly. Furthermore, the adaptation of secret operations techniques derived from intelligence operations to political operations is hindered—at great cost to the political objectives—if the philosophy and techniques of information for information's sake govern. Similarly, it is out of the question to engage in secret intelligence operations on a purely political basis.[5]

In the 1961 Cuban affair, for example, it was impolitic—to put it mildly—to attempt the political overthrow of Castro with Right-wing Cuban politicians; it would likewise be inefficient to limit our intelligence sources about Cuba to Center or Left-wing Cubans. In the one case the political objectives are gravely jeopardized; in the other, possible valuable information is rejected. Nevertheless, the national interest requires that we use all three. How to reconcile them? Particularly when a Left-wing politician, co-operating in a political operation, objects to the use of a Right-wing politician in an intelligence operation as implying political support for the latter —an interpretation favored and probably even expounded gratuitously by the Right-wing politico? This problem in secret operations is inevitable and eternal. No secret service has solved it perfectly yet. In the United States, unfortunately, the solution has weighed predominantly on the side of information for information's sake, to the great detriment of our political operations, our power, and our prestige. The problem will be examined in detail elsewhere.

1. According to a letter from Louis Kruh in the January 1986 issue of *Foreign Intelligence Literary Scene*, McGeorge Bundy, Stimson's biographer, replied to a query about this quotation with the statement that he "had checked the book [where the quotation first appeared] closely, and he now concluded that 'it [the use of single quotation marks around the quote in the Stimson-Bundy book] means that Colonel Stimson used that description of his thinking in his discussions with me' when we were preparing the book." In short, the quotation appears to be considerably ex post facto. A 1954 letter from Herbert Hoover on the subject says that Stimson explained that he had to denounce telegraphic intercepts "in order to preserve his relations with various embassies," and that he, President Hoover, "took no part in this matter. It was the Secretary's responsibility to conduct his department." Whatever Secretary Stimson's words at the time, he *did* close down the American "Black Chamber" in 1929.
   2. This is a curious paragraph. Where it ran somewhat off the track, I think, is the point at which it began the comparison between the artist and the criminal. The original point, resentment against the informer and secret agent, is valid. Certainly there is resentment against the criminal. But it is difficult today to discern "resentment" against the artist for his independent outlook—except among those Mencken labeled the "booboisie," and the lunatic fringe who decorate some areas of our public life. The final statement gives it away: clearly, the criminal is not attempting "to achieve the society's aims"—except as the aim of amassing riches happens to coincide with a number of individual aims in the society.
   3. This discussion of "control," valid as far as it goes, is at fault in omitting any mention of the social or political implications of control. It is one thing, for example, for Hitler and Ribbentrop to withhold from their Ambassador at Moscow their intent to attack the Soviet Union. It is quite

another for the Chief of Staff of the President of the United States, or the President's National Security Advisor, to withhold vital information affecting foreign policy from the Secretary of State—or, let us face it, for the White House to make a fool, if not a liar, of Adlai Stevenson before the Security Council of the United Nations with respect to the Bay of Pigs action. The health of constitutional government depends very largely on observance of democratic procedures, onerous as they frequently are in foreign relations.

4. It is only fair to quote at this point from a review of this book by a Commander Robert E. Bublitz, USN, then on duty in the Foreign Intelligence Division of the Office of Naval Intelligence, in the July 1964 *Proceedings* of the United States Naval Institute: "From a critical point of view, there are a few points with which the military reader might disagree. The assertion that 'military doctrine resorts to an extrapolation of intentions from capabilities, based on an underlying assumption that intent is always hostile . . .' might, for instance, provide the basis for a warm debate. Frequently, those with long service in the civilian branches are wont to aim an occasional indirect slap at the 'military.' Mr. Felix is no exception, but he criticizes the deficiencies of civilian policy and working-level types more directly . . ."

5. This dichotomy is as lively as ever—as those dealing with Afghanistan, El Salvador, Nicaragua, and sensitive spots in Africa and the Middle East in the Eighties certainly must be able to attest.

CHAPTER III

The Spy and His Master

In likening secret operations to an octopus, it is clear that the tentacles are made up of the chain of human relationships linking the direction of the operations to even the most remote agent. The muscles guiding each tentacle are, in turn, made up of the responsiveness, the discipline, which characterize each of the relationships in the chain. Of all these relationships—which include, of course, auxiliary services such as logistics, communications, and administration—there is one which is at the very heart of secret operations. It is the critical relationship, dictating in many cases the success or failure of the operation. It is that between what are called—in American terminology—the agent and the case officer.

It is the agent who acts and who is directly in touch with the enemy, the "opposition." The agent is exposed and visible; he operates "outside." The case officer directs the agent. He is invisible and works only "inside." The relationship between these two is the bedrock of all secret operations. Most human and organizational connections in secret operations can, in fact, be defined basically in terms of this one fundamental relationship. It is possible, for example, to visualize the entire "inside" establishment of the CIA as constituting a collective case officer and all those "working" outside as making up a collective agent. Such an image, while accurate, is meaningless, however, because it does not convey any idea of the variety, complexity, and individual elements which govern the relationship.

What is involved here is the ability of the case officer to insure that the agent's actions advance the objectives of the operation, that none of the agent's actions hinders the attainment of those objectives, and that the agent exerts his best efforts. This clearly requires domination of the agent by the case officer. The possibilities of this domination are reinforced at the outset by the fact that the case officer represents the authority which defines the objectives of the operation, and he controls the resources which make the operation possible. But woe to the case officer who relies only on these two elements to achieve his mastery. In doing so he immediately forfeits the confidence of the agent as well as his essential willingness. These two elements are implicit in the relationship, and if the relationship is properly developed in human terms, their explicit use should not be necessary, or can be kept to a minimum.

It is just here that an American weakness occurs. Time and again I have seen American case officers resort to cutting off funds to enforce discipline over an agent. One effect of this maneuver, if successful, is ultimately to reduce the agent to the status of a mere pensioner. In espionage operations this can, and often does, result in highly unreliable information; in a political operation it can be fatal. As one disgusted Cuban exile said of the CIA after the Cuban affair, "They have no idea how to work with political allies. They think in pennies."

Often this matter of funds is permitted to become an irritant in the relations between the case officer and agent simply because of American suspicion about money and fear of being victimized. Whatever may be the public impression of what the CIA does with its vast unvouchered funds, the fact of the matter is that behind every case officer is a squadron of bookkeepers and accountants, sniffing hungrily for a wrongfully diverted penny.

One highly qualified agent not many years ago worked out with the Americans a complex political operation which included considerable mailing, for which he was given a specified budget. His headquarters were in an American cover organization and, early in the operation, before he had actually received the promised funds, he had to absent himself for ten days. He told his secretary to continue the mailings, using the organization's postage meter and keeping a record of postage as obtained. In his absence a bookkeeper complained of his unauthorized use of the postage meter and immediately, without any opportunity for explanation on the agent's part, the case officer was required to cancel the operation. Funds were never even granted for expenses, fairly considerable, already authorized and incurred. When the agent told me this story, almost a year later, he was still paying off the debts with which this episode had saddled him. He was not enthusiastic about working with Americans; as he put it to me, "In your system every bookkeeper is a comptroller, and every agent is required to be a bookkeeper."

Often also the American difficulty with the agent and case officer relationship is simply a reflection of the bureaucratic approach to problems and the disproportionate influence of the fetish for administration in American operations. I was once charged with the planning and direction of the American part of a combined Anglo-American operation, similar in nature to the Cuban operations, but smaller and more tentative in scope. (It also failed, with some loss of life, but at least the failure was not public.) While I was still casting about for the most qualified personnel—the area was fairly exotic, and very few Americans were at all acquainted with it—I was summoned to a conference in Washington. On entering the room I remarked an intricate organizational chart on the wall. One of my colleagues—I didn't know he was even interested in the operation—rose and then started his discourse by pointing to the chart and saying, "I have now worked this all out, and, as you will see, you need 457 bodies for this operation." He then spoke for forty minutes, without ever once even mentioning the country with which we were concerned. I confined myself to remarking that I didn't think we could find 457 "bodies" and that I would happily settle for six brains.

By way of contrast, I went to London a week later and observed the British approach to the same problem. After sitting around a table in desultory fashion for an hour or two, one Englishman finally said, "I say, why don't we get old Henry up here? He knows about this." A day or two later old Henry showed up from down in Sussex, and when the problem was put to him, finally agreed to undertake the task, although, as he said, "This will wreak havoc with the garden, you know. Just getting it into trim." He then added that he would do it only on condition that he could have six persons, whom he named, and that they be responsible solely and directly to him.[1]

Apart from the purely personal elements in the relationship, one of the principal tools in the case officer's hands for establishing and maintaining his dominance over the agent is greater knowledge. He has, after all, national resources of information behind him, and he must use them. One of the most brilliant agents I ever "ran"—as the professional saying has it—was a Rumanian Socialist who had certain definite objectives of his own. My interest in him had to do with his usefulness in the international Socialist and labor movements; his consuming interest, however, was anticolonialism. His very brilliance made him difficult to control, and his initiative in pursuing numerous of his own objectives could have involved me in activities which I had no intention or authority to support. I achieved a certain balance in our relationship, however, by dint, not only of heavy reading of dossiers, but also by talking at every opportunity with people who had known him in his early life, long before we became associated. In this manner I accumulated quite a store of information about him, which he did not suspect. Occasionally, when reminiscing, he would discuss some incident in his early political life. At these times I would invariably also adopt an air of reminiscence—not of knowingness—and exhibit as detailed a knowledge as possible of the time and persons of whom he spoke, usually capping it off by some misinterpretation of his own role in a particular event which would require him to explain, to excuse, or to deny. The point was made. When, therefore, in order to present me with a *fait accompli,* he embarked on some delicate negotiations which he knew very well I did not desire, and about which I heard

only by the sheerest accident, no lecture or confrontation was necessary. Over a drink I brought the conversation around to the
objective he was pursuing, and then merely remarked that the negotiations which he had undertaken were bound to result in failure.
He never knew how I knew; it was sufficient that I did. He made
no excuses, but tacitly accepted the seeming—but actually dubious
—fact that he could not get around me. Accordingly, he brought
the subject out in the open, argued its merits, and ended by acced-
ing, even if reluctantly, to the point of view I was required to
express. Every case officer must have a bit of Stephen Potter's
Oneupman in him—but it is best to be able to back up a ploy.

Obviously the case officer's authority, at least vis-a-vis the agent,
must be unassailable. This means ideally that the agent's contacts
with the organization should be limited to the case officer only.
This is usually possible in espionage operations, but in political
operations it is much more difficult. In many American political
operations the agents—even if they are political allies they are still,
in the terminology of secret operations, agents—are often in touch
with several persons in the CIA, as well as with appropriate policy
officials in the State Department. The possibilities of end-runs in
such a situation are endless. Whatever may have been his other
difficulties, in this respect one can only sympathize with the position of Richard Bissell, the CIA deputy director in charge of the
1961 Cuban operation, and his aides, when it is realized that the
members of the Cuban Revolutionary Council had simultaneous
access to Adolf Berle, Jr., in the State Department and Arthur
Schlesinger, Jr., in the White House. In a quite different type of
operation, I once had the ground cut out from under me very
effectively by just this kind of multiplicity of contacts. Following
an exploratory conversation with a prospective agent, the agent
was dissatisfied at the conditions I posed, under instructions, for an
agreement, and called several days later at the State Department.
He mentioned my conversation to an official there, who quickly
replied, "Mr. Felix's conversation with you was unauthorized."
Whether the official merely intended to rebuke his caller for mentioning something the official could not properly admit to knowing,
and did so clumsily, or whether he intended to sabotage the operation, I never found out; I had no choice but to quit the operation.

However imperative the need for the case officer to dominate the
relationship with the agent, there are major and intrinsic obstacles
to his doing so. For one thing, the relationship is not that between

employer and employee, particularly in political operations, nor is it the military one between superior and subordinate. In its theoretically ideal form the case officer would be master and the agent servant. The case officer would define the objectives, and the agent would obey unquestioningly, his skill completely—and successfully —at the disposition of the case officer. Obviously, no human relationship attains such barren simplicity. The military system is an attempt to approach such a relationship, but every new officer in a military service soon learns that it is not sufficient merely to give an order for leadership to be real and effective. How much more so is that true in secret operations, which exist in an unrecognized sphere, a sort of tacitly unobserved shadow world which is nonetheless starkly real, and in which the generally accepted constraints and values of conventional relationships do not apply. And how even more true is it in the case officer-agent relationship, in which the unavoidable fact is that it is the agent who acts. To this extent every agent is a free agent. The case officer can neither be present at the action, partake of it, nor supervise it on the spot. A man thus dependent upon another is not in an intrinsically good position to dominate their relationship.

This basic problem is intensified by the fact that communications between the case officer and agent are frequently highly tenuous: there may be long intervals between meetings, or communication may consist of no more than occasional radio signals. In a great many cases even where liaison is more immediate than by radio, personal contact between case officer and agent is rare or nonexistent. Where it is nonexistent, contact is maintained by "cut-outs."

A cut-out is a person, also an agent, who acts as intermediary between the case officer and his agent. Cut-outs serve one or both of two valuable functions. They permit oral contact between a case officer and an agent when actual physical meeting would be excessively dangerous and written communication undesirable. They are also used in situations where it is desired that the agent not know the true identity or even appearance of the case officer or principal agent. It not infrequently happens that even the cut-out does not know the true identity of either agent or case officer. In one case in my own experience I was saved great embarrassment by the fact that the agent had no knowledge of the true identity of either myself—as case officer—or of the cut-out. Some months after giving him some money and a mission—via the cut-out—this agent

defected to the Soviets. Thanks to the cut-out device, all he could
inform the Soviets was that a man he knew only as "Mike" gave
him money and instructions on behalf of a man named "Ray"
whom he had never seen. No great loss.

When conditions permit, the cut-out may be a device such as a
"drop," a person or place by means of which written communications can be safely exchanged without personal contact. Drops are
an opportunity for real ingenuity: a classic device involves sending
a theater ticket to the agent; his neighbor, sometimes the case officer, more usually a cut-out, then exchanges documents with him
in the darkened theater, often without a word passing between
them.

Where personal contact is dangerous or impolitic but nonetheless imperative, resort is had to the "safe house." The safe house is
a place where personal contact can be made under circumstances
and precautions which minimize risk. Brothels were at one time
traditionally favored as safe houses; nowadays, however, they are
professionally regarded as booby traps, the inmates usually having
been corrupted by the police into becoming informers.

A further difficulty in the relationship stems from the recruiting
process. The fact is that as often as not the initiative comes from
the agent. He proposes a course of action which he is, or claims to
be, equipped to carry out. In effect, he is offering a special skill.
This gives him some bargaining power; he can negotiate, even if
only within small limits. In the operation in Hungary which is
described in Part II of this book, the entire escape chain worked
through one agent who proposed to me its organization—at a time
when he could well guess that I must have been casting about for
such a mechanism. He could accordingly negotiate with me the
conditions under which we would work together; my sole initial
card in playing out our relationship was my ability to turn down
his proposition—certainly not in my own interests. The agent's
ability, in the case of his own initiative, to bargain, rather than
defer to commands, rests on his uniqueness, real or alleged.

If, on the other hand, the initiative comes from the case officer,
who has presumably made a choice of the best available and possible person for the mission, the agent's uniqueness is immediately
conceded and underscored. He has even more leverage than the
agent who takes the initiative. If the case officer permits himself to
feel uneasy about these basic facts, if he handles them awkwardly
in an attempt to suppress them, the relationship can be overbur-

dened with duplicity from the outset. In place of the confidence which should characterize it, both case officer and agent are in danger of behaving like a pair of irascible spouses, each trying to impress the other with his greater indispensability to the relationship—to the detriment of its true purposes.

There are ways, of course, of overcoming some of these initial advantages of the agent. American practice has achieved a certain sophistication over the years in this respect. Faced with a specific task, the CIA will usually make a considerable effort to determine who is the best qualified man. They will then study the man's chain of friendships, and more often than not it is possible to reach one of the man's friends in such a manner that, if he does not do the recruiting himself, at least the official who does so approaches the prospective agent with the benefit of the friendship. Another tactic is to overwhelm the prospective agent with rank; an approach by a "high official" is not only flattering to the vanity, but is an implicit mark of confidence.

Unfortunately, American practice may be well conceived but often falls down badly in the execution—in this as in so many related fields where what matters is not so much what you do but how you do it. A friend told me he had finally refused to arrange any more contacts for the CIA because, in too many cases, having been importuned by the agency to speak on their behalf to some important friend, the CIA either never followed through or spoke once with the man and left him awaiting a further word which never came. Another friend, whom we shall call Frank, recounted to me his own experiences in this regard. He had worked in the CIA for several years and had left—in a far from satisfied frame of mind. Nevertheless, about three years later he was approached and asked to act as agent in an operation which would have meant completely altering some urgent and, to him, vitally important plans. He explained his difficulty but said that he would be willing to undertake the operation anyway in view of the importance they seemed to attach to his participation, adding only that he must know definitely about it within two weeks. He heard nothing further, ever. But about two years later he was at a cocktail party in Washington, talking with a Cabinet officer, when Allen Dulles, Director of the CIA, walked up. The Cabinet officer turned to Mr. Dulles and said, "Allen, you know Frank, don't you?" Mr. Dulles responded heartily. "Why, of course I do," he said. "I've been trying to get Frank back into our work for the past five years." As

Frank, later explaining to me his stupefaction, said, "I guess the explanation is simply that it's a very big organization." He added moodily, "At least, I hope it's no worse than that."

A further basic difficulty in the case officer-agent relationship is the question of objectives. The case officer has usually received his objectives from above; they are expressions of national policy or interest. As such, they are also subject to change. The agent, on the other hand, has generally defined his own objectives; his service is for the purpose of accomplishing certain aims which are of personal merit to him, and his objectives are less flexible. An agent is chosen for a particular operation because of his abilities to achieve the case officer's objectives. But it is a rare occasion when the purposes of the agent who possesses the necessary abilities are identical with those of the case officer. Some coincidence there may well be, but in that case the case officer has to reflect carefully on whether the agent's purposes other than those which coincide with his own might not be the source of conflict at a future crucial moment. A community of interest may also exist, but the very phrase requires that the case officer weigh the possibility of achieving his objective against the fact that in a community of interest specific objectives and means must usually be negotiated. Negotiation there must be, and most often is, but it is never without some cost to the case officer's ability to dominate the relationship and the operation. What the wise case officer seeks is an agreed reconciliation of purposes.

To accomplish this, however, he must know as much as possible about the agent and all of the agent's aims, but people do not often go about openly proclaiming all of their purposes—particularly not if they understand them clearly themselves. Nevertheless, the motives of agents—and, it should be added, of case officers as well—fall into identifiable categories. The most accurate assessment and fullest understanding of which of these motives or combinations of several of them moves the agent must supplement the case officer's greater knowledge of the field of operations and detailed knowledge of the agent's history and talents, in order for him to establish and maintain maximum control of the agent. In ascending order of desirability and dependability, these categories of motives are money, compulsion, personal gain, ambition, political support, and duty.

The agent who operates only for money certainly exists; cities like Vienna, Beirut, Hong Kong, Zurich, trading places of information and centers of maneuver for both sides in the secret war, are full of men attempting to glean a living from selling their services, without regard for nationality, as agents. Obviously, however, the provider of secret services for money is all too prone to the temptation to overstate his accomplishments, if not deliberately to falsify them, both in advance of any arrangement and in practice. More importantly, he must always be assumed to be available to the highest bidder; and it is always obligatory to assume that the highest bidder will be the opposition. In periods of great confusion and violent transition, such as existed in Europe immediately following the Second World War, agents operating for money are frequently able to make a success of their work. Networks are disrupted, former relationships are altered, patterns of movement and communication are in chaos; in such circumstances a secret service, for lack of anything better, will buy an agent. Likewise, in cases of very limited actions requiring special skills or local knowledge—a guide in the mountains or jungles, a clandestine boat trip, a difficult border crossing, a particular document sought from the confidential files of a bank—a hired agent may be used. But generally a competent secret service avoids, as much as possible, the agent working for money. It is worth noting that there has seldom been a Western trial of a Soviet agent which revealed anything more than relatively trifling sums to have been involved. It is not that the Soviets are penurious in these matters; they simply observe the classic principle that a hired agent is the least desirable.[2]

Compulsion to force an individual to act as a secret agent takes many forms and is not infrequent. Blackmail is one form of such compulsion, and it is a favorite Soviet technique. It is by no means limited to sexual matters. But it is a regrettable fact—accurately understood and utilized by the Soviets—that Americans, and to a lesser extent the English, are particularly subject to blackmail in this sphere, profusely decorated as it is by a rich welter of complexes among so many Anglo-Saxons. However, at least one of my American colleagues in time past gave the right answer when confronted with the problem. Shown a series of highly compromising photographs of himself with a lady not his wife, he was threatened with transmission of the photographs to his wife and—notable Soviet deduction from American sociology—to his mother and father. His answer was brief. "Superb photography," he cried. "I'll take a dozen copies." He at least understood that if you're going to go out, it may as well be laughing; the tears are for later. In his case, interestingly enough, they weren't; neither he nor his family ever heard of the matter again.

In the period immediately following the Second World War the Soviets were able to recruit a number of agents in Europe among former fascists or collaborators, by means of either threats of revelation or promises of immunity from prosecution—depending on the individual circumstances and the extent of Communist power in the given country. Another favorite Soviet device is the holding of hostages, usually family, in order to compel service as an agent. One of the strange elements in Soviet behavior in this connection is the fact that almost uniformly they hold to promises made about members of a family held as hostages—release from imprisonment, special privileges, or even release from Soviet territory—although they are notorious for not honoring promises to the victim of compulsion himself.

It is also a fact that compulsion is not limited to the Soviets. In many Western European countries it is made perfectly clear to resident foreigners, particularly refugees in difficulties, that the necessary permits and facilities for work and residence are dependent upon their reporting regularly and fully to the intelligence authorities. And American officials are far from immune to the temptations which are offered by the possibility of having a hold over a man. Nevertheless, it stands to reason that the recruitment of an agent by compulsion is a very limited technique. An agent moved only by fear of punishment is certainly lacking in initiative —perhaps one reason the Soviets favor the technique—and is in no frame of mind to exploit his own skills or possibilities to the fullest. The most important limitation on such an agent is his lack of reliability: hidden betrayal is a constant possibility, even when the hold over the agent still exists, and it is pretty much of a certainty when the hold is relinquished. It is also fairly certain that if the agent is uncovered by the opposition he will co-operate fully with them.

The agent who is moved by prospects of personal gain is a more subtle and sophisticated variant of the agent who seeks only money. He is similar to the latter in that personal enrichment is his ultimate goal. He is dissimilar, however, in that his scope is wider since he knows and acts on the principle that secret information is power. His intent is to turn that power to personal profit. It is extremely rare that an operator of this type is so crude as to hope to extract profit from the blackmailing possibilities which secret operations may give him. He usually counts on his participation in a secret operation either to give him access to information otherwise unobtainable or to put him in a geographical location or social position, any or all of which he can turn to good account. The good account is usually expressed in money, but it may also be influence or position or merely opportunities. His intent is seldom to profit from the operation itself; on the contrary, he generally renders reasonably good service up to a point. His personal gain comes more or less as a sideline to the operation, a calculated windfall, a sort of fringe benefit. The limitations of such an agent in terms of control and dependability are obvious: since the fringe benefit—never acknowledged by him to be paramount—is to him the important part of the arrangement, his participation in the operation has an element of falsity which, if not recognized and compensated for by the case officer, can lead to serious errors. Furthermore, his mobility is affected, since he is in fact tied to objectives which are not those of the operation; most importantly, the extent of his reliability—though not necessarily his loyalty—is questionable for the same reason.

At first glance ambition seems like a strange motive to associate with secret operations. It is not readily clear what ambition can be satisfied by work in a field hidden from the public gaze and without philosophical or aesthetic rewards. It nevertheless does play a valid role, largely because of developments in the past twenty years. Prior to the Second World War the secret war was limited in scope and intensity. Its professionals were men who performed valuable services for their governments, but their influence was by and large limited. A particularly capable official might be respected and his counsel sought on a variety of problems, but in general the professional of secret operations remained a technician playing no role in the process of decision. Today, all over the world, on both sides of the Iron Curtain, that has changed. The real power which is now wielded by the upper echelons of secret operations is no less considerable for being unadvertised to the public.

In Communist countries the men who control the secret operations apparatus are high Party functionaries and participate in major decisions. It is noteworthy that as time goes on more and more of these men achieve their high Party rank via advancement in the secret operations apparatus and not the reverse. Secret operations have tended to become a career, an accepted path to governmental power. The infamous Gabor Peter, Chief of the Hungarian State

Security Authority, the AVO, and master of a reign of terror engulfing tens of thousands of victims, was a major power in the Hungarian Government until his fall; he had spent his whole adult life in the Soviet secret operations apparatus; only ten years before his fall from power he had been a Soviet line-crosser, that is, an agent maintaining continuous clandestine liaison between case officers in Soviet-controlled territory and Communist agents in enemy-controlled territory. The ultimate achievement of power is by no means limited to the control of secret operations themselves. Two British former secret operations officials with whom I collaborated in postwar operations are now increasingly influential Members of Parliament. One of President Kennedy's ambassadorial appointments was a man who made his mark in Washington through some years of outstanding work in the CIA. No one familiar with Washington in the decade of the Fifties discounts the heavy weight of the CIA complex in the important American foreign-policy decisions of the period. No one familiar with the realities of what C. Wright Mills has styled "the power elite," or what Richard Rovere has more lightly but as penetratingly dubbed "The American Establishment," discounts the pressures and influence the CIA can bring to bear in the private sectors of the American scene. In the United States the possibilities are formally recognized in a system whereby "outside" agents are brought into "inside" posts in the CIA Washington hierarchy, and vice versa, all the while advancing in their careers.

Ambition, therefore, has become a real motive for entering into secret operations. It is obviously a reliable motive for an agent—or for a case officer. Its drawback is that of all bureaucracies: the desire for advancement tends to cloud the judgment, impair initiative, and stifle the willingness to risk controversy in favor of conformity and the path of least resistance.

Political support is a highly reliable but varied and complex motive. It transcends limitations of nationality and is a prime mover in the secret war. For it to constitute a motive, however, there must be a political conviction, consciously and independently arrived at. This makes it differ markedly from patriotism—although patriotism may be an element in arriving at a political conviction. The agent or case officer moved by patriotism is not acting on the basis of an independent political conviction. He is a product of the system in which he has been raised; he accepts, in greater or lesser part, and without doubt or challenge, the tenets of that system; and he is prepared to act on them. A man moved by the desire to give or obtain political support, on the other hand, is acting on the basis of a political conviction he has arrived at personally and independently; his objective is political, but defined by himself.

In 1961 the British discovered that a Foreign Office official, formerly British Consul in Seoul at the time of the North Korean invasion of South Korea, had for ten years been acting as a Soviet agent. His motive was solely political support, arising from his conviction, arrived at while interned in North Korea, that the Soviet system deserved to win. But an outright defector is far from being the sole example of an agent so moved. It was an earnest—but unfulfilled—hope of the dissident French Army generals and colonels in Algeria, long before the attempted putsch of April 1961, to enter into working relations with the American CIA. Their motive was to gain secret American political support, and indeed they tried hard to press their viewpoint that any solution of the Algerian problem other than their own was dangerous to the interests of the United States as well as to those of France. But even the judges at the trial of General Challe and his collaborators publicly recognized that these were patriotic Frenchmen.

For the secret services of all the great powers, the most frequent opportunities for the establishment of effective espionage nets in a foreign country come from citizens of that country who seek in exchange support for their particular domestic political objectives. Most of the agents in a network I directed in Hungary immediately following the Second World War were moved solely by their hope that they could thus help to bring about effective American support against the Hungarian Communists and their Soviet backers.

But political support as a motive does not necessarily mean full collaboration. On the contrary, a case officer using agents whose motive is political support must have the clearest possible understanding of precisely what is being offered and demanded. The Polish anti-Communist emigration, for example, is composed of a variety of political groups holding widely divergent views on Polish domestic affairs. Some consider American support detrimental to their own Polish interests and therefore withhold co-operation in American secret operations. Others take an opposing view, but in differing degrees. Not even those most eager for American support, however, will collaborate in any American enterprise which involves so much as a tacit acceptance of American policy toward certain German problems, in particular that of the Polish-German boundary. On this point, all Polish exile groups are one with the Warsaw Communists in insisting on full recognition of the Oder-Neisse frontier—a problem in which the United States, by its public position in favor of postponing this question for decision in a peace treaty, appears to all Poles to be supporting in fact the West German claim for boundary revision.[3]

Notwithstanding such limitations and complexities, which result in a certain independence in the agent, an agent whose motive is political support is among the most dependable. He is often the most competent as well, since the process of personally defining his own objectives produces both self-reliance and clearheadedness. Such motivation is particularly valuable for an agent operating in his own country's secret service; he then has what the Soviets term —and lay great stress upon—political consciousness.

In the international conflicts of our times nationalism is the great wellspring of a sense of duty. As a motive for an agent, a sense of duty ranks high. It insures his reliability, and it eliminates any necessity for bargaining about objectives. Since the fulfillment of a sense of duty provides its own rewards, the agent thus moved is devoid of any falsity in his position; anonymity, lifelong if necessary, is acceptable. The sense of duty is the single great advantage of military intelligence services. In the period prior to the Second World War the American intelligence organization was limited to the Army and Navy and a few officers in the Foreign Service. These men are by and large unknown and unsung today; in almost all cases their devotion to secret operations meant a sacrifice of their careers as military, naval, or diplomatic officers—the concept of the "well-rounded" officer as being the only one meriting the posts of highest responsibility is no new invention. But these officers nonetheless performed highly valuable services for the country, and the fulfillment of their sense of duty in doing so left them, with few exceptions, personally content. An agent moved solely by a sense of duty suffers only one potential impairment. Since he accepts unquestioningly the objectives he is to serve, it is possible, and does happen, that he has no genuine understanding of these objectives. To this extent he is sometimes lacking in imagination in technique and in the fullest and best comprehension of the circumstances in which he finds himself.[4]

Nobody enters into the world of secret operations as a lark. The demands are too rigorous, the issues too weighty and complex, for a mere adventurer. Some men in secret operations have indeed a strong sense of adventure; some relish the feeling of being privy to secrets; some experience personal satisfaction at being thus able to operate outside the framework of normal order and society—but these are attributes of the life, and as reasons for adopting it they are insufficient. Some men and women even become involved in secret operations unconsciously, so to speak; a chain of circumstances ensnares them without a clear or definite realization or decision on their part. But sooner or later understanding of the nature of their work comes to them. At this point, if they go on, it is with awareness, and it is in response to the motives described above.

It is rare, however, that an agent—or case officer—is moved by only one of these motives. Such purity of motive does not correspond to the complexity of most human beings. When it does occur, it is usually for special reasons, generally of short duration, and often results in fanaticism—not a desirable quality in a field where coolheadedness and breadth of view are prime qualities. In the vast majority of cases motives are mixed, and if properly understood by the case officer the mixture can contribute to the usefulness of the agent. The value of one highly useful American agent in Latin America, for example, for years depended upon his ability to move freely among the very wealthy. The fact was that he was a social snob, addicted to a form and level of living for which he would otherwise have needed vast personal resources which he did not have. His functioning as an agent was, therefore, to some extent an example of the agent working for personal gain, in this case the connections and standard of living which his cover required. However, he had also a strong sense of duty—perhaps it compensated him for what would otherwise have been a parasitic existence —and his reliability was therefore not at all in question. Similarly, his very interest in the kind of life he led contributed to his usefulness and success in his circumstances, to an extent that could probably not have been matched by an agent moved by duty alone.

In the matter of mixed motives the Soviets do not hesitate even to attempt seemingly impossible mixtures, as, for example, the effort to inculcate, in a prospective agent whose basic motive would be compulsion, some motive of political support. In 1945 the Soviets promised safe-conducts to sixteen leaders of the non-Communist Polish Resistance for purposes of negotiation, but when the men arrived they were arrested, taken to Lubianka Prison in Mos-

cow, and ultimately tried for alleged anti-Soviet activities. Before
the ultimate decision was made to stage trials, however, there were
the usual long interrogations. Zgygniew Stypulkowski, one of the
sixteen, shows in the following extract from his account of his
interrogation the mixture of motives suggested by his interrogator
(italics are mine):

The [interrogator] had, in my opinion, in the first stage of
investigation, three tasks. The first was to get from me all the
details of my life, and of the life of my family; to judge my
intelligence and find out my weaknesses, my ambitions and my
will-power. The second task he had to perform was to put into
my mind the idea that the most important task for me was to
defend myself; to be free at any price—*that was my duty for
myself and also for my family and for my country. My country,
he said, badly needed my support, my work.* Finally he had to
destroy my mental balance by throwing me constantly from optimism to deep despair. . . . *He expressed regrets about my
family, but he insisted on knowing where my son was.* I said I did
not know. *He tried to convince me that it was my duty as a good
father to find him,* and that he would help me. . . . At 4 a.m.
one day . . . we talked about books . . . he tried to soothe
me, and succeeded. . . . Then he took my arm, looked in my
eyes and said, "I am sorry for you. I regret very much that you
are in such a bad state, and sitting here in this Lubianka Prison.
But I am very happy to be able to tell you that my Government
is not interested in having your head or in putting you in one of
the labor camps in Siberia. *On the contrary, we need you because
Russia's historical task is to rule over Europe.*"

Pretty crude, one might say. In Mr. Stypulkowski's case the
method definitely didn't work—he is today a distinguished Polish
exile leader. It has nevertheless worked in an astounding number of
cases.

The agent's motives are not only important in establishing and
maintaining the case officer-agent relationship; they also play a role
in terminating that relationship, a process and problem referred to
in American parlance as—the word never failed to strike me as
unnecessarily macabre— "disposal." There is a popular belief that
once a secret agent, always a secret agent. This is not true. There
are always men who are called upon from time to time for special

services—the CIA maintains a regular, formal list of such personnel, whose clearances are always kept up to date—but there are
equally those whose usefulness is ended with a particular operation. This sometimes poses an economic problem for the agent; it
always at least poses a security question for the case officer. In
estimating the degree of risk involved in disposing of an agent his
motives and personality will obviously play a role. As importantly,
however, this is another one of those questions where it matters
more how you do it than what you do. In brief, insight and tact are
of the essence. This is especially true of political operations, where
the consequences of termination may seem to an agent to involve
vital questions of policy as well as the purely personal question of
his living. However, even in these cases, most people don't mind a
"No," but much depends upon how it is put. About the worst way
to put it is not to put it at all.

As in the matter of recruitment, bureaucracy impedes American
practice in this sphere as well. Often arrangements are canceled
without notice or explanation, as in the case of the man who fell
afoul of the postage meter and the bookkeeper. Even less justifiable
is the tendency, all too often indulged, to frame an agent, or publicly to besmirch his reputation, as a means of disposing of him. A
ludicrous case of this sort occurred some years ago when an American agent who was also the beneficiary of one of the great American fortunes was charged with diverting funds to purchase an automobile for himself—an unprovable assertion in the particular
circumstances of his work and ridiculous on its face—and was
hastily dismissed in disgrace. As a colleague remarked at the time,
"At least the Russians wait until a man defects to our side before
they falsely accuse him of embezzlement." Slander and smear are
too often used by the CIA in these matters, and all too many
American agents have left its service dangerously embittered.

While these techniques of "disposal" may be the expected responses of moral people who, when faced with an amoral problem,
cannot understand the category and therefore behave immorally,
this is no justification for ineptitude. And not all of the ineptitude
is accompanied by immorality. One of the most violent and influential critics of the CIA in print in the United States today is a
man who worked for almost three years for the Agency on highly
important matters. The case officer handling him—himself a senior
official—had great difficulty doing so, and finally decided to abandon the operation. Instead of talking it over with the agent, he sent

a minor functionary to inform him brusquely that he was fired. The official—and the CIA—have paid needlessly and many times over in the years since in blood-inked editorials and in jeopardy to the security of some of their operations. None of this excuses the agent's petulance—but the responsibility to dispose of him smoothly was not his; it was the case officer's.

Sir Francis Walsingham's secretary oversimplified things considerably; there is much more to it than simply going out and hiring "a base fellow."

1. This seems to have become a popular story. Phillip Knightley's *The Second Oldest Profession* (New York: W. W. Norton, 1987) states, pages 286–287: "Early in 1956 CIA officers in London remember listening in dismay as an SIS representative outlined a plan to engineer a coup in Syria. . . . Following yet another meeting, this time in London, the CIA officers reported to Washington: 'After sitting around a table in a desultory fashion for an hour or two, one Englishman finally said, "I say, why don't we get old Henry up here. He knows about this." A day or two later old Henry finally showed up from down in Sussex and agreed to undertake the task, although as he said, "This will wreak havoc with the garden, you know. Just getting it into trim." ' " Knightley (whose 1968 *The Sunday Times* Insight team book on Kim Philby spoke of "Christopher Felix") footnotes the source of this story as "Unsigned article, *New Statesman*, 7 July 1978." The meeting was not in 1956, did not concern the Middle East, and the remarks were not "reported to Washington."

2. The 1986 trials in the United States of the Walker ring—Soviet agents in the U.S. Navy—revealed more sizable sums at stake (the prosecution charged receipt by the principal of some $1 million over a number of years, and of sums around $350,000 for subordinate members of the network over shorter periods). Perhaps this should be modified to say that, although generally penurious taskmasters, the Soviets are willing to accommodate greed if the circumstances give cause for confidence (i.e., the agent's hopes for pay are combined with sufficiently professional performance), and, obviously, the results are worth the cost.

3. This has been overtaken by events. West Germany's *Ostpolitik* brought the first Western concession to the Russian-dictated Polish western border (agreed to at Potsdam by the British and Americans under the impression, according to Churchill's memoirs, that the Neisse River mentioned was the eastern, not the western, branch of the river, whereas the Russians intended, and got, the western branch). The 1976 Helsinki Accords on Security and Cooperation in Europe, with the United States as a signatory, confirmed those borders (and acted, in effect, as the peace treaty

the United States sought). But later events have shown that all this has given neither Russians nor Poles contentment in Poland.

4. Much of this is still true, but as November 1986 showed, concerning dealings with Iran in the White House itself, the United States is not at all immune to the confusion arising from varying interpretations of the obligations of "duty." The duty of an officer of the American Government (including the Armed Forces) is to the Constitution. But once into the body of that document, and under the influence of the American mystique of the Presidency, many an officer will identify the President—the Commander in Chief—with the Constitution. The tradition (for the private citizen and the Executive Branch) has been that you do not refuse a request of the President. But this is custom, not law.

CHAPTER IV

The Art of Cover—I

As open warfare depends upon weapons, so does the secret war depend upon cover. Weapons are not in themselves the purpose of war, but they shield the soldier and enable him to advance to his objective—or they protect his retreat. Cover shields the secret agent from his opposition. It puts him into position to accomplish his mission. Ideally, it should also protect the mission against at least the worst consequences of the agent's being uncovered. Dealing as it does with human beings, their relations to each other, with what they feel and believe, with their habits and impressions, their insights and their actions, cover is an art.

During the Second World War an Englishman whom we shall call Geoffrey was living in Tangier. As a mildly eccentric bachelor whose small private income enabled him to indulge his liking for the climate, the good life, and a certain sense of the exotic, Geoffrey had already spent some years there. In peacetime, he was no different from the majority of other members of the Tangier British community. In other words, his cover for his work as a British intelligence agent—which he was—made sense precisely because he didn't stand out.

The outbreak of war changed that. In fact, the problem became exactly the reverse. For Geoffrey to continue and to cultivate those Axis contacts which were desired, he now had to have a cover which would isolate him from his fellow Britishers. It had to be one which would explain his continued presence in Tangier and would make him acceptable to his German, Italian, and Spanish sources. It would certainly not be sufficient for him merely to pose as a pro-Axis Englishman; it is the fate of turncoats, usually unforeseen by them, to be regarded with double suspicion by their new-found friends. There is always a counterespionage official somewhere who continues to suspect that even the most sincere defector is a double agent.

Something was needed which would lend authenticity to Geoffrey's banal—in the eyes of covert operations professionals—protestations of pro-Axis sentiments. Like most Englishmen of his class Geoffrey had had various scrapes in his past and was given to occasional hell-raising of sorts. It was decided to play up this aspect of Geoffrey; in fact, to put on the act of the Englishman going native, running to seed in his exile—a sort of Somerset Maugham China Seas character in a North African setting. But it had to be authentic; Geoffrey had to live his cover, as the professional saying has it.

He did so. He went from women to men, from alcohol to drugs, and from bad to worse. Geoffrey perfectly fitted the Nazi preconceptions of the errant, degenerate Englishman. He was not simply isolated from his compatriots. He lived in a sea of their opprobrium. In London his superiors had an easy check on his progress simply by reference to the number and the violence of denunciations of Geoffrey by Britishers—some themselves agents, but unwitting. But Geoffrey successfully accomplished his mission. He never once gave away his cover. Even after it was all over he didn't give it away. And it killed him. It wasn't just the drugs and alcohol; the hatred and contempt of people one likes can easily be physically unbearable.

Not all cover is as dramatic, or as damaging, as Geoffrey's. But all good cover owes its success to the element which made Geoffrey's so effective: it reaches into the mind of the opponent, thinks as he would think, and then creates a combination of fact and fancy, of actual arrangements and contrived impressions, which the opposing mind is prepared to believe. In all human conflict the stronger man is he who can think as his enemy thinks—can read his mind, as we say—and the victor is he who seizes the advantage this gives him. Hannibal at Cannae, Nelson on the Nile, Togo at Tsushima, Bradley in Normandy—all demonstrated and then exploited this ability in its most dramatic form. Its value is as true in covert operations as in commercial competition, in secret as in open warfare. Good cover cannot be created without this ability. The competent agent knows that, in this sense, good cover is an intimate relationship between deceiver and deceived. And in the strangely altered world of covert operations, in which real and unreal change places hourly, the deceived are necessarily both friend and foe.

Cover takes an infinite variety of forms. Certainly the commonest—and widely used by people outside of covert operations, including bankers, ambassadors, and lovers—is the large cocktail party or diplomatic reception. At these affairs, meetings and conversations which would be for one reason or another undesirable if deliberately arranged elsewhere can take place seemingly casually —under the cover of the cocktail party.

The budget of the United States Government is itself a cover. Buried in it is the budget of the Central Intelligence Agency, whose funds are nowhere publicly recorded but are instead scattered about through the appropriations of the rest of the Government in a manner that is reportedly proof against even the closest scrutiny. In other words, the Central Intelligence Agency receives its appropriations under the cover of the Federal Budget.

Cover may be no more than a story. The cover story is most frequently used to explain the visible evidences of a clandestine operation or to provide an explanation when an operation encounters difficulties. The U-2 flights, for example, operated—at least on their own bases—under cover of meteorological research. When the Soviets protested what turned out to be Powers's violation of their frontiers, a previously prepared cover story was given out by the NASA, stating that these were meteorological research flights and that on this occasion the pilot reported having difficulty with his oxygen equipment while on a triangular flight course within Turkey, one leg of which brought him close to the Soviet border. The story went on to state that it was therefore assumed that the pilot lost consciousness and, while unconscious, inadvertently crossed the Soviet border.

The failure of this cover story illustrates—among other things—several points about cover stories in general: they should not be too precise or too detailed, and they should not be forthcoming too quickly or all at once.

When Bulganin and Khrushchev paid their official visit to Great Britain aboard a Soviet heavy cruiser, there was great Western interest in the ship itself. In the midst of the visit the Russians protested that the ship had been attacked in Portsmouth Harbor by a frogman. Whatever was the true mission of Commander Crabbe, the British Admiralty's underwater expert, it was clear from the Soviet protest at the time, and from the Commander's disappearance, that the Russians had caught him. British official announcements on the subject were quite some time in coming. When they came, they came piecemeal. First there was an announcement about the mysterious disappearance of a man who had registered at a Portsmouth hotel. It was some time before a further announcement gave his name. Then a newspaper reporter uncovered the fact that he had arrived in Portsmouth with underwater diving equipment. To this there was an official announcement, eventually, that investigation showed Commander Crabbe occasionally did some research on underwater work for the Admiralty, under contract. This was followed, later, by a denial that Commander Crabbe had been on official business when he visited Portsmouth, and that was the last officially spoken on the subject. Throughout all these statements there was an air of vagueness, implying alternatively that Commander Crabbe didn't exist or that he was such a tremendous enthusiast for underwater diving that it was highly probable he had gone to Portsmouth on his own for several days of his favorite sport.

To be too precise in a cover story qualitatively increases the chances of repudiation of the story; to be too detailed increases those chances quantitatively. To speak out too fast is to show your hand before you know all you can about what your opponent is holding in his; and to tell all in one bleat eliminates your chances to improvise as the situation develops. The proof of this British pudding lay in the fact that the Soviet visit went on to its planned completion, and, following their single protest, the Russians dropped the matter.

It is typical of the peculiar combination of drama and irony characterizing covert operations that, at the same time that Commander Crabbe was being discovered by the Russian watch aboard the *Sverdlovsk* in Portsmouth Harbor,[1] a Soviet espionage ring was functioning smoothly ashore in the British Underwater Detection Establishment at Portland. The principal agents were a couple who conducted their operations under the cover of a bookshop; they were well and favorably known in the neighborhood where they lived. They were uncovered and arrested only years later, in 1961. And when this finally occurred there was considerable doubt as to their true nationality and identity. Their personal cover of false identities and Canadian citizenship held up even for a time after their arrest, until American authorities came forward with a positive identification of them as American citizens with past records of Communist activity in the United States.

This couple, the Cohens—alias Kroger—lived in a quiet residential section in a house in which was found, after their arrest, a radio transmitter and other clandestine equipment. In fact, the only proof of their involvement in espionage was radio signals from the house to the Moscow area. They themselves never received documents from the sub-agents working at the Portland Naval Base. These were transmitted to the Cohens by a cut-out who was in due course brought under British security surveillance. Even after arrest, however, the Cohens produced a cover story. It was that they had lent their house several times in their absence—as in fact they had—to friends, among them the cut-out, and they denied knowledge of the hidden equipment or of those friends' activities, or indeed any responsibility for them.

The effectiveness of the Cohens' cover story was of a very high order. It endured for a considerable time by professional standards, and even continued to confuse the investigators after the couple's activities had been revealed. (The Cohens' true identity was not uncovered until about a month after their arrest; the true identity and nationality of the cut-out—a Soviet citizen—was not actually announced until some ten months after his arrest.) Furthermore, it was not a defect in the cover which destroyed the operation; it was the matter of those radio signals. The camouflage and detection of radio signals is a separate, highly technical aspect of covert operations. Furthermore, the effectiveness of the final cover story, given after their arrest, is not to be measured by the fact that the court, in convicting and sentencing them for espionage, rejected it. Its effectiveness is more properly measured by the extent to which

other agents and activities of their group were protected by the
story and its accompanying delays and confusion. And who knows
who and what these other agents and activities were? Moscow
does; London and Washington do not. Who can properly estimate
the true extent of the defeat represented by the arrest of the Cohens? Only Moscow can. This is good cover at work.

Cover is not created by recourse to a theatrical supply house.
Disguise is rarely feasible. Exceptions always exist, of course, and
the outstanding one in my experience is a non-mustachioed British
general who periodically operates disguised as a woman. As he
once said to me, "Not flashily attractive, you understand, but not
motherly either. Just chic, don't you know."

In covert operations, including cover itself, that which is false is
called notional. The nonexistent intelligence network and false reports created for his superiors in London by the hero of Graham
Greene's *Our Man in Havana* were notional—and are a far from
rare occurrence in espionage. An entire U.S. operation was once
financed by a notional oil millionaire, for whom a life history and
personality, complete with foibles and eccentricities—including his
adamant refusal to see persons whom he was aiding financially—
had to be created.

That which is true is called legitimate. (This word has been
extended into a somewhat dubious phrase used by CIA insiders to
describe someone not in the business, as "Oh, he's legitimate.")[2]

The best cover is that which contains the least notional and the
maximum possible legitimate material. Probably one of the most
dramatically successful covert operations of modern times was the
Soviet espionage ring in prewar Manchuria and Japan headed by
Richard Sorge, who operated as a German journalist. Everything
about Sorge's cover was legitimate; its sole notional feature was his
explanation of his whereabouts in the years when he had actually
been living and training in the Soviet Union. He set something of a
record in the realm of cover by successfully maintaining his without a single respite for nine years. In his case, as in the Cohens', his
arrest was not due to the breakdown of his cover, but to his radio
transmissions to the Soviet Union.

Aside from the mission itself and the circumstances in which it
is to be accomplished, the most important items in creating cover
are the history, talents, and personality of the agent himself. An
agent without journalistic background cannot use journalistic

cover. The saying, "Do not send a boy to do a man's job," has a literal meaning in the art of cover.

During the Occupation of Germany, we sent a man there whose cover was a job in one of the numerous Occupation Government offices. More than that, however, it was essential to his mission that he appear to be a low-level, obscure employee, although he was in fact a high-level covert operations official with considerable authority (and is today a high official of the U.S. Government in a quite "legitimate" field). We wanted no attention drawn to him which would interest Soviet agents in his activities or which would make it difficult for our own agents to contact him quietly. In brief, we had left him his true identity, but we had given him a notional personality. As it turned out, his notional personality was inescapably in conflict with his true personality and talents. He hadn't been in Germany more than a few months when our mistake became obvious. Driving about in a large red convertible, he was soon immersed in every American group activity up and down the Rhine. He was president of the American Ski Club, he was a trustee of the American Church, his wife was president of the American Women's Club, his office was one of the liveliest in Germany, and his house was overrun with people gaily planning charity bazaars and Hallowe'en dances. We wanted a self-effacing, invisible man; we got a prominent community leader. The mistake could probably have been avoided if we had attached more importance to the fact that he had been president of the student body at his university.

Perfect cover is an ideal, rarely achieved in practice. Necessity imposes something less than perfection, and so it is sometimes necessary to resort to such a dangerous device as a notional identity. Notional identities obviously depend upon the histrionic ability of the agent and his capacity to believe, think, eat, sleep, and live his false identity. The famous Sorge, although operating under his own identity, nonetheless possessed this capacity to a high degree. A heavy drinker, he one night ran his motorcycle into the wall of the American Embassy in Tokyo. Taken to a hospital, he emerged from a coma some days later, but was delirious for several more days. Not once, even in his delirium, did he ever say anything which could arouse the slightest suspicion—a fact respectfully noted in his report by the Japanese official who finally tracked him down.

In the world in which we now live, notional identity also depends upon the forger. All covert services of the great powers maintain special offices for the forgery of documents and seals of all kinds. (This is one reason the U.S. Department of State gets very upset when American tourists lose their passports.) Immediately after the Second World War, before the U.S. had adequate facilities for forgery, American operations depended heavily upon private enterprise in this field. I had a man in Rome who for $500 would deliver a Venezuelan passport which he proudly said was "valid anywhere, Signor—except Venezuela." I also had a Hungarian refugee in Salzburg who, when he finally received his visa to the U.S., with which I had been able to give him some help, gratefully delivered to me his entire remaining stock, which included identity documents and border guard seals for every country in Eastern Europe except Poland and the Soviet Union itself. Unfortunately, my Salzburg friend was not available when I once had to move an agent through the Soviet Zone of Austria. It fell to me to forge the name and date on an expired Soviet pass—the forgery was nothing compared to the problem of erasure.

Cover cannot always be created quickly in a desirable form. It is often necessary to resort to the process known as building cover, which is nothing more than engaging in actions which will increase the plausibility of the cover. I once sent a man wandering aimlessly about Europe for eight months looking for just the right place to live, so that his final choice—a particular house in a particular city —would not seem prearranged.

Cover is not a durable commodity. By its very nature some people have to be privy to the secret—to them cover is revealed, meaning disclosed under authorization—and obviously the more people who know, the greater danger of the cover being blown—meaning discovered or unauthorizedly disclosed. (It is this fact which causes cover to be described as light or deep; obviously, the fewer persons to whom the cover is revealed, the deeper the cover.) The fundamental rule in all cover arrangements is that if cover is endangered, the operation is suspended until cover can be rebuilt or new cover developed. I once lost five urgent weeks obeying this rule.

Assigned temporarily to a foreign capital, my work necessitated my presence in one office, but my cover required my presence in another. This was solved by revealing the cover to one secretary in the cover office, who was supposed to take all my calls, state that I was out, and then give me the message where I was really working. When the inevitable happened and the secretary fell ill, her temporary replacement took a call for me with the cheery remark, "Oh, he doesn't work here. He just comes in and picks up his mail occasionally." As the caller was a Belgian diplomat, it was decided to suspend the operation temporarily and rebuild the cover by the simple expedient of having me spend a suitable time in the cover office. So I spent five empty weeks there, lunching twice during the period with the Belgian diplomat and making sure that on both occasions he came to the office to pick me up.

At that I fared better than a colleague in neutral Turkey during the Second World War. A former journalist, he was working for General Donovan's organization in its formative days, when it was still the Office of the Coordinator of Information. My colleague showed up in Istanbul as a journalist. His second morning there, he came down to breakfast at his hotel to find the Turkish police awaiting him. They simply sat him down in a corner of the lobby and asked, "What is your connection with General Donovan?" After giving him plenty of time to protest that he was a journalist, had previously been in Turkey as a journalist, as they well knew, and had no connection with General Donovan, the police quietly handed him a long telegram. It was addressed to my colleague and was composed entirely of five-letter code groups, except for the signature which succinctly read, "Donovan, Coordinator of Information." Within an hour he was on the train to the Syrian border, with plenty of time to visualize a new secretary in Washington, eager to please, obeying quite literally the order to "get that off to him in Istanbul right away."

The Turks can scarcely be blamed for being alert, even nervous. Only six months before, the British Minister to Bulgaria had arrived at the same hotel, with his entire staff, following the rupture of British-Bulgarian diplomatic relations. When the British diplomatic baggage was all finally assembled in the lobby, at least one part of it—to the mortification of one Britisher a bit negligent about technicalities—exploded and wrecked the place. It had only just been repaired when my colleague came to town.

On occasion, even blowing cover can be—don't anyone lose the thread here—part of cover. I once encountered an Englishman in Greece during the Civil War whom I had good reason to suspect was a covert agent—and he the same of me. He mentioned that he was working in a bank, and when I politely asked which one, he left in confusion. He came back to the same bar the next day—it's true what they say about some bars—and glancing at a piece of paper, said proudly, "About that bank. It's the Royal Corinthian Island and Specie Bank." (Or some such obvious concoction.) An intramural joke, of course—provided we were working to the same end. But if his mission was also to uncover and report on our activities, his cover could logically include partially blowing it to us to inspire our confidence. This kind of non-elevating thinking is necessary in the part of cover, but it is a poor agent who shows he is engaged in it. People do get suspicious, particularly of suspicion.

1. In March 1963, Mr. Larry Cott, of Honolulu, Hawaii, kindly corrected me—in what he politely called "minor errors," which "someone could use to try to challenge your overall accuracy"—as follows: "In the Commander Crabbe [other authors spell this Crabb] incident you have Bulganin and Khrushchev arriving aboard the cruiser *Sverdlovsk*. If memory serves, B & K came in the cruiser *Ordzhonikidze*, and she was the ship involved in the underwater incident. *Sverdlovsk* visited England, but that was in June 1953 at Spithead, Southampton, for the naval review following the Queen's Coronation. *Sverdlovsk* aroused considerable interest because she steamed into harbor, backed down at her assigned berth, put over her chain to the buoy and secured from mooring in something like eleven minutes. It was an impressive display of seamanship." Both Mr. Cott and I indulged in another error: the proper name of *Sverdlovsk* was *Sverdlov*.

2. I assume the jargon in this as in other respects has probably changed in the past twenty-five years.

CHAPTER V

The Art of Cover—II

The lone agent, operating under a personal cover, à la E. Phillips Oppenheim, is certainly not extinct, but he is fast becoming an anachronism. In a world of organization men, the best cover for an agent is to be an organization man. The adventurous explorer has been converted into an executive of a large travel agency; the writer in quest of stories and color has been replaced by the administrative director of a large private educational mission abroad; the independently wealthy expatriate with friends in high places everywhere has become the vice-president of a great corporation; and—alas!—Mata Hari works from 9 to 5 as a research assistant on the staff of a mass-circulation magazine.

This melancholy development is known as organizational cover. At the very outset of developing organizational cover a vital decision must be made. This is whether or not the use of the organization as cover will be revealed to one or more responsible officers of the organization itself. General practice is to try to sanction the arrangement wherever possible. This is a practical matter, since an agent bound by the full-time work requirements of an American company is pretty well hamstrung in his ability to do anything else. It also is preventive medicine against possible future embarrassment, of a type I know from experience.

After a particularly grueling two-year stint, I arranged to take a brief respite in the form of an overt and "legitimate" six months' job in an eminently "legitimate" Government office in Europe. My chief took an instant dislike to me since, as I eventually discovered, he suspected that I was there to engage in skulduggery beyond his control, and most likely to report on him. With patient effort and some show of frankness I finally began to ease his suspicions, and life became a little more restful. At this moment, unfortunately, my successor in my previous operation ran into some trouble which he felt warranted a message to me. In it came, addressed to me via my chief, but in a code which he could not break. The temperature in his office as he handed me the telegram made me think I was picking up my mail in the deep freeze. I apologized, went to my office, deciphered the message, composed a reply including the request that I be left alone, enciphered it, and then returned to the deep freeze to ask that he transmit the reply. I explained what had happened, without going into detail, reassured him as best I could, guaranteed it wouldn't happen again, and finally felt that he was mollified. Even more unfortunately, my restful life had softened my brain so that, while I deciphered well enough, I had forgotten how to encipher. My message was unreadable at the other end. Back came another message, by the same channels as the first. Protesting my innocence, I knew what George Washington would feel like if, returning to life and remembering that he hadn't chopped down the cherry tree, he had to read American history books. As I was innocent nothing was lost but my brief respite. However, much could be lost by an agent at a crucial point in his operations whose unwelcome true status was uncovered by his superiors in the organization. And their feeling of having been tricked would be fairly sure to make his true status unwelcome.

Most organizations take a co-operative and responsible view of these activities. However, there are some which, either because of the nature of their work or their vulnerability to charges of providing organizational cover or simply because they do not agree with covert operations in principle, will not sanction such arrangements.

The Russians have serious problems of their own in this field. Since almost all activity in the Soviet Union, and certainly all Soviet foreign activity, is organized and directed by the state, no Soviet agency can provide plausible organizational cover. Consequently, they most often use foreign organizations, obviously without sanction. It is this which explains their inability to resist the temptation offered by the UN as cover for some of their agents.

Cover is by no means confined to the problems of individual agents or of espionage operations, or to the concoction of stories to explain mishaps. More effort is probably expended today—at least by the Soviet Union and the United States—on cover organizations than on single agent cover. Cover organizations—let the reader beware—are not to be confused with organizational cover.

In contrast to organizational cover, which uses legitimate agencies for cover purposes, cover organizations exist solely for the purpose of providing cover. They are an enabling and protective device, usually for large-scale operations. Their great advantage lies in the fact that, once established, no further cover for the individual agents who make up the organization is necessary. In fact, a great many people who need not even know that they are functioning as agents can be brought into an operation. The purpose is simply to set in motion, under ostensibly independent auspices, activities for which the government does not wish to avow responsibility. It is not, therefore, the activities themselves which are covered, but only the link between them and the government.

Cover organizations are usually an expensive matter. Furthermore, they are, for the most part, suited only to political or paramilitary operations and not to espionage. Consequently, they are usually reserved for activities which are direct expressions of a government's foreign policy. They are infinitely more complicated than the Israeli Government's feeble attempt in 1960 to disguise a nuclear energy establishment by the simple statement that it was a textile plant.

Cover organizations are no new device. Americans can reflect on the historical fact that American independence is in large measure due to French ingenuity and success with one cover organization. In 1777 Louis XVI was persuaded by his ministers that it should be French policy to support the fight of the American colonists for independence from Great Britain. The French Government, however, was not yet prepared to put such a policy into effect openly. While Lafayette and scores of other young French officers, inspired by libertarian sentiments, volunteered for service with the Continental Army, this was by no means the type of significant aid that was needed or that the French Government contemplated.

The answer was found in the person of Pierre Auguste Caron de Beaumarchais, poet and playwright, author of *Figaro* and a man well known for his espousal of the ideas of the Enlightenment. Beaumarchais, a wealthy man, was granted letters patent to found a private trading firm in Paris, under the name of Hortalez and Company. This firm promptly entered exclusively and actively into the promotion of North American trade. It was well equipped for the purpose by the presence among the principals of Silas Deane—whose qualifications, besides being an American, were that he was an agent of the Continental Congress. The doors of the French Treasury and of the French arsenals were quietly opened to Hortalez and Company, and the firm forwarded on to America vast and decisive quantities of arms, munitions, textiles—and money. Among many other things, these supplies included nine-tenths of the arms and munitions used by the Americans at the Battle of Saratoga. (It is sad to be obliged to add that Beaumarchais, who was himself out of pocket for considerable expenses, was eventually forced to protracted litigation to recover these sums. The case was only solved in 1835, when the American Congress finally reimbursed his heirs.)

The range of cover organizations is vast. They embrace activities in every corner of the globe—save for that cold exception to the Cold War, Antarctica. They exist in all fields of international life: political movements, youth organizations, religious groups, the arts, publishing, education, labor, professional societies of all kinds, banks, foundations, and friendship societies. Some are very

large organizations, playing a genuine role in their particular fields.
Others are merely support agencies, usually for funding purposes;
people everywhere are interested in money, where it comes from
and how much, to the extent that the transmission and provision of
funds is one of the most difficult aspects of covert operations. Some
are, by now, long-established, permanent features of the international scene. Others come into existence for a specific, limited purpose and are disbanded when their function is accomplished.

Some are highly successful in their maintenance of cover and
indistinguishable from genuine institutions; others carry with them
an aura of falsity. One significant feature of the present situation is
that this aura of falsity does not affect the value of the organization; even the opposition accepts the legend of the cover since it
accords with their interests. One very large American cover organization, in existence for some years now, is well known by everyone in its field to be a Government operation, even though it cannot be proved. Nevertheless, on the Western side this is accepted
and the cover honored because it serves a useful co-ordinating
function, and it is accepted on the Soviet side because it is recognized as a major Western gambit, for the abandonment of which a
price will have to be paid—the problem on both sides is how much.

A general acceptance of transparency in cover organizations is a
fair indication of international tension and of a situation of crisis.
During the Greek Civil War I journeyed to Lake Prespa, a large
body of water in the middle of which the Greek, Albanian, and
Yugoslav borders intersect. At that particular moment in history
the Yugoslavs were still aiding the Greek Communists, as were the
Albanians, but the Yugoslavs and Albanians were on bad terms
due to the Tito-Stalin rupture, and the Greeks, except for the Communists, were obviously hostile to both the Yugoslavs and the Albanians. In addition, there was considerable intrigue among the
Greek Communist rebels, as pro-Yugoslav and pro-Cominform
agents sought to sway them in that dispute.

By day the lake was an idyl of mountain beauty. The still waters
lay undisturbed, and the mountains rose blue and brown in the
hazy sunlight. Nothing moved. But when darkness fell, hell broke
loose.

From the north shore of the lake the put-put of a Yugoslav boat
heading for Greece or Albania could be heard; and then from the
western Albanian shore more boats would put out; and finally,
traffic of all factions would embark from the Greek southern shore.

A machine gun would open up; rifle fire crackled all around the lake and on the waters. Tracers would tell the direction of fire, but not who was firing at whom. An occasional flare would give just enough light to distinguish a boat, but nothing about its occupants. A respite meant everybody was landing successfully, but it would be followed by even more vigorous boating and shooting. Lake Prespa was the Grand Central Station of secret agent movements of Southeastern Europe. The trouble was that all the commuters were armed and had nervous trigger fingers.

Into this muddle of peace and war the British covert services had sent a mission to check on the traffic and perhaps do a little commuting of their own. For some obscure reason of propriety, London had decided to cover the mission as being a British Consulate at a town near, but not on, the lake. For me to proceed further on my journey it was necessary for me to have my passport stamped by the Consulate. I waited one entire day and never saw a soul. On the second day, late in the afternoon, the "Consular" staff came in to replenish their ammunition. Roaring up in a jeep, as fine a "Consular" group of fighting men as I have ever seen entered the Consulate, armed to the teeth. When I explained my need, the "Consul" looked blank. "Jarvis," he called out, "where's that blasted Consulate seal? I saw it a couple of weeks ago." Jarvis, chewing on some tinned beef, went to a corner piled high with heavy wooden cases. "In with the Sten ammo, I think," he muttered.

When I had my passport duly stamped, and had brushed Jarvis's corned beef out of it, I congratulated the "Consul" on his cover. "Hah!" he said. "We haven't got time for that in this show. They'd have done better to make this a branch Naval Attaché's office and send us a gunboat—with searchlights." With that, he and his "Consular" staff were off to the lake for a night's work. The "Consul" was right. The secret war had become a shooting war, and nobody really cared about his cover. Nevertheless, this indifference to cover can only be indulged in by the West in times and areas of gravest crisis. It is one of the seeming inequities of the secret war today that, in general, world public opinion does not permit such transparency in Western political cover organizations while it is often indifferent to such transparency in Soviet political cover arrangements.

To many this indifference to the unmasking of Soviet political cover, this seeming inequity in judging Soviet and American actions, is an affront. At best they regard it as the mark of deceived or misguided minds, or Communist dupes. To be sure, this is sometimes the case. But I personally believe, on the basis of not inconsiderable experience, that this is a very defeatist view of our situation. If it is true that, for example, the millions of supporters of the Communist Peace Campaign were all, or even a majority, Communist dupes, or that everyone who agitates against nuclear testing or nuclear warfare is a Communist dupe, then we may as well throw in the towel throughout the rest of the world. The dupes have us badly outnumbered.

But I do not believe that is the case. The Peace Campaign was launched initially, in 1948, as a Soviet cover organization aimed at reinforcing Soviet policy concerning Western defense. The U.S. Government reacted with statement after statement showing conclusively that this was a Soviet initiative, in support of Soviet foreign policy. The technique didn't work. The Campaign succeeded beyond the Russians' fondest hopes, even to the extent that years later, when they intervened in Hungary, they had to pay a high price in loss of prestige with the very people they had won in the Campaign. In brief, people were indifferent to the unmasking of the Peace Campaign as a Soviet initiative. I do not believe it was because they were dupes; I believe it was because people—in this specific issue—liked what was offered. In large areas of the world the mere word "Communist" did not—and does not today—automatically close people's minds to the subject matter. The fundamental question is, what is being offered? And because we failed to understand this, we were outmaneuvered on this occasion.[1]

Very well, it will be said, but then why are we the Americans, required at the same time to be so careful about our cover? To my mind, the answer is a double one. For the first part, it is simply that if we come up with as good an idea as the Peace Campaign we won't have to worry too much about our cover. The second part is what I believe to be the fact that more people than we realize judge the Soviet Union and the West, particularly the United States, on our own estimates of ourselves. The Soviets do not pretend to a distinction between public and private initiative in foreign affairs. People accept this and ask only, what is being offered? But the West claims there are, or should be, large areas of private initiative, including foreign relations in the broadest sense, in a well-ordered society. People assume we practice what we preach. More sophisticated opinion, aware of our problems and needs, realizes we cannot always, in this period of conflict, do so. Naïve opinion censures us for the unmasking of our cover; more sophisticated opinion merely expects our cover arrangements, by and large, to hold up. In short, we are not being unfairly penalized in the secret war; we are merely paying a price for what we say we believe in.

It is possible that political cover organizations are more numerous today on the Western than on the Soviet side. This is not to be taken as an indication of greater skulduggery on our part. On the contrary, the proliferation of such organizations in the West is a measure of the intensity of the secret war and of Soviet aggression. It is, encouragingly, a barometer of our response in that conflict.

Some observers hold that, from the point of view of international relations, the Soviet Government, and its imitators, are a cover for the Russian Communist Party—whose name, Vsesoyuznaya Kommunisticheskaya Partiya (Bolshevikov), All-Union Communist Party (of Bolsheviks), contains nothing except the language to label it as Russian. From the viewpoint of cover experts, the purpose of this cover is not secrecy; it is to obtain international privileges, immunities, and powers to which a political party has never before been entitled. In other words, it launches on the international scene, as the equal of governments, what was a domestic political party. Political parties are instruments for advancing particular viewpoints on the organization of society. A government which is merely a cover for a political party is, in its international relations, moved to interfere in its neighbors' forms of organization of their societies. This is the ideological war.[2]

In nations with more than a single political party, it is only the duly elected government which can act nationally and internationally. Consequently, the rallying of democratic public opinion to action short of war is a difficult process. It can really be accomplished today, on the necessary scale, only by government. Furthermore, in a world of acute tension, private organizations cannot be permitted to undertake international actions which affect the relations between states and the balance of power. Such actions must be reserved to governments. However, many such actions, particularly political, would lose their effectiveness internationally if it was known that the action was sponsored and directed by a foreign government. Or the action might, if undertaken overtly by the government, risk bringing into play opposing forces which would either defeat the action or seriously alter the international political balance. For the West, the answer to this dilemma is the cover organization. It is a means for organizing and utilizing valuable but diverse public opinion in the common national or international interest.

Once this problem is understood, the necessity and usefulness to the West of the cover organization becomes clear. It can also be seen that the West is better equipped in this game, by reason of its greater variety of views and interests, than the Soviet Union. However, this is not necessarily comforting news, for whatever their problems with organizational cover and with cover organization, the Russians suffer no impairment of their ability to exploit another important and common variety of cover for political operations—the front organization.

The difference between cover and front organizations is the subject of some argument among professionals. Cover experts agree that differences exist, but they are often blurred in practice. Many organizations contain features of both, and some cover organizations grow into fronts, and vice versa. Briefly, however, a front organization goes a step or two beyond a cover organization in complexity. Whereas a cover organization exists to mask government involvement in an activity, a front organization hides not only the government involvement, but also the true purpose of that involvement.

Let us suppose that it was suddenly reported from Antarctica that penguins can talk—Penguinese, an ancient Romance language —and have certain plans of their own for the continent. A delegation of Penguins would be seated in the UN, and the powers interested in Antarctica would agree that, pending further discussion and negotiation with the Penguins, the present treaty renouncing national territorial claims on Antarctica would continue to be honored.

The first thing that would happen would be the simultaneous establishment of (1) a Soviet-Penguin Friendship Society—Antarctic Branch headed by four Penguin Communists secretly trained at the Soviet South Polar station at Mirny; (2) the Royal Society of Penguin Lovers—Honorary President, Lady Florabella Ffinch-Hyde, noted linguist and bird-watcher; (3) The Penguin Educational and Development Corporation—a private, nonprofit New York corporation headed by a retired Admiral who commanded the last four expeditions to Antarctica; and (4) La Société Francaise pour la Diffusion de la Culture parmi les Oiseaux Parlants—Monsieur le Président, Guy Pamplemousse, former Socialist Governor-General of Indochina and myna bird collector. All cover organizations.

When interest in Antarctica was at its height, the cover organizations were stumbling over each other's missions to the Penguins, and a summit conference had agreed to keep the Cold War out of Antarctica, a Uruguayan named Schmidt would suddenly issue a call for the founding of an International Union of Antarctic Veterans (IUAV)—purposes: pensions for Antarctic veterans, the exchange of reminiscences among Antarctic veterans, and the provision to the public of factually objective information about Antarctica. The organization would be formed, and at its first Annual Congress, held in Tahiti, the Union would send greetings to its Penguin friends, call on the UN to demand pensions for the membership, and authorize the publication in Greek, Tamil, Swahili, and Guarani of fourteen booklets on life in Antarctica. At the second Annual Congress, held in Accra, Ghana, Schmidt, by now permanent Secretary-General, would point out that no pensions had yet been granted, but that the booklets had sold like hotcakes, and he therefore proposed to distribute a dividend to the membership. Proposal warmly accepted, and Schmidt's suggested resolution on keeping the Cold War out of Antarctica passed unanimously. Fifty-eight additional booklets authorized, this time Urdu, Tibetan, and Gaelic being added to the list of languages.

At the third Annual Congress, held in an oasis in Baluchistan, Schmidt would deliver a ringing speech about pensions, noting that the membership was pretty seedily dressed this time—except for the members from the Soviet Union and the People's Democracies. Sitting down without comment on how the year's booklets had gone, or any mention of a dividend, he would be succeeded as speaker by a Norwegian whaler who had only learned to read the year before by setting type on the booklets. Consequently, he would read his address in broadly accented Swahili, to the gratification of various African members. Translation would show that it was a fiery resolution condemning United States imperialism in Antarctica. Before the resolution could be brought to a vote, Schmidt would deliver a report on the year's activities, showing booklet sales at an all-time high, and announce a dividend, payable at the close of the Congress. The resolution, strengthened from the floor, would then pass by a large majority—and be headline news all over the world the next day. A Penguinese edition of *Pravda*, carrying the resolution on page 1, would be distributed free by the Soviet-Penguin Friendship Society in Antarctica.

Only *The New York Times* would report—besides the resolution on page 4—the interesting information, on page 97, that the American membership, and most of the British and French members, had walked out of the Union, and borrowing carfare home, had established the Free International Union of Veterans of the Antarctic (FIUVA), with headquarters in Arkansas. It would also carry the new organization's announcement that investigation showed that Schmidt, although a Uruguayan, had a Swiss grandmother who had been Lenin's laundress in Zurich in 1912. Furthermore, except for eight library sales and three private purchases of the Greek editions, all of the booklets, to the tune of 1,480,000 copies, had been purchased by SOVEX-IMPORT and used as fill in the Aswan High Dam. FIUVA's announcement would also charge that IUAV was a Soviet front organization. They would be right.

This story—which, except for the Penguins, is by no means as ridiculous as it sounds—illustrates an important difference between cover organizations and front organizations. In a cover organization most of the responsible personnel are aware of the true nature of the organization—of the link to government which is being hidden. In a front organization there may be relatively few of the leading personnel who know; their link to government is hidden—frequently by personal cover—and their true mission is carried out behind the front of the organization's ordinary functions, and behind the front provided by the unwitting personnel.

To some persons all of this has an unsettling ring to it. I know of directors of cover organizations who have resigned on learning officially that they were serving a government-financed and directed group, even though, on accepting appointment, they heartily approved the organization's aims and activities. With all due respect for the scruples and principles which have moved such people, I personally believe that their viewpoint is outmoded by events and by urgent needs. I myself join in their longing and nostalgia for the private initiative, independence, and spontaneity of the nineteenth-century ideal. But, after all, that same ideal, in allegedly more halcyon days, encompassed the Panamanian Revolution, which produced both Panama and the Panama Canal, and for which the United States Congress ultimately paid an indemnity of $8,000,000 to Colombia, the Revolution having been managed by the New York law firm of Sullivan and Cromwell under a fee from the U.S. Government—then without a CIA.

We live in a period of sharp conflict in which, for the moment, the driving forces are two great centers of power. Both powers proclaim their desire to avoid open conflict of the kind which would call into play the ultimate weapons; but they also for the moment feel obliged to continue steps to maintain or gain overt military advantage. Steps of this sort such as nuclear testing are bad enough, but they are hostile only implicitly and by indirection. A step such as the Soviets' 1962 attempt to station their missiles in Cuba, however, was an act of overt, direct hostility; it could barely be dignified as even clandestine, and that only to the point of a rashness which suddenly faced humanity with destruction. It is this kind of direct and overtly hostile confrontation of the powers, whether in Cuba, Berlin, or elsewhere, which covert operations— competently conducted, of course—are historically designed to avoid. To this extent—and in more than one sense—we might all pray for more and better cover.[3]

1. I have seen no evidence in the past twenty-five years suggesting that this is not still the case.

2. The late Dr. Graham Stuart, Professor of Political Science and International Relations at Stanford (under whom I had studied in the late 1930's), wrote me in 1963 that he felt this paragraph embodied the crux of the problem of the Soviet Union and the international community. He did not (nor did I in the paragraph) mention China. China too has a government that is merely a cover for a political party, and while the Chinese have in the past interfered widely abroad (cf. Zanzibar, 1964), their effectiveness seems limited by their vast domestic problems. With increased economic development and strength the Chinese may, of course, assume as troublesome an international role as the Russians have played for six decades now. Nevertheless, and notwithstanding Professor Stuart, I feel that something should be added to the formulation here. The fact is that there are one-party governments that are not internationally disruptive, or not seriously so. What is missing in the formulation, therefore, is the combination of one-party government with messianic zeal and nationalistic expansionism. The Russia of the Tsars had an abundance of the latter two characteristics (cf. "The Third Rome"), which contributed to more than two centuries of territorial conquest. That territorial expansion only became international disruptiveness on a worldwide scale, however, when the ingredient of the Bolshevik Party's seizure of the Russian Government was *added* to the preexisting recipe of messianic impulse and hegemonic ambitions.

3. There seems to have.been a sea change in this respect since the 1960's. The Cubans, as surrogates for the Russians, acted openly in Angola from 1975 on, as did the Russians themselves in Afghanistan in 1979 and subsequently. The response of the United States in both Angola and Afghanistan, frequently debated openly in the Congress, cannot be qualified as covert, any more than can the Reagan Administration's open embrace of the Nicaraguan "contras." Sometimes this kind of flouting of good sense on both sides is deliberate: the justification is the desire "to send a signal" to the other side. A properly designed covert "signal" is, of course, just as effective as open bellicosity (assuming that the "signal" is intended for the other side, and not just to enhance domestic appearances).

CHAPTER VI

The Open-faced American

While cover is an art it is also an American weakness. The weakness is both conscious and unconscious. Its conscious aspect is summed up in the reaction of a young and able Harvard graduate whom I had employed for a covert operation in the Mediterranean area. His cover was to be a minor starting clerkship in a shipping firm. When this had been explained to him, he responded, in tones of shocked protest, "But you've got to give a man a cover he can be proud of!"

The unconscious aspect is typified in the experience of a New York corporation executive with whom I was once discussing these problems. A cultivated and elegant man, he was once a guest in a London club. He repaired his first afternoon to the steam room, where he found himself alone and, except for wisps of steam, completely without "cover." He was, he thought, indistinguishable from any Britisher in a steam bath. A club member, a total stranger, entered and, sitting down next to my friend, said, without preliminaries of any kind, "I say, so nice to have an American here."

In the conscious department we must recognize the influence of the Horatio Alger legend and its modern-day Organization Man version. Success is not its sole component; success must also be visible, even conspicuous. The American dream can be a serious handicap to the American agent. Most Americans in the CIA view their work as a career. Its ultimate rewards for them are certainly not financial; but they are matters of recognition, of advancement in the hierarchy, and of power and influence as a high Government official. Very few men are willing to spend long years under cover outside of the Government; the few who do so are remarkable.

I refrain from any estimate of the number of Americans who might be willing to undertake an assignment similar to that of Rudolf Ivanovich Abel, a Colonel in the Red Army who, having succeeded in entering clandestinely into the United States, operated a very successful Soviet spy ring in New York. Separated from his wife and children in the Soviet Union, he for years lived obscurely in New York making an ostensible living at various small odd jobs. And when finally apprehended, he denied all and took his sentence stoically. (His exchange in 1962 for Powers was not his doing, but that of his American lawyer.)

I referred to the question of how many Americans might be *willing* to undertake an assignment like Colonel Abel's. There is also the problem of how many Americans might be *capable* of undertaking such an assignment. In the unconscious department it is a sad fact that all too often American agents look and act like American agents.

Any big-city dweller by his twenty-fifth year—and often earlier —can instinctively spot a plainclothes policeman or a detective. Connoisseurs of that subject can even distinguish between city detectives and private detectives. Similarly, in the world of intelligence, FBI agents—that is, career FBI men who have been through the FBI Academy, as distinct from subagents who only work outside the Bureau—stand out just about like pink carnations in a vase of red roses. Perhaps the widespread comments on their heavy preference for gabardine have now led to the Bureau's agents to change into less uniform garb. But experience tells me no one has been able to do anything about their expressionless faces and their transparent reticence. They are of a mold—not unlike the comic strip's Dick Tracy, who any fan knows only laughs once a year and can keep his counsel for as long as five years at a time, no matter how baffled his Chief becomes.

Unfortunately, the same is all too often true of American agents abroad, even if for less obvious reasons. As a nation we may still be maturing, but by now the American has become a readily identifiable physical type abroad. It is not only his appearance; there are such things as gait, manner, and, above all, accent which weigh heavily. Then there are intangibles such as psychological reactions, the approach to facts and situations, the content of idle conversation, daily habits. I myself have passed as an Englishman—but in not very discerning company, obviously never in England, and only by denying indignantly that I was English and claiming proudly that I was a Welshman.

This is about the maximum available to most American agents. There is an obvious logical exception which strangely often fails in practice. These are first- or second-generation Americans. Their principal and most obvious asset is language—the Achilles heel of countless American officials and agents abroad. Apart from the language, however, two things count against them. The first is that the emigrant from a smaller country is easily traceable and even recognizable in his native land—and suspicion, at least on the part of the official authorities, attaches quickly to him. Elsewhere than his native land his situation is better, but, in these days of rapid communications and countless dossiers, his cover story frequently has as many difficulties to overcome as that of a native-born American. An Eastern European exile, for example, who fled Communist persecution in his native land may encounter a sympathetic reception in India or parts of Southeast Asia, but the way is open for the local security or counterespionage authorities to find out much about him from his original country.

All this applies mostly to first-generation Americans. Second-generation Americans suffer some of these handicaps, plus a special one. Sociologists have long remarked the features of American society which produce a desire on the part of second-generation Americans to be more American than the Founding Fathers. This is a goal, represented usually in terms of material gain and community standing, that they will not surrender lightly—indeed cannot, without serious internal conflict, surrender at all.

Notwithstanding these difficulties, the principal exceptions to

American agent cover weaknesses are first- or second-generation Americans. One of the most astute and effective American agents I know—political, not espionage—came to this country as a child from Russia. (In fact, in one of CIA's rare gestures of gratitude, he was awarded a medal and citation. Called to Washington, he was summoned to the Director's office, where Allen Dulles read the citation, bestowed the medal upon him, talked warmly with him for a period, and then, at the conclusion of the ceremony and interview, took back the medal and citation for safekeeping in the vaults. Still and all, it was a nice gesture.) It must be admitted, however, that this agent's accomplishments are more distinguished by virtue of his ability to deal with a very touchy, temperamental, and diverse group of people in difficult circumstances rather than by any particular mastery of unusual cover problems.

All this should not be taken as indicating that the American problem with agent cover is simply that Americans cannot pass as foreigners. It is more subtle and complex than that. From the cover point of view, there is nothing wrong in giving an American agent abroad an American cover; in fact, as implied above, it is the only practical course. But to be an American abroad in itself presupposes—for foreigners—certain things, all of them the result of the modern impression held by foreigners of Americans—whether justified or not. One is the American pride in remaining conspicuously, even aggressively American.

This is expressed in more than PX's and American cars. It is implicit in the American prejudice against "expatriates," a prejudice remarked by knowledgeable foreigners and not held, for example, by Dutchmen or Swiss or Norwegians or Chinese or Japanese toward their own compatriots abroad. In 1958 an American general stationed in Orléans, France, issued a public statement to the effect that he wanted no American in his command who had been abroad longer than four years as he felt they could no longer be good Americans after such an extended exposure to foreign influences. He then suited action to word by departing for the United States shortly thereafter, at the end of his own four years—but not before he had backed down from the ensuing hue and cry by explaining that he had meant that his personnel lost touch with the latest American technical developments. Whether the general meant that or not, I was once told by a high Presidential adviser, who disagreed with my views, "That's the trouble with you Americans who live abroad so long. You become un-Am—" He had the grace to pause and amend his sentence, if not his thought. "You have to adapt too much to the circumstances you live in," he concluded. Foreigners know that, in American eyes, the American has to have a good reason for living abroad.

Related to this is the American view that life abroad, even in the world's most civilized countries, is a physical, psychological, and cultural hardship. This view, known to foreigners not only from their reading, but also from the complaints, clannishness, and attitude of superiority of all too many Americans, reinforces the general belief that an American abroad must have an especially good reason for being there. Lastly, the well-known American addiction to material success, status, and recognition further presupposes a compelling reason for residence outside the United States.

Occasionally the interrelation of what the American is, what the foreigner thinks he is, and what the American thinks the foreigner ideally ought to think he is produces some unexpected results. It was, for example, and still is widely assumed by professionals that a certain bank in a European city is a Soviet cover organization. As U.S. operations in Europe grew in complexity, and their financing became a real problem, it was at one point decided to follow the Russian lead and to take over a certain old-established but relatively inactive bank in a large American city, revise its charter, and establish a branch in Europe. Apart from the fact that the new board of directors was almost too distinguished to be believable, the operation failed because the man chosen to lay the groundwork in a peculiar way overdid his cover.

The local government was not, at that time, issuing charters for new banks; it was necessary to purchase the charter of an existing bank. As it happened, I knew of a small bank that was willing, for a reasonable sum, to sell its charter, subject, as required, to the Finance Ministry's approval. Unfortunately, the emissary from America talked too much. Instead of saying merely that his principals in America wanted to enter banking to make money, he talked incessantly and widely about how local interest rates were usurious. It was his principals' intention, he said in noble, ringing tones, to introduce modern banking practices, to put credit within reach of everyone, for the ultimate benefit of the entire local economy. While he was delivering these sentiments, of course, his hearers, many of them bankers, hastened to the Ministry to protest strongly in advance against the approval of any charter for such disruptive elements. (As a colleague of mine remarked at the time, "A good example of all cover and no agent.")

The conscious and unconscious elements in the American character and personality have led, at least in the domain of agent cover, to two defects. One is excessive use of Government cover abroad; the other is a certain transparency in private cover arrangements.

The use of Government installations abroad as cover is not necessarily a defect in itself; it is a matter of proportion. The proportion applies both to the number of covert operations officials in relation to the number of legitimate officials, and to the number of covert personnel under Government cover in relation to the total covert personnel in any area. Too many covert officials masquerading as legitimate Government officials increases enormously the risks of embarrassment; it also undermines the reputation and effectiveness of the legitimate officials. In addition, it subjects the CIA to a charge which in its own interest, and that of all American covert operations, it ought to avoid: that of exercising a disproportionate influence over United States policy. And finally, too many covert officials working under Government cover, in relation to the total number of covert personnel, produces too great a uniformity of point of view in intelligence reporting and diminishes the scope and effectiveness of covert political operations.

The general situation was described clearly by Thayer Waldo, an American reporter, who wrote in the *San Francisco Chronicle* concerning the Cuban operation:

This reporter spent the first half of last year [1960] in Cuba. At that time, with the U.S. Embassy still in operation and fully staffed, eight of its personnel were CIA agents, three worked for the FBI, and each of the Armed Services had from one to five operatives assigned to intelligence work.

No special effort was required to learn these facts or to identify the individuals so engaged. Within thirty days of arrival in Havana, their names and agency affiliations were made known to me, without solicitation, by other correspondents or Embassy employees.

The latter included one CIA man who volunteered the identities of all three persons accredited to the FBI; and a Cuban receptionist, outspokenly pro-Castro, who ticked off the names of six CIA agents—with entire accuracy, a later check confirmed.

In addition to Embassy staffers, the CIA had a number of operatives (I knew fourteen, but am satisfied there were more) among the large colony of resident U.S. businessmen. One of these, a roofing and installation contractor, had lived in Cuba from the age of six, except for service with the Army during World War II—as a master sergeant in G-2, military intelligence. Predictably, that known background made the man a prime target for observation by Castro's people when U.S.-Cuban relations began to deteriorate seriously. He was shadowed day and night, his every contact reported. Yet the CIA made him its chief civilian agent in Havana.

The American dilemma which all of this reflects can be handled in three ways. The first is by the classical rule of covert operations: if cover is blown or even seriously endangered, suspend the operations until cover has been rebuilt or a new cover developed. The second way is simply to ignore the problem, hoping to get by. The third way is to rely heavily upon agents of foreign nationality. The third way, which has, of necessity, been widely used in American operations, poses problems other than cover—chiefly political —which are discussed elsewhere. In describing cover as an American weakness I had in mind chiefly our heavy preference for the second solution over the first. It is a root cause of our troubles.

In the course of the 1961 Cuban operation, a recruiting office for the anti-Castro forces was established in New York. In due time, the press uncovered this center. At the appearance of the very first article on the subject, the recruiting office was closed. Correct procedure—even if the reason was the proximity of the United Nations rather than a breach of cover. At the same time, however, stories began to fill the newspapers of the training and preliminary operations taking place in Florida, Guatemala, and elsewhere around the Caribbean. The operations continued unchecked. To complain later that the American press was unpatriotic or irresponsible in publishing these stories is unworthy petulance.

This lesson was brought home to me succinctly, if painfully. I was once in immediate charge of an operation similar to, but considerably smaller than, the Cuban operation. To my chagrin, I picked up a leading American newspaper one morning to find that one of the better-known American foreign correspondents had the

entire story, with shattering accuracy, starting on page 1. When I
saw him shortly thereafter I gave him the usual bureaucratic re-
proach for irresponsible journalism. His answer was quick. "Look,
friend," he said, "that story didn't come to me from any confidential briefing. If I could put it together so could the Russians and a
lot of other people. Take it as a measure of how well your arrangements are working." I found the logic irrefutable.

Knowledge of the projected Cuban operation was by no means
confined to American reporters. Was Castro's Foreign Minister,
Dr. Rau, also unpatriotic when he presented these same stories
before the United Nations? Can anyone believe that Dr. Rau's sole
source was American newspapers? That Castro sympathizers and
foreign correspondents of all nationalities didn't know what was
going on, once the cover wore thin? The responsible party in this
situation was not the American editor; it was the American official
who, knowing that cover exists to mask connections and activities
from the press just as much as from anyone else, and that the cover
on this operation had been blown, decided to go ahead anyway. In
other words, he consciously chose the second solution over the
classical rule.

To state that an official was responsible is not necessarily tantamount to saying that he was wrong. For a variety of reasons I
personally believe the decision in the 1961 Cuban operation was
gravely wrong. But this does not vitiate the principle that, in any
given situation, the ultimate authority, recognizing that perfect
cover is an unattainable ideal, can weigh the risks and decide,
without being either arrogant or irresponsible, to ignore the classical rule.

The U-2 case illustrates the point—plus a few specific weaknesses.

Faced with the implications of our cover difficulties, the Government made a concerted study in 1954 to find new ways of meeting
our needs for intelligence about the Soviet Union. The U-2 was one
result of this study. Its primary appeal was, of course, the unques-
tionable veracity and reliability of the information it could produce.

So far as the basing of the planes and the transmission of the
collected information for processing were concerned, the operation
used American and allied airbases as cover, plus a cover story that
the planes were engaged in meteorological research. The flights
over the Soviet Union were, however, clandestine rather than co-

vert. There was no conceivable story which could cover the presence of the airplane 1,000 miles from the nearest Soviet border nor,
with the photographic and monitoring equipment aboard, explain
the role of the pilot as being other than what it was. If there was
any cover for the flights themselves, it lay in the technical performance of the aircraft—its ability to fly above the range of Soviet
anti-aircraft weapons and at a speed which guaranteed it could
outdistance any pursuers.

This protection, however, was subject to two risks: one, mechanical failure; and two, Soviet development of weapons which could
intercept the aircraft. It is still not clear which of these eventuali-
ties materialized. In any event, the decision was made that the
potential results justified the risks. General Eisenhower has stated
that the operation was justified on exactly these grounds, namely,
that the advantages outweighed the risks. The four-year history of
the operation certainly seems to support this decision. So far so
good.

However, responsible cover for the operation would not be limited to these considerations. It would also of necessity have to
embrace the steps to be taken in the event of an interception of the
aircraft. Clearly this had been taken into account in the U-2 operation. How well it was taken into account is another matter.

When Powers's flight was overdue, the cover story was issued.
Its announcement by the National Aeronautics and Space Administration was authoritative reinforcement for the story that these
were meteorological research flights. The story itself, of a flight
over a triangular course within Turkey, with one leg approaching
the Soviet border, of a message at about this point from the pilot
reporting difficulties with his oxygen equipment, and the suggestion that the pilot must have lost consciousness and inadvertently
crossed into the Soviet Union while in this condition, was adequate. The accompanying bellicose assertion that the Russians
must have outrageously destroyed the airplane was gratuitous and
politically inept. It was not, however, the fundamental defect of the
cover story.

The defect was simply that, at the very least, for the story to be
at all plausible, the airplane had to be totally destroyed. And for it
to be a fully valid cover story not only would the airplane have to
have been destroyed; the pilot would also have to be dead. Even
with only the wreckage of the aircraft, the Russians—as was
shown—could make a mockery of the cover story. But with only

the wreckage, public opinion would be inclined to believe that the Russians were lying in their charges of deliberate overflights for reconnaissance purposes, and the issue would ultimately have been obscured in dispute. With the pilot alive, however, the possibility of clouding the issue was materially lessened. Powers could certainly not have hoped to pass as anything except an American pilot. But if he himself had maintained the same cover story as that given out by the NASA, it is possible, though not certain in the face of the evidence the plane wreckage provided, that the issue could have been kept sufficiently in doubt so that Soviet ability to exploit the incident would be kept to a minimum. This is what might be called the last-ditch function of cover.

But Powers talked. (According to CIA announcement in March of 1962, at the time of Powers's appearance before the U.S. Senate Armed Services Committee, this was in keeping with his instructions.) Naturally, the same people who thought all signers of the Peace Appeal were Communist dupes alleged that Powers was a Soviet agent. This again is a defeatist view which clouds the true problem. Personally, I wonder about the role of the American Dream in this case. From Powers's public statements in Moscow and from his published letters to his wife, it appears that his chief motive in his work was to save the money to buy a house.

There is evidence that the role of both plane and pilot had been thought about in advance. The Russians claimed that the U-2 was equipped with a button which, when pressed, would totally destroy the aircraft and the pilot, and that Powers had been told only that it would destroy the plane after the mechanism had first ejected him. This is open to conjecture, in view of Powers's statement that the destruction switch was designed to eject him first, and that, prevented by gravity from reaching it, he was only able to eject himself but not to destroy the plane. If the Russian version is true —which we will never know—the question whether or not Powers knew the true function of the button is immaterial. If Powers knew, then the cover for the operation ultimately depended upon his suicide. If he did not know, it depended, in effect, upon his murder. It is axiomatic among covert professionals that a cover which depends for its success upon the suicide of the agent is not reliable. It is only slightly less accepted that a cover which depends for its success upon the murder of the agent, even by mechanical means, is also not reliable. Victims have a way of behaving unpre-

dictably and thereby unconsciously outwitting even mechanical devices.

But regardless of advance provisions for plane and pilot, we
come back here to a fundamental weakness of American cover
practice. The cover for the U-2 operation was good as far as it
went. My own view is that the cover did not go far enough. It
could have gone farther, far enough to preserve the reputation and
prestige of the United States Government, not to mention the stature and capacity for maneuver of the American President, but only
by one means. That sole means was the story the agent himself
would give to his captors. The CIA public statement on the case
does not mention whether Powers was told of what the NASA
cover story would be in the event of disaster. The point is far from
academic. If Powers's instructions were as stated by the Senate
Armed Services Committee ("pilots should . . . adopt a coopera-
tive attitude toward their captors [and] are perfectly free to tell the
full truth about their mission . . .") the question arises of why the
detailed and belligerent NASA cover story was originally issued
when Powers was missing.

Our problems and weaknesses with cover do not stop with the
difficulties of adapting the American personality to this work or
with a recurring slipshod tendency in our arrangements. The basic
weakness is a heavy preference for the alternative of hoping to get
by over the well-founded rule of pausing when cover is endangered.
It is tantamount to downgrading cover as an element in covert
operations, which is, in turn, like playing baseball without a bat.
One of our fondest national legends is that if you want success
enough, success will come. But in covert operations, even more
than in open war, it is vital to plan for both success and failure.
Cover is the realm where this is done.

On April 15, 1961, three B-26 bombers—a type of plane then
still in Castro's Air Force—raided military targets in Cuba, mostly
airfields around Havana. The planes then flew to Florida where,
upon landing, one of the pilots was permitted to see the press. He
gave out a laboriously detailed account of how he and his companions, who he said were all officers in the Cuban Air Force, had
planned to defect from Castro for months. Fearing detection of
their plans, the group had taken to their planes that morning, he
said, and, as a final gesture of resistance, had bombed military
targets on their way to exile in the United States. This was the

cover story—for, as a quick count of his Air Force told Castro, the bombers had come from outside Cuba.

The bombing had a twofold purpose: militarily it was supposed to cripple Castro's Air Force in preparation for the invasion, planned for forty-eight hours later; politically, it was supposed to create the impression before Cuban and world opinion—including American—of a mounting opposition to Castro inside Cuba. The military success of the operation did not depend in any way on the cover story. Its political success, on the other hand, was totally dependent upon the cover story. As anticipated, the press—particularly the American newspapers—gave a big play to the cover story. Castro's denial that any of his Air Force had defected was thrown into doubt. The impression was created of strife, potent opposition, and turmoil in Castro's Cuba. So far so good. In the hue and cry the basic defect was barely visible.

But it was there, all the same. It was simply that there was a definite time limit on this initial success. That limit was the day when a foreign correspondent left Cuba and reported the truth. For world opinion, that day would occur when any reputable correspondent filed his story supporting Castro's denial; but the effectiveness of this eventuality, at least for American opinion, could—unfortunately all too easily—be sharply limited by denunciation, and the limit put off until an American correspondent returned with the true story—as later happened.

Those responsible for this operation could not but be fully aware of this time limit. They were also aware that the invasion was scheduled for forty-eight hours later. Since the blowing of this cover story would seriously compromise the U.S. Government's reputation and integrity—not the least with the American press itself—there had to be an assumption that the cover would hold beyond the obvious limit. There were only two possibilities which would have produced such a result. One was that the invasion would succeed, in which case the true story would have been suppressed or overlooked or even condoned in the aura of success. The other was that the invasion would be partially successful and the story forgotten in the drama of civil war. It is impossible to know which of these alternatives weighed most heavily; most probably both weighed equally in deluding the authors of this scheme that it was usable. The fact that certain Americans in New York were approached—by American officials—prior to the Cuban invasion and offered jobs as advisers to a new Cuban Government-to-be suggests that not much distinction was being made between total and partial success. And in making a judgment about cover it doesn't matter. For any operation which relies on success for the preservation of its cover, or presupposes that success will obliterate the fact of blown cover, is not a covert operation. It is not even clandestine. It is a gamble.

American weaknesses with cover will not be solved by looking for scapegoats. The problem is more complex than the individual responsibility of some official and more profound than the organizational chart or allotted powers of some government agency. It is compounded of three main elements.

One is, as was suggested by the Powers case, the psychological limitations on Americans acting as agents.

Another is a certain slipshod quality at the professional level, which is not so much a lack of thoroughness as it is the hope to get by. In the summer of 1960 two young Americans, traveling ostensibly as students gathering materials for treatises, were arrested by the Russians in the Ukraine on charges of espionage. (It is worth noting that each denounced the other and that they were forthwith released and expelled from the Soviet Union.) They were traveling, they said, on grants from the Northcraft Educational Fund, of Baltimore, Maryland. An American reporter, hoping that the Fund itself would be able to refute the Russian charge, uncovered the fact that no such organization existed in Baltimore or anywhere else. In this case, a minor expenditure for a one-room office and a telephone listing would have saved the U.S. Government considerable embarrassment.

The other main element in our difficulties stems from the highest levels of Government. At these levels decisions are made on whether or not to proceed with those operations which engage the world-wide power and position of the United States. No one who has observed this decision-making process can be other than sympathetic to those who carry the burden. But it is my impression that where those decisions have led to difficulty or even disaster, it is because at this level there was too little understanding of the nature and importance of cover. A certain desperation governs such decisions; there is a feeling that political and power considerations outweigh cover. When, for example, the overthrow of the Arbenz regime in Guatemala was decided upon in 1954, and the highest levels of Government insisted, over the vigorous protests of CIA professionals, on the use of aircraft in the operation, no serious observer—and there were millions in Latin America—believed that Colonel Castillo Armas just happened to be the owner of a number of American bombers. The question can properly be asked whether we would not have had more Latin American support in the Castro problem if we had not been so flamboyant in Guatemala. Cover certainly does not outweigh fundamental considerations of politics and power; but in covert operations it is an integral part of the international political results of those operations.[1]

Whatever may be the shortcomings of the open-faced American in this work, they are never ameliorated by Americans either overconfident of or desperate for success.

1. A remarkably classic example of the flow of consequences from this relationship is provided by the Reagan Administration's operations in and with Iran. There was abundant secrecy (a good deal where it should not have been), some rather successful clandestinity, and covers so ill-conceived and flimsy as to leave, in the sad end, only two alternative views of the President of the United States: either a rash and clumsy schemer, or a cheery dreamer unaware of the realities about him.

official mission to Egypt, arrested six days earlier, appeared on
television to confess to charges of espionage against the United
Arab Republic on behalf of the French Government—the confessions amounting to admissions of "routine political and economic
reports" sent to the French Foreign Ministry and including a report of the possibility of an Israeli attack on the U.A.R. In Washington and Bonn the United States State Department released a 21-
page document analyzing Communist espionage activity in Berlin
and Germany, including the case of an American woman Armed
Forces employee who had been, under the guise of a romance with
an ostensible American citizen whom she met at the American
Embassy Club in Bonn, the victim of a fairly crude Soviet attempt
in East Berlin to blackmail her into passing secret documents to
the Soviets. And finally, in probably the day's most plaintive note,
Prime Minister Nehru of India told his Parliament that "international spies" outnumbered the normal population of the Himala-
yan border town of Kalimpong. "Every important country has
espionage agents functioning there," he said, with what one can
only imagine, in the absence of further details, must have been a
catch in his throat.

A fairly representative daily selection. The Russians accuse the
Americans, incidentally dragging in the West German problem; the
Americans accuse the Russians, mixing in the East German problem for good measure; the Arabs accuse the French, sideswiping
the Israelis in the process; and neutral Nehru, without being specific, accuses everybody, thus by implication correcting the day's
omissions of mention of Britain and China. Without judging the
merits or validity of these particular cases, and leaving aside their
self-righteous exploitation by prosecutors and propagandists, the
question can fairly be asked as to what all this activity is about.
Assuming, justifiably, that the number of espionage agents caught
is at any given moment only an infinitesimal fraction of the total
operating, what are these thousands upon thousands of people
looking for? The answer is: secret intelligence.

The official American definition of intelligence is "evaluated information." The evaluation simultaneously concerns both the credibility of the information itself—a process involving a check
against information already in hand and an educated guess as to
the new information—and the reliability of the source. The two
cannot be totally divorced from each other. Obviously, a report
that the Moroccans are mobilizing 30,000 men for an attack on the

Spanish territories bordering Morocco is one thing if it comes from a taxi driver in Casablanca and quite another thing if it comes from the official in charge of mobilization in the Moroccan Ministry of National Defense. All other things being equal, the official source will be evaluated as of high reliability, and—in the present state of affairs—the information being credible, the report will be considered valuable intelligence on which some action may be based. If, however, the taxi driver's report is supplemented by, say, forty similar reports from merchants, including army suppliers, from families whose sons have allegedly been among those thus conscripted, and from a variety of citizens throughout Morocco, then the information takes on the status of a widespread rumor. In this case, the problem becomes that of assessing the credibility of the information itself: Was the rumor deliberately circulated, and if so, by whom and why? Is it a reflection of a state of alarm among the Moroccan populace? Is it an implied threat to the Spanish by the Moroccan Government to hasten negotiations? Did the Spanish spread the rumor to provide a justification for some action they plan? Or is it simply a genuine Moroccan action which could not in the circumstances be kept secret? While the lone taxi driver's report would warrant no action whatsoever, the widespread rumor would require action to provide answers to this whole series of questions—would require action, that is, of an intelligence service whose government felt it had an active interest in Moroccan-Spanish affairs.[1]

The matter of the authoritativeness of the source can never be ignored, but it is sometimes overdone in the light of the credibility of the information. In the summer of 1945, the Soviet passenger-freighter *Balkhash,* of 15,000 tons, and bound for Vladivostok, was proceeding at night through the Straits of La Perouse from the Sea of Okhotsk to the Sea of Japan. As the Soviets were not yet at war with Japan, the ship's lights were blazing and the large red Soviet flags painted on the hull, together with the letters "U.S.S.R," were floodlit. Sometime around midnight the *Balkhash* was torpedoed and sank in a very few minutes, with some loss of life. The survivors were rescued by Japanese fishing vessels and coastal craft during the night and the following morning. Several weeks later I forwarded to Washington a report concerned not with the fact of the sinking, but with the reaction of Soviet citizens to the sinking of a Soviet ship by an *American* submarine—which was withal remarkably philosophical—since it was accepted by Soviet maritime authorities that, in the then state of the Japanese Navy, the submarine could only have been American. The result for me was a peremptory query from my superiors as to the basis for my assumption that the submarine in question was American. When I replied that I was reporting a Soviet reaction to a Soviet assumption, based on logical deduction, that the submarine must be American, I was coldly reminded that I was reporting mere rumor without labeling it as such, and thereby casting doubt on the reliability of my reports. (Much later, in Washington, I got to the bottom of this one: my chief acknowledged that it had in fact been an American submarine, but added, "You didn't think we were going to admit it to you, did you?" Nevertheless, I took the reprimand so to heart at the time that when, several months later, a reliable Soviet source informed me, twenty-four hours in advance of Moscow's declaration of war, that the Soviet Union was already at war with Japan—which I reported with all haste—but then six hours later, fearing trouble for himself, denied his earlier information, I canceled my original message, only to awaken the next morning to Moscow's announcement.)

The question of what is authoritative and what is not is also relative. A highly authoritative source may convey eminently credible information, but the question must always be asked—most particularly in the case of highly authoritative sources—"Why?" The danger of planted information—a complex subject covered in the next chapter—is always present. To this extent, a stolen document is often intelligence superior to a gratuitously conveyed secret from whatever source, since it obviates the risk of deliberately misleading information. The "why" does not apply only to the danger of planted information, however. It must also be asked of the source whose bona fides are beyond question. The danger here is of an intelligence headquarters believing what it wants to believe—a failing that has affected almost all the world's secret services and governments at one time or another. The outstanding recent example was, unfortunately, provided by the American Government in the 1961 Cuban affair. There was neither malice nor an effort to mislead in the reports of anti-Castro Cubans—nor in those of American agents in Cuba tied to American commercial interests undergoing expropriation—that an invasion of Cuba by anti-Castro exiles would result in an uprising of the Cuban people against Castro. This was their natural, human, logical bias, reflecting hopes which touched the very core of their beings. The fault was not in the bias of those so reporting; it is a rare man who in their circumstances would have done otherwise. The fault lay with those who, in evaluating these reports, gave them too much weight. They did not accept fully the logical answer to the "why" of these reports—perhaps because the answer countered their own hopes; they discounted more dispassionate, even if unpopular, reports of observers such as Claiborne Pell, a politician with considerable experience at the working level in foreign affairs, who, while still Senator-elect from Rhode Island, visited Cuba privately and quietly, and reported that hopes for an anti-Castro uprising were, at worst, wishful thinking and, at best, premature.

The problem of the bias of the evaluators is one that is unavoidable in intelligence; it extends even to information of fullest credibility from the most reliable sources. There was a story circulating just after the Suez invasion of 1956 which I have never verified, but which, even if only apocryphal, is still plausible. According to this story, a Secretary of the American Embassy in Israel—no secret agent by any means—stumbled onto the fact of the forthcoming Franco-British-Israeli action against Egypt by the simple expedient of an accidental but friendly conversation with some French Air Force pilots who were in Israel with their Mystere jet fighters to aid the Israelis. It was alleged that the Secretary's report of this information was not only suppressed, but he himself was reprimanded. The story could well apply to any country. After all, the German High Command in World War II had at least three reliable reports stating the date and place for the Allied invasion of Normandy, but they chose to believe in a later date and, even after the landings had taken place, that the real Allied assault would take place in the Pas de Calais. And Alexander Foote, in his remarkable account of his World War II experiences as a Soviet secret agent in Switzerland, has pointed out how Red Army intelligence, suspicious of what appeared to be too great ease and rapidity, month after month rejected his network's greatest achievement of almost daily detailed reports of battle order and plans straight from the Headquarters of the Wehrmacht, the German Navy, and the Air Force, in favor of banal reports from a man who was in fact a German agent.

Bias in evaluation can never be fully overcome in an intelligence service and, more importantly, in supreme government councils; it cannot even be tempered by shuffling and reshuffling the organizational charts; and it can only be compounded by creating evaluators to evaluate the evaluators. Within the intelligence establishment, the only effective safeguard lies in the individual competence and qualities of its members. Doctrinaire partisans, superpatriots, men of provincial outlook, bureaucratic climbers—all are, in this field, dangers to the national safety, however comfortably they may accord with the popular temper or ethos or with the preconceptions of legislators and of the Administration in office. Perspective, perspicacity, worldliness, a soundly philosophical outlook, the knowledge and sense of human history—these are the individual qualities which minimize error in the interpretation and evaluation of information. (Contrary to the tenets of the majority of American administrators, intellectual brilliance—even if eccentric, troublesome to the organizational charts, or occasionally shining through a bottle of whisky—is also a valuable asset. A sense of humor, on the other hand, may be of no particular national interest, but is an essential prop to the sanity of those who work in intelligence.) Professional excellence inside the intelligence establishment is but half the story; to be effective as a safeguard it must be complemented by international political sagacity in the nation's foreign affairs leadership.

The definition of intelligence as "evaluated information" does not, unfortunately, touch upon the most important element which confers value on intelligence—and which also explains the true objective of all secret agents. The objective is secret intelligence, as stated above, but the emphasis is on the vital element contained in the word "secret."

The need for intelligence is an effect, not a cause. It is the result of situations of human conflict or competition which, between nations, run the gamut from the inescapable frictions and rivalries among allies, through the wary maneuvers of potential enemies and the covert clashes of the secret war, to open hostilities. Whatever the degree, the essence of the situation is human conflict. In any such situation, as we have seen previously, the most potent and useful information about an opponent is that which he does not know you possess.

Thus the meaning of "secret" in the phrase "secret intelligence" is precise and specific. It does *not* mean that the opposition does not possess the same information. By definition, since the information came from them, they do. What is secret, what is unknown to the opposition, is the fact of your possession of the information. The contrast between Pearl Harbor and the subsequent Battle of

Midway is an obvious example. American possession of the Japanese codes prior to Pearl Harbor yielded only the information that a carrier task force was on the high seas operating under radio silence—with the results known to history. The Japanese had to consider the contingency that the Americans had broken their codes, but the very fact of their victory at Pearl Harbor was, to them, important evidence that we had not succeeded in doing so. Accordingly, Japanese radio traffic prior to the Midway battle, only six months after Pearl Harbor, revealed not only the whereabouts and destinations of two Japanese striking forces, but also (correctly interpreted) showed that the northernmost of the two fleets had a principally diversionary purpose. Admiral Nimitz was thus enabled to concentrate his defending forces at the point of maximum danger—with the resultant decisive U.S. victory at Midway. Needless to say, only one ill-advised public statement by a member of the commissions investigating the Pearl Harbor debacle, or by any of the principals in the disaster, to all of whom our possession of the Japanese codes was known, would have sufficed to make the Midway victory impossible.[2]

This is not to deny either the existence or value of non-secret intelligence, i.e., intelligence which the opposition either knows or must assume you possess. In fact, the great bulk of intelligence is obtained overtly from a vast range of sources. The study and analysis of publications, broadcasts, statistics, diplomatic and military reports yield an enormous amount of basic information. (Such research and analysis is the overt function, in the United States, of the intelligence branches of the State Department, the Defense Intelligence Agency, the armed forces, the Atomic Energy Commission, and the CIA.) Furthermore, a great many of the new scientific intelligence operations, such as communications analysis and nuclear explosion detection, are overtly acknowledged; only the scientific devices or techniques are secret. (In the detection of nuclear explosions, even the end result is made public, since, in this almost unique case, the national power is reinforced and not weakened by demonstrating knowledge of enemy actions.) The remainder of intelligence—including that universal governmental prop, the routine surveillance of cables, telegrams, and mail—is secret intelligence, i.e., intelligence which the opposition assumes you do not possess. Such intelligence is, at a guess, quantitatively no more than 20 per cent at maximum of the total intelligence available to a major government. Yet, whether political, military, economic, or scientific, it is intelligence of the highest value.

It is this very precise meaning of the word "secret" in "secret intelligence" which dictates some of the fundamental characteristics and techniques of secret intelligence operations. It is, for example, the basis of a perpetual misunderstanding between the public, the press, and legislatures—particularly the American—on the one hand, and the executive branch of government, including the intelligence services, on the other. This is the misunderstanding which arises when a secret agent is caught. In such cases, it is fundamental secret intelligence practice on the part of the capturing government never to reveal publicly what it was precisely that the agent had obtained. (This is why the legal indictments of captured secret agents are always couched in broad, vague terms, and the evidence made public generally limited to proving the activities of the accused without specific reference to information he obtained. Such trials frequently cause almost as many headaches to the intelligence authorities—particularly in America, where the statutes and precedents in such cases are of fairly recent origin—as capturing the agent in the first place.) It is at this point that an article usually appears somewhere pointing out that the Russians—or the appropriate nationality—already know what the agent knew, so what is the Government being so tight-lipped about? If the Russians know it, why can't we? Even an editor so personally experienced in secret intelligence operations as the Englishman Malcolm Muggeridge recently expressed pique on this subject. "Secrets which are known to have leaked, far from being written off, are guarded with particular ferocity," he wrote in the *New Statesman*, and added, in evident exasperation, "The most wonderfully complicated locks are put on the stable door after the horse is gone."

If it is remembered that the secrecy which is at stake is not whether or not you know something, or even whether the enemy also knows the same thing, but the more complicated fact of knowing whether the enemy knows you know it, the reason becomes apparent. It is simply that any public discussion of the information obtained by a captured agent risks conferring validity, for the enemy's benefit, on that information. In effect, you risk evaluating the information for the enemy. The public statement, "The Government is embarrassed that the recently apprehended enemy agent discovered the location of our 27 secret missile bases," or "The Prosecution demands the death penalty, the accused having stolen and transmitted to the enemy the Army's war plans," obviously confirms to the enemy that what he has is of prime value. Silence, on the other hand, downgrades the information in the enemy's possession. He is left to follow the course of the public trial, while wrestling with several vital and unanswerable questions: How much of what our agent transmitted to us do they really know was transmitted? The plans for the East Coast antimissile defense system, for example? Will they change them, knowing we know them, or do they not suspect we do, and therefore will leave them as they are? And what about that purported summary of a meeting of the National Security Council? Their silence certainly gives us nothing concrete with which to evaluate that report —which we were doubtful about anyway. And so on. Silence may not undo all serious damage, but it is the only way to minimize it. (Silence also has a positive aspect. For years following the surrender of Japan, American authorities refused any official mention of the case of Richard Sorge, Soviet agent who operated in Japan until his arrest in 1943, for the reason that the ramifications and techniques of that network were of great value in uncovering other and subsequent Soviet operations—a fact dependent in large measure on the Soviets not knowing how much we had learned from the Japanese archives.)

Similarly, the concept of secrecy as hiding from the enemy your possession of information, more than the information itself, dictates, in the reverse case, the practice of secret agents in the field and the preparations they must always make for the eventuality of capture. The cardinal principle in secret intelligence operations is the observance of priorities of expendability in the event of compromise, discovery, or arrest. The first and easiest thing to dispose of in case of danger is money and property. (One of the many reasons why secret intelligence is an expensive business.) The very next thing is the individual agent himself. While it is obviously incumbent on every agent, as a matter of primary personal and professional interest, to observe meticulously all possible security precautions concerning himself, it is a bald fact that, when the choice must be made, the national interest dictates that the agent himself has a high priority of expendability.

After the agent himself come the "lines of communication." This phrase can be taken to include a clandestine radio transmitter or codes, but it more usually refers to the human connections, the prearranged relationships and contacts in the field and running back to the headquarters, which make up a secret intelligence network. The lines of communication are the entire conspiratorial apparatus which links all the individual agents together to form a functioning network, ranging from the "place of conspiracy"—a predetermined time and place of meeting between agents who have lost contact—to the methods of transmission of intelligence to headquarters. (It can easily be seen that, faced with the choice between the loss of a single agent and the compromise or destruction of an entire network, the single agent is the more readily expendable. There are, of course, sub-priorities here: the loss of a cut-out who knows no true identities is much less serious than the arrest of the principal agent. But the point is that without "lines of communication" there is no secret intelligence network; there is only a useless number of unconnected, unco-ordinated, and unresponsive individuals.)

The least expendable asset is information already transmitted to headquarters, or anything which will provide a clue to that information. It is the agent's ultimate duty, in the event of danger, to insure, by any and all means, that the knowledge of information already transmitted does not, either directly or indirectly, become available to the opposition. (There is obviously a time limit to this necessity, but it depends entirely on the merits of each individual case and is not a matter which a single agent is usually equipped to judge.) It is bad enough to lose a functioning intelligence network to the enemy; it is a double or triple loss also to have all the operation's previous work wiped out at a single blow—for if the enemy knows what information you already possess, it is, by definition, no longer secret intelligence. This point is all too infrequently understood even by secret agents themselves. They are often under the illusion that, in the event of danger, they burn their papers or swallow scraps containing cipher keys or make other such heroic gestures to hide proof of their illegal activity or to protect the government they are serving. These are desirable objectives, certainly, but they are very much secondary to the fundamental necessity to preserve the secrecy and hence value of secret intelligence already obtained.

The matter of codes illustrates the point clearly. The secret breaking of a code is a major disaster (or triumph); the opposition's possession of the code, being unknown or unsuspected by the user, is secret intelligence of exceptionally high value. However, this eventuality is not and cannot be the responsibility of the agent, provided he observes all necessary precautions in the use of his codes. The fundamental utility and security of codes is the function of the headquarters' cryptographic staff. But mere compromise of a code—that is, any set of circumstances which leaves unresolved the question of whether or not the opposition benefited from those circumstances to obtain or to break the code—can be almost as damaging. (There is no practical difference so far as countermeasures are concerned between knowing the opposition has obtained the code and the obligation rationally to assume they have it. Once, at the outset of a mission traveling across Communist territory, my pockets were picked and my wallet stolen in, of all places, a circus. Besides money and personal documents, the wallet contained—I am ashamed to say—a scrap of paper on which was written an unidentified random phrase which happened to be the key to my double transposition code. It was highly likely that I was merely the victim of a hungry and light-fingered citizen; I nevertheless had to assume that the security police were light-fingered, if not hungry, and that any cryptographer, looking at my quite innocent scrap of paper, would have no choice but to try it out as the key to a double transposition code. Even though I could remember the phrase, I still completed the rest of the mission in silence —which did nothing for the timeliness of the information I was seeking and for which my base was waiting.)

The possession by the opposition of a code has effects both forward and backward in time. If you do not know your code is broken, the opposition has the entire backlog of the network's efforts, plus the ability to monitor the entire operation into the future. If, however, you know the opposition has the code, or are obliged to assume they have it, their advantage over future operations can immediately be canceled either by substitution of another code or silence until an alternative code is obtained. But nothing can repair the damage done to the intelligence already transmitted: it simply ceases to be intelligence. For this reason a secret agent has no better ally than a good memory and no more dangerous enemy than a nice, orderly, complete set of files.

Finally, and most importantly, this precise definition of secrecy in the phrase "secret intelligence" means that intelligence, to be secret, must be obtained in such a way that the opposition does not know what is being obtained. The steps the agent takes to mask his activity are merely elementary security; his main concern must be to keep the enemy from knowing what he knows, rather than the mere fact that he knows something. This is one reason a micro-filmed document—obtained without anyone's knowledge—is more durable intelligence and superior to information obtained, no matter how secretly, from a secret, even if genuine, sympathizer in the enemy camp. But since such uncompromised opportunities for obtaining information are extremely rare, the standard procedure in all intelligence services is to seek wherever possible to establish lines of communication in such a way that persons providing information do not know its ultimate destination. More than one potential purveyor of secret information—even for the highest motives—has been bewildered to find his sincere advances rebuffed by the very services he hopes to assist. The rebuff arises, however, only partly from possible suspicion of his motives. An additional reason for rejection of his offer is the fact that to accept it puts him in the position of knowing the identity of the end-users of the information; this knowledge on his part increases the risk of the enemy being able to invalidate all previous information passed by him if they uncover his activities. In brief, if you know the recipient, you can sometimes deduce what information he has received.

Similarly, it is this distinction between the act of obtaining secret intelligence and the sure knowledge of what is being obtained which explains in part the international tolerance of military attachés. While a part of this tolerance is due to the "I'll accept your legitimate spies if you'll accept mine" theory, it is also just as firmly based on the conviction of the receiving government that it can control—that is, know—what information an attaché is obtaining. In most countries this is done by discreet surveillance. In the Soviet Union and its satellites, however, the surveillance is done with the heaviest and most obvious possible hand—not only as a control measure, but also as a forthright obstruction to any activity at all by the diplomat or attaché being so conspicuously and ubiquitously "tailed."

It may seem superfluous, even banal, to point out that the information sought in secret intelligence operations is originally in the possession of foreign nationals. In brief, the sources of secret intelligence are, by definition, foreign. However, this pedestrian but fundamental fact has important consequences for the conduct of such operations. Foremost among these is the constant necessity to gain and hold the co-operation of foreign nationals who have the essential access to the desired information—even if such a foreign source is hostile. There are secret intelligence operations which do not involve foreigners; I suppose the U-2 operation could be counted as one, although even here the co-operation of foreign governments was required for the basing of the airplanes. Nevertheless, the overwhelming majority of operations depends heavily upon foreigners for their ability to produce anything of real value. The complex of Soviet operations designed to obtain information about nuclear weapons would have been impossible without the co-operation of American and British personnel.

The vital question of whether a foreign source is willing, whether he knows and understands what he is doing, is one on which a clear and precise decision must be taken at the very outset of any operation. It is here that a most accurate assessment of the foreigner's motives, capabilities, and general emotional and intellectual posture must be brought into play. A man thoroughly disaffected with the regime under which he lives may regard services to a foreign intelligence service as fulfilling a higher duty to his own nation. If such a feeling is genuine, his knowledge of what he is doing it for may be an essential part of his co-operation, even if it does constitute an added risk to the security of the operation and the secrecy of the information he provides. Here the Soviets have a valuable asset in the ideological loyalty of foreign Communists to the Soviet state. However, they also suffer compensating liabilities. The facts of life under Soviet power provide plenty of disaffection which can be exploited by others for secret intelligence purposes. This is patently true of the satellite countries; but even in the Soviet Union itself, with its rigid safeguards, its xenophobia, and its security mania, there is exploitable disaffection. (This is not to lend the slightest credibility to the fantastic Soviet charge that Lavrenty Beria, Stalin's long-time secret police head, was an American agent. Even Trotsky, hounded and persecuted—and ultimately murdered—by Stalin, would have balked at any kind of co-operation with capitalist intelligence services. However, in my own experiences with the Russians I found a sufficient, even though always limited, number of useful Soviet sources, although I admit that to do so I became a temporary expert in fence-climbing, back-alley skulking, and general dodging. I never recall without a twitching of my nostrils one source whom I always met in a particularly filthy and foul-smelling public toilet. For a long time I hoped that my superiors would someday comment that "This information stinks," thereby giving me an opportunity for a witty and pungent rejoinder, but my chance never came.

An intelligence service cannot, however, limit itself to using dis-affection on the part of foreign nationals for its sources of informa-tion. Furthermore, if at all possible, it is desirable—and sometimes necessary—that the foreign source not understand clearly what he is doing or for whom. The most desirable such situation is one in which the source does not know that he is in fact providing infor-mation to a foreign intelligence network. This ideal was achieved by Richard Sorge—the Soviet agent of German nationality work-ing in Japan during the Second World War—who achieved the position of Press Attaché of the German Embassy in Tokyo. The Embassy staff naturally were under the impression that they were talking with a loyal Nazi colleague, and many—though not all—of Sorge's Japanese sources believed they were working with a Ger-man ally. A variant of this situation consists in the source knowing that he is providing information, while laboring under a carefully sown misapprehension as to who is really benefiting thereby. Let us take the hypothetical case of an Iraqi Government functionary who is profoundly disturbed by a flirtation between the dictator, General Kassem, and the local Communist Party. He may genu-inely fear the possibility of eventual Soviet domination of Iraq and the danger of ultimate loss of the Kurdish territories in the north. At the same time, the Israeli Government, in the interests of ele-mental survival, must have all information possible about their Arab neighbors. The Iraqi official, as a patriot and as a good Arab, would never consider for one minute aiding the Israelis. But, in his concern, he would consider entering into a working relationship with the Americans, who would constitute, in his mind, the logical counterweight to Soviet influence in Iraq. The simple solution to this problem is that the Israeli agent who recruits this official poses as an American agent. It is sad to have to relate that this technique enjoyed, at least during the Fifties, a certain vogue in many parts of the world, with the Americans as the favorite substitution. We were not without our faults during that agitated decade, but not all the faults ascribed to us were really ours.

An even more frequent variant is the situation in which the source knows for whom he is working, but is necessarily and delib-erately misled as to his true purpose. Shortly after the Second World War American intelligence entered into a working relation-ship—reasonably productive for a period—with a monarchist group in an Eastern European country. These people were under the impression that this was a co-operative arrangement in which the Americans were supporting their political aim of restoration of the monarchy—which was definitely not U.S. policy. Nonetheless, American support for the group even included a clandestine radio over which political messages were broadcast to the population. The group's operations inside the country also produced considerable intelligence, which they gladly turned over to the Americans as a by-product of what they regarded as a political collaboration. It was, of course, the intelligence which was the true and sole interest of the Americans. Needless to say, bitterness and recriminations filled the air the day American support ceased—even though its termination was alleged to be based on the political and realistic grounds that the cause was hopeless. (While I personally believe that this particular operation went too far, my opinion is based on specific political grounds. It is irrelevant to apply a moral or an "American" standard here; the same story could be told of the intelligence services of any of the major powers. Even more pertinent is the fact that sincerity of purpose or nobility of motive does not exempt those who enter into the life of conspiracy from the rules and risks of that life.)

From this frequent necessity to disguise motive, purpose, and even identity flows one of the major and identifying characteristics of secret intelligence operations—the existence of a potential or actual element of falsity, marked specifically by duplicity and deceit, in the basic case officer-agent relationship.

Contrary to general belief, the major difficulty in secret intelligence operations is not the actual laying hands on "the loot," so to speak (or, as French gangster argot mysteriously has it, *"le grisbi"*). As often as not the moment of acquisition of information, whether it be in written or spoken form, is a mere mechanical detail or a matter of wit and patience. It is generally a phase of relative calm, a lull, so to speak, sandwiched between the two principal difficulties besetting the gathering of secret intelligence. In a well-conceived and skillfully executed operation the information which is sought should be obtained almost automatically—as the result of prior successful solution of these two major problems.

Of these problems the most difficult is chronologically the first. It is that of placing the agent in a position and a role whereby the information comes to him with a minimum of risk and as a natural by-product of his position. This is, of course, a major function of cover, and here, as usual, one aims for perfection and seldom achieves it. It is one thing, for example, to be Cicero, the valet of the British Ambassador to Turkey during World War II who was an agent of the Germans and whose position enabled him clandestinely to rifle the contents of the Ambassador's safe while the latter slept. An eminently successful operation. But how different and better a thing to have been the Soviet agent Sorge in Japan, with automatic and unquestioned access to both German and Japanese information sanctioned by his role as a German official—and flavored, perhaps even improved, by his affair with the wife of the German Ambassador.

It is in this matter of maneuvering one's agent into position that skill, judgment, ingenuity, and keen understanding of other peoples are called for in the highest degree. The classic method is "penetration," meaning, in its historic form, the placing of the agent within the structure from which it is desired to obtain intelligence. Obviously the flow of defectors back and forth between East and West in the secret war affords numerous opportunities for such direct penetration. Precisely because this is so obvious, however, it is a difficult technique, risky, and not usually productive. Barring unusually suspicious circumstances, such as exist at the outset of or immediately following a war, for example, the technique of direct penetration generally requires time, and plenty of it, for success. Clearly, if you want to put an agent into the Central Committee of the Soviet Communist Party, you are going to have to wait a long time while he fights his way up the ladder of the Communist hierarchy. (There is a recurrent story, for which I have no means of vouching, that the Poles did in fact achieve this with Stalin's prewar Politburo.) Furthermore, while you await your agent's maneuvering into the desired position, you risk his ultimate success if you use him. This difficulty has led to the technique of the "sleeper" agent, whose tasks are defined in advance to fit a certain eventuality; meanwhile, no matter what the period of time, he is not used. A notable example of the "sleeper" agent was the innkeeper whom the Germans introduced into the British Naval Base of Scapa Flow not long after the First World War. He didn't stir during all the years until the outbreak of the Second World War; he was then able to provide the information which permitted a Nazi submarine to sneak into Scapa Flow early in the war, torpedo the aircraft carrier *Ark Royal,* and escape untouched.[3]

Security measures being what they are in our times, direct penetration poses extreme difficulties. Accordingly, a favorite—can one say popular?—technique, and far from a new one, is that of indi-

rect penetration, also known as subversion. The advantage of subversion is that it avoids the complications of choice of agent and
the preparations and delay which are part of direct penetration,
since it utilizes someone who is already in position to obtain the
desired intelligence. In subversion the problem is not that of tailoring the agent to the task, it is that of tailoring the method of
recruitment to the character, disposition, and motives of a selected
potential agent. The continuous Soviet efforts to blackmail U.S.
Government employees into their service is but one form, albeit
crude, of subversion. A more refined form was evidenced in the
case of the British diplomat who was persuaded, as a result of
reflection during a period of internment in North Korea during the
Korean War, that "the Soviet system deserved to win."

Another alternative to direct penetration is to have someone else
in a more advantageous position do the work for you. In secret
intelligence operations this means, as a practical matter, working
relationships with other intelligence services. The intelligence services of many smaller nations do not, by the simple fact of nationality difference and because of lesser prominence as leaders in the
secret war, suffer the disadvantages of the great powers. Furthermore, they often hold unique assets, as witness the very large Polish population in France or the Greek populations in Bulgaria,
Rumania, and the Soviet Union. The result is a constant and vigorous competition among all the great powers for strictly exclusive
working relationships with the services of lesser powers, which
relationships most often turn into a control of the lesser service.
Thus the immediate postwar period saw a lively scramble by all the
great powers for exclusive dominance over the intelligence services
of the smaller nations. There was, of course, no doubt anywhere
that the services of the Eastern European states, with the exception
of Yugoslavia, were not merely controlled by, but were to all practical purposes integral parts of Soviet intelligence.

The other major problem in secret intelligence operations is
chronologically the second, but involves more danger than the
first. This is the problem of how to get the information, once obtained, back to the headquarters. The most significant secret intelligence in the hands of an agent who cannot transmit it to the sole
place where it can be used is, of course, valueless. But this is no
easy trick. The comparison drawn above between the case of Cicero, the German agent who was the British Ambassador to Turkey's valet, and that of Sorge, the Soviet agent in the German

Embassy in Tokyo, pointed out that, in the light of the classic criteria, Sorge was much better positioned than Cicero. Yet Cicero was never caught, whereas Sorge was arrested and executed by the Japanese. The difference lay in the means of transmission of information. Cicero passed his information to the Germans in a series of clandestine meetings in Istanbul and Ankara, and by means of letter drops; Sorge relied on a clandestine radio transmitter.

Here is the source of another salient characteristic of secret intelligence operations. No matter how covert an operation may be, no matter how carefully devised and skillfully executed the cover, the precise moment of transmitting the information is, in almost all cases, clandestine. It is thus the moment of greatest danger in such operations. The great majority of secret intelligence agents who are caught are apprehended at the moment of passing information. (In the Portland Royal Naval Base case the arrest of part of the network took place at the moment of passing documents; the other members of the network were apprehended as a result of monitoring and then locating the source of clandestine radio signals to Moscow—both being the actual moments of passing information.) The reason for this is not because security services hope to improve the chances of prosecution by evidence obtained *in flagrante delicto;* it is quite simply that, being clandestine—there is no cover which can adequately explain the illegal transmission of documents or information to unauthorized persons, whether it be hand-to-hand, by letter, or by radio—this action is the most vulnerable in the entire operation and is often the only moment when agents can be caught. Secret inks, letter drops, and an everchanging series of devices, including the constant development of techniques to obstruct the location of clandestine radio transmitters—all are part of the continuous effort to transform this vulnerable moment from clandestine to covert, or to minimize the clandestine risk. However, defense techniques are also constantly being devised, improved, and revised, so that the problem remains a major one. For this reason—and because, as stated earlier, a clandestine act is internationally interpreted as a hostile act—such risky methods as illegal radio transmissions are generally kept to a minimum in peacetime. The prevailing solution to the problem the world over in peacetime is usually a series of cut-outs and letter drops by which the information ultimately comes into the hands of agents having diplomatic immunity and is then forwarded on in an embassy's regular diplomatic mail or telegraph traffic.

From the viewpoint of the over-all national interest, there is another characteristic of secret intelligence operations which weighs heavily, above all in the balance and outcome of the present East-West secret war. It is that the need for intelligence cuts across all political lines. We have already noted that, for intelligence to have the needed quality, variety, reliability, and breadth of coverage, it cannot be limited to sources chosen solely for their political ideology or compatibility with one's own political aims. West Germany's Gehlen Organization is a case in point.

General Gehlen held high responsibilities for German intelligence on the Eastern Front during the war. With the collapse of Germany in 1945, Gehlen salvaged the records of his extensive networks throughout Eastern Europe and the accumulation of years of intelligence about the Soviet Union, the Red Army, and its leadership. All this mass of material Gehlen hid in various places in West Germany. He also gathered a group of his best subordinates and instructed them to go into secure hiding. He then did the same, waiting a sufficient time until it became clear to the American Army that what they lacked most of all was any real and detailed knowledge of the Red Army which faced them across a long border and with which they were constantly being called upon to negotiate and solve an infinite variety of problems—from the regulation of Allied communications with Berlin to the repression of Peasant Party leaders in Bulgaria. When, in due course, General Gehlen emerged from hiding and presented himself to the Americans, an agreement was reached which permitted the Gehlen Organization to function as a unit, under the command and direction of Gehlen himself, even though at the outset for the sole benefit of the United States Army. In the temper and climate of postwar Europe and in the light of Allied political aims, such an agreement was politically indefensible; indeed, Gehlen had succeeded where all the rest of the German political and military hierarchy had failed, namely, to persuade the Western allies, or at least a part of them, to co-operative action against the Soviets. From the viewpoint, however, of the national security of the United States, of its armies in Europe, as well as of the security of Western Europe itself, the agreement was not only justifiable but essential. (This arrangement, it might be added, was as weak consommé compared to the witches' broth of Soviet collaboration with the Germans in wartime in the apprehending and execution of the Polish Underground connected to the Polish Government-in-Exile in London.)

Here arises the crucial conflict between the requirements of secret intelligence operations and the aims and methods of political warfare. This conflict never ceases. It goes beyond the question posed in an earlier chapter of how to reconcile, as an example, the need for full and reliable intelligence about Cuba with the political aim of assisting anti-Castro but also anti-Batista Cubans in their action to free Cuba from Soviet influence. For the consequences of this conflict will still continue to appear even after a policy decision, designed to regulate or compromise the conflicting interests, has been made at the highest level.

At one point in the postwar period, for example, a political operation was undertaken in the West which had as one of its objectives the creation of political unity among the Albanians in Western countries—a sizable number in proportion to the million-and-a-half population of Albania itself—excluding, quite naturally, pro-Communist Albanians and those with records of collaboration with the Italian or German occupations of the country. So far so good. But as it happens, by the simple facts of geography, a goodly number of Albanian exiles, including some of the most capable leadership, resides in Italy. It was perhaps understandable that the Italians should take a position strongly in favor of the inclusion, in any unified group, of the Albanians who had in the past loyally served Italian interests in Albania, and it was equally understandable that such a course would prejudice the potentialities of any such group in Albania itself. What complicated the operation throughout was that American intelligence, as distinct from American political agents, tended—naturally enough—to regard the advantages of close relations with the Italian intelligence services as outweighing the objectives of the political operation, and were therefore inclined to favor the Italian point of view in purely political matters. Needless to say, the Greeks, working through the British, had similar objectives—equally repugnant to the Albanians of Albania, who are quite aware that the Greeks regard most of Albania as a Greek province called Northern Epirus. (This particular soufflé rose to new heights when Marshal Tito of Yugoslavia—feuding then as now with the Albanians—announced the formation of an Albanian Committee in the Kossovo region of Yugoslavia, where there live some 500,000 more Albanians.)

It could be argued, of course, that this type of conflict could be resolved by more vigorous action with allies and more rigorously enforced policy decisions within a government. The argument has some merit, but only to a small degree, for the conflict is inescapable. For one thing, the Western world is organized as an alliance, not a train of cowed satellites. For another, even with their supreme word within their empire, the Soviets have the same troubles: one of the all-time feats of political tightrope-walking and agitated duplicity was performed by a high Soviet official who once found himself caught on a festive occasion between the East Germans on the one hand and the Poles on the other, with both demanding contradictory assurances about the Polish-East German border.

At the level of secret operations, the Soviets themselves recognize the perpetual conflict between intelligence requirements and political action, and rigorously separate the two insofar as that is possible. (Local Communist Parties may provide a recruiting base for Soviet intelligence, but it is only in rare cases of need that active Communist Party members will be found to be functioning as integral parts of an intelligence network.) This separation is in fact only for convenience and security at the lowest working levels; above that level in the Soviet hierarchy, as everywhere else, the decision must be taken in favor of either political objectives or intelligence interests when, as inevitably happens, the two conflict.

The American Government has experimented back and forth between separation of these two principal branches of secret operations—which is wasteful, expensive, and often produces worse collisions of interest in the field than at headquarters—and integration of the two branches—which fails to safeguard the legitimate interests of either—and a series of compromises between the two. Here again the best solution is in the last analysis dependent upon the breadth of view and the ingenuity of the men who must make it work.

1. The fact that today Polisario or Polisario/Algeria must be substituted for Spain in the equation does not eliminate the equation.

2. A number of studies and memoirs, too lengthy to catalogue here, which have appeared since this was written suggest that this brief summary of a complex subject is oversimplified, and that the principal emphasis should probably be put on what I only inserted in parentheses; i.e., *"correctly interpreted."*

3. The same reader in Hawaii who corrected me on the Russian cruiser in Portsmouth Harbor (see the notes to Chapter IV above) also pointed out that the aircraft carrier torpedoed at Scapa Flow in 1939 was not the *Ark*

Royal but the *Royal Oak.* The late Ladislas Farago, who served in the U.S. Navy under Admiral Zacharias in World War II, asserted (in his book, *Burn After Reading)* that no such German spy (whether an innkeeper or a watchmaker, as he has also been described) existed at Scapa Flow, and I believe it is now generally accepted that he was myth, not fact. Some "sleepers," however, *are* fact.

CHAPTER VIII

CE versus Security, and Other Devilry

Counterespionage, usually called simply by its initials CE, is a widely misunderstood branch of secret operations. Its purpose is not to apprehend enemy agents—that is an aim of the security forces. It is the word "counter" which causes the trouble, since it is generally interpreted to mean "against": a defensive operation against the enemy's intelligence operations. Quite to the contrary, CE is an offensive operation, a means of obtaining intelligence about the opposition by using—or, more usually, attempting to use —the opposition's operations. CE is a form of secret intelligence operation, but it is a form so esoteric, so complex and important as to stand by itself.

The flavor of CE operations was caught to hilarious perfection by Peter Ustinov in his *Romanoff and Juliet.* In the play Ustinov, as the Prime Minister of a small, neutral nation squeezed between the giants of East and West, calls on the American Ambassador and learns that the Americans know about a secret Soviet maneuver in the contest to dominate his country. After a bit of reflection the Prime Minister—crossing the stage—calls on the Soviet Ambassador. After some preliminaries he says to the Soviet Ambassador, "They know." The Soviet Ambassador replies calmly, "We know they know." Back to the American Ambassador goes Ustinov. "They know you know," he says conspiratorially. The American Ambassador smiles confidently. "We know they know we know," he answers. Ustinov returns to the Soviet Ambassador. "They know you know they know," he says. To this the Soviet Ambassador replies, triumphantly, "We know they know we know they know." Once again the Prime Minister calls on the American Ambassador. "They know you know they know you know," he says, weary and curious at the same time. The American Ambassador repeats it after him, counting on his fingers. "WHAT?" he suddenly cries in horror.

The ultimate goal of all CE operations is to penetrate the opposition's own secret operations apparatus: to become, obviously without the opposition's knowledge, an integral and functioning part of their calculations and operations. CE thus differs from other general secret intelligence in having a single, specialized target.

The superior interest of this target—the opposition's secret operations—over most others in intelligence is marked. A successful penetration of an opponent's secret operations organization puts you at the very heart of his actions and intentions toward you. You share his mind and thinking to an intimate—and reliable—degree impossible in any other secret operation. This means that so far as intelligence is concerned, you know what he knows. You have thereby annulled, in one stroke, the value to him of his secret intelligence about you; you have neutralized the power of his secret knowing. Even more importantly, through your knowledge of his intelligence interests and of his political operations, as revealed in his policy papers and instructions, you are in possession of the most reliable possible indications of his intentions. Most importantly, you are in a position to control his actions, since you can, by tailoring intelligence for him to your purposes, by influencing his evaluation, mislead him as to his decisions and consequent actions.

The above, of course, describes the ideal. The actual practice of CE moves along for the most part at a level of compromise well below such total success—although it is the ideal which forever animates both theory and practice.[1] The kind of total success which is the ideal of CE is more or less ruled out by the facts of human conflict and organization. Even if it were true, for example, as has been alleged, that Admiral Canaris, chief of the World War II German Abwehr, was in fact a British agent, this still did not prevent various Abwehr subordinates from achieving a number of genuine and striking successes in their operations against the Allies. And even between friendly or allied secret operations organizations there are distinct and specific limits to the degree and substance of co-operation—in other words, to the easiest kind of penetration and control. Secret services may sit on the same bed together; they may even turn back the covers part way; but they never actually get into the bed. Even at a partial level of fulfillment, however, CE operations (unlike the demi-vierge) can be enormously effective.

Penetration is the technique par excellence of CE operations. But much of their complexity arises from the fact that effective and successful penetration is not limited to the single possibility of introducing one's own agent into the enemy's operations. The same effect can be achieved in many substitute ways—and most often is, if for no other reason than the imposing difficulties and length of time which are the usual prospect for planting an agent in another service.

The commonest substitute for planting one's own agent is the "turning" of an enemy agent. Turning an agent, that is to say, convincing a man working in another cause that he should change sides and continue active in the conflict, with all the added risks involved, is clearly a psychological operation of immense complexity. As if this were not enough, the operation has the inherent weakness that what can be done once may perhaps be done twice. In a recent British case of this sort, on which the British Government has understandably refused all comment, all the pitfalls were demonstrated. A British agent, working in Germany against the Soviets, was approached by the Soviets to serve them. He agreed to do so—which made him a double agent, i.e., an agent who is working on two sides, but to the knowledge of only one, each side believing he is working exclusively in their behalf. Then, however, as a part of his operations on behalf of the Soviets, he informed the British of the Soviet approach to him and agreed to act as a double agent on behalf of the British. The British were thus led to believe that he was also acting as an agent of the Soviets but was really serving Britain. In fact, however, the man was a triple agent: from the British point of view he was a British agent who had falsely agreed to work for the Soviets—a standard penetration double agent, unturned from his original loyalty. But from the Soviet point of view he was a British agent who had agreed to do his real work for the Soviets and then had, in a second, false turning, honored his first turning. The latter was the truth of the case, as eventually the British discovered. So long as the man was a double agent—turned once, but falsely, as the British thought—he was valuable to the British; but his value to the Soviets rested on the fact that he was really a triple agent—a man turned twice, in this case once genuinely and once falsely. In brief, once turned makes a double agent; twice turned makes a triple agent, and so on. The decisive question is precisely which turns are genuine and which are false. This is but one of the problems which makes CE an extraordinarily complex affair; the determination of which turns are genuine and which false is a painstaking exercise in the control of information, of who knows what when, that requires constant alertness and a simultaneous grasp of both large perspective and detail. It is obviously an intellectual exercise of almost mathematical complexity.

The problem is further complicated by the existence of another kind of multiple agent, that is the triple—or even quadruple—agent working for three, four, or more different services. This type of multiple agent is generally a lone operator working for his own profit, and the question of turning is not as important with him. I once knew of a Viennese hotel porter who was working simultaneously for—and being paid by—the American, British, Soviet and French services, and who also—without pay—did his duty as an Austrian citizen. This kind of agent is usually something of a freak, however, and appears as a phenomenon only under very special circumstances, such as existed in Vienna at the end of World War II with four powers in occupation of the city. It is a dangerous gambit—even though my porter friend still is a leading fixture in Vienna—and is not of the same quality of professional interest, because of its patent unreliability, as the agent genuinely turned as between two conflicting services.

It is not unnatural that men who specialize in affairs of such complexity should regard themselves somewhat as the Cabots of the intelligence world, speaking only to God. CE practitioners do in fact believe, with some justification, that CE is the queen of all secret operations. This view is based on the undeniable fact that, for the mere conduct of their daily work, CE men must of necessity know more than anyone else, not only about enemy operations, but also about the operations of their own service as well. It is this greater and broader knowledge which leads CE specialists to the belief—often, but far from always, mistaken—that they can and do control all other secret operations. In the sense of control of knowledge as used in Chapter II—knowing who knows what—the control is real; in the sense of direction of operations, the control is real only in proportion to the lack of alertness of their colleagues, allies, or enemies.

CE's spread of knowledge extends also to all relations with any other services. CE men do not conduct the relations with other services, generally speaking. But they must be fully informed about the extent and substance of them. If, for example, it is decided, as a policy matter, to consult with the French services or to act jointly with them in a certain operation, it is of utmost importance that the CE men know the substance of the contacts with the French. The fact of French possession of a particular item of information may mean nothing to a political agent working with them; to a CE officer, however, it may well constitute decisive proof of enemy penetration of the French services or of secret French actions of particular interest to us.

This ubiquity of CE interest and activity can sometimes be a bit jolting. I once conducted a political and highly secret operation in an area in which it was decided, for political reasons, to exclude a neighboring but friendly service from both participation and knowledge. The first step in the operation involved the passage of a boat, at night, through waters adjacent to this friendly country, and the discharge, in a nearby hostile area, of several infiltration agents. My agents reported success, and I went about my business fairly calmly. Fairly calmly, that is, until one of my CE colleagues called on me and read to me, at great length, the report—alarmingly accurate—of the passage of the boat, its passengers, their destination, their equipment, and, unkindest cut of all, a somewhat detached professional critique of the operation. My operation had been penetrated by the friendly but excluded country; their service, at the same time, was penetrated by our own CE man—with the result that I had quite a bird's-eye view of my own operation.

Such information can be highly useful and even reassuring, however. I was once obliged to engage in some very ticklish and difficult negotiations with a political group thoroughly under the domination of the local intelligence service. For weeks on end we met daily and pursued our talks. In the evenings members of the group with whom I was negotiating would report to the local intelligence service. During the night our own agents in the local service, the result of penetrations and turnings by our CE officers, would report what my fellow conferees had commented and what their reactions and plans were as a result of my day's work. In the early morning this information was passed to me by our CE agents. I thus entered each day's talks with a quite accurate and highly useful idea of what faced me across the table.

It is perhaps understandable that the ideal of all CE operations is a form of penetration in which the intervening factor of an agent is removed. This occurs when an enemy network is captured—intact and in its entirety. Such cases are rare and are most often the result of a lucky accident—but this doesn't stop CE men from forever trying to achieve it. The most notable example in recent history of such an operation was the German Operation North Pole in World War II. Early in the war the Abwehr arrested two Dutch underground agents infiltrated from England at the moment of their arrival in the Netherlands, but after they had already given the signal of safe arrival. The Germans were lucky in that these two agents were the first of a projected series; they had as yet no connections in the Netherlands who could relay the word to England of a mishap. The agents were secretly imprisoned and no mention made even in German Army reports of their capture. Then by a combination of information found on the captured agents, of deductions from radio signals intelligence, of threats to the prisoners, and—unusual for the Abwehr—of the ability to think as the enemy would think, the Abwehr succeeded in entering into contact by radio with the agents' British headquarters and passing themselves off as being the agents.

For two years the Germans were able to maintain this tour de force, organizing in conjunction with Dutch-British headquarters in England ever new secret forays into the Netherlands of additional agents—all of whom were met on the beach or on the landing grounds by the Abwehr and imprisoned. The falsification was so perfect that on various occasions the Abwehr itself—acting as the Dutch underground—sent out "escaped" Allied prisoners to Spain through the channels indicated by London; the Abwehr even once blew up—over the understandably irate protests of the local German commander—several German barges in Rotterdam in order to prove to the British how well the "underground" in the Netherlands was working. The entire operation was a rare achievement, but to CE men it excites that admiration which only the professional ideal can arouse.

Men dedicated to a profession are susceptible to seeing themselves in terms of fulfilling exactly the image of the profession. Intelligence officers are no exception. Malcolm Muggeridge, writing in the *New Statesman,* said on this subject,

> The identity of "C" (head of the British services) was also disclosed, along with other unpublished information about MI-6, in an article in the New York *Herald Tribune* by Stewart Alsop. I asked Alsop subsequently whether his disclosures had any repercussions. He said there had been some rumblings in Anglo-American intelligence circles, but that Menzies himself had been appeased by the epithet "legendary" which Alsop had, with sagacious forethought, applied to him. "Legendary" was precisely what, in my experience, all Intelligence Brass wanted to be.

I have only one clue as to what this image might be in the case of CE officers. It came during a visit to France. I called on a high French CE officer, bearing, among other things, friendly greetings to him from an American CE colleague. On seeing the Frenchman I was instantly struck by his extraordinary physical resemblance to the American officer. The same long, thin face, elegantly pointed chin, aquiline nose, sensuous but disciplined mouth, sunken cheeks, deep-set eyes illuminated by a kind of controlled fire, thick black hair surmounting an aristocratic forehead. I immediately conveyed the greetings of Mr. X. The Frenchman acknowledged them with just a trace of a smile, but with an air of respect. "Ah, oui," he said. "Monsieur X." A moment's reflection, then—gracefully, even appreciatively—*"Un homme macabre."*

It can be seen that CE operations are offensive operations which depend for their existence as well as success on constant, if controlled, contact with the enemy. Security, on the other hand, is a defensive operation which seeks to destroy the enemy's operations and to cut off all contact with him as dangerous. Here lies one of the classic conflicts of secret operations. With the discovery of an opposition network, security will pause only long enough to seek to uncover all members of the network and will then call for its obliteration. CE will insist on exploring the possibility of exploiting the network, of—as the phrase has it— "playing it back" to the enemy. I remember discussing an American operation which had been penetrated by several foreign services, including the Soviets, with a security officer and then with a CE official. Referring to the operation's headquarters, the security man said, "Good Lord, stay away from that place. It's a catastrophe. There are more foreign agents in there than our own people that we can count on." As he spoke, his genuine worry was evident. The CE man, on the other hand, spoke calmly, almost wistfully. "Quite a sponge that place. We've picked up a lot of interesting threads there," he said.

As with the conflict between political and intelligence objectives —and techniques—there is no master solution for that between CE and security. Each case must be handled on its merits. Since there is no impartial authority which can decide these cases in the event of disagreement, however, and as there is often no time for such bureaucratic procedures, it is often found that CE and security are in practice working at cross purposes, even though in the same field and on the initial basis of much the same information.

Counterintelligence is generally used as a synonym for counterespionage. Despite the sanction given it by the U.S. Army's Counter-Intelligence Corps, the term is a misnomer. It suggests, in its strictest sense, an impossible kind of exchange of volleys, in which the lethal bullets are bits of evaluated information. There is, nevertheless, a secret operation which could conceivably be described as counterintelligence—although it is not. This is the deliberate planting of information with the enemy or the undertaking of an act or series of acts which will create a desired impression upon him.

When the purpose of such an operation is to test the opposition's reaction to a given piece of information, whether true or false, it is a simple intelligence operation. It is the intelligence equivalent of a military probe or of a political trial balloon.

When the same operation is undertaken with the purpose of tracing the course and ultimate destination of the planted information, it is a CE operation. It provides the vital information about who is in touch with whom and who knows what. If, for example, American agents plant with the Soviet Military Attaché in London a secret and ostensibly reliable report that in ten days the Americans will deliver an ultimatum to Pakistan to open its ports to transshipment of Afghan goods, and two weeks later the French Military Attaché in Kabul questions his American colleague as to why the reported action did not take place, it does not mean necessarily that the French Military Attaché in Afghanistan is a Soviet agent. It does mean, however, that there is a connection, however tenuous, between the Soviet Attaché in London and the French-

man in Kabul. It could mean any of a number of possibilities, from
mere idle leakage, to a Communist cell in the French Defense
Ministry, or a Soviet network in Afghanistan with some connection to the French Embassy. It is one of the functions of CE to
trace these possibilities whenever they seem promising enough.

When the purpose of planting of information or the taking of
actions to create a desired impression is to influence the enemy's
decisions and actions, they become one of secret operations' most
vital and complex activities—deception. Although good cover de-
ceives, this is not what is meant by the technical term "deception."
One of my colleagues once spent nearly a year trying to devise a
good definition of deception, and finally concluded that it meant
merely luring your opponent into doing voluntarily and by choice
what you want him to do. The history of human conflict is filled
with the use of deception, such as the crude but effective Trojan
Horse, or the famous gesture of the Dame de Carcas, who, when
her citadel was under siege in the Dark Ages, threw her last remaining food supplies over the walls to the hungry besieging army,
which thereupon, in the discouraged—but false—realization that
she could not be starved out, withdrew. (The ensuing victory celebration, with unceasing ringing of bells, changed the citadel's name
to Carcassonne, of modern tourist fame.)

The Second World War provided recent history's most classic
known example of deception in the Allied invasion of Normandy.
In his superb *The Struggle for Europe,* Chester Wilmot wrote of
the prelude to Operation Overlord:

> All the guile and ingenuity of . . . Intelligence were being
> turned to the devising of a scheme of strategic deception, far
> more subtle in technique, far more sinister in design. The object
> of this plan, which carried the code name FORTITUDE, was to
> convince the German High Command *before D-Day* that the
> assault would come in the Pas de Calais, and *after D-Day* that
> the Normandy landing was a preliminary and diversionary oper-
> ation, intended to draw German reserves away from the area
> north of the Seine so that the main Allied attack might be deliv-
> ered there at a later date. By this bluff it was hoped that an army
> of a quarter of a million men might be kept, idle but expectant,
> between Le Havre and Antwerp until the Battle of Normandy
> had been won. . . . The seeds of deception was sown in fertile
> ground. . . . To the Germans the Pas de Calais was of vital

importance and they made the common German mistake of assuming that it must therefore bulk equally large in the eyes of their adversaries. In working to strengthen these preconceptions, the British played upon the notorious tendency of German Intelligence Officers to approach problems with a card-index mind, indefatigable in collecting information, but incompetent in assessing it. . . . The aerial plan was shaped accordingly. For every reconnaissance mission over Normandy, two were flown over the Pas de Calais. For every ton of bombs dropped on coastal batteries west of Le Havre, two tons were put down on batteries north of it. In the bombing of railways 95 per cent of the effort was directed against targets north and east of the Seine. . . . The impression created by these operations was confirmed by information which came from the English side of the Channel—from [German] air reconnaissance, wireless interception, and the reports of spies who were surreptitiously provided with appropriate data. . . . Preparations in the southeast [of England] were discreetly revealed, but those being made in the south-west were hidden as carefully as possible. . . . The presumption that the main invasion forces were assembled in the south-east was reinforced by deceptive wireless traffic. By another radio subterfuge the idea was conveyed that the two follow-up armies (First Canadian and Third American) were in fact an assault force destined to land in the Pas de Calais. The Germans were allowed to learn that this Army Group was under the command of Lieut-General George S. Patton, who was an ideal bogey . . . [and] this set-up carried conviction to the logical German mind.

Wilmot, writing in 1952, still did not have access to the operation made public later which was a notable feature of the same Allied deception. This was the famous and delicate British operation of putting ashore on the north coast of Spain a corpse clothed as a British officer carrying secret papers—containing false information, naturally—concerning the forthcoming invasion, which the Spanish, as foreseen, quickly turned over to the Germans. Here was proof, if ever needed, that there are an infinity of ways of reaching and influencing the enemy's mind.[2]

Deception, like CE, is concerned with intimate, controlled, and purposeful contact with the enemy. While its objective is more specific than CE, it is a broader type of operation, being aimed at the total range of elements which make up the opposition's thinking and decisions, rather than only his intelligence organization. It therefore frequently happens that the ultimate stage of a CE operation, the ability to mislead the enemy, is subordinated to the requirements of a deception operation. In this case, the CE operation becomes known as a deception channel.

Deception, because of its immediate relevance to action, is probably the ultimate secret operation. But even if this evaluation is not universally accepted by professionals of the secret war, there is no doubt that strategic deception, whether in peace or in war, is the most secret of secret operations. Accordingly, the less said about it here the better.

1. While I was doing this annotation, a retired CIA friend, of a theoretical bent, said to me (the quotation is *verbatim* because, not understanding it when spoken, I wrote it down): "The ultimate philosophical rationale for intelligence as a function of government would lead inevitably to the hypothetical establishment of liaison between the Russian and American intelligence services," and quoted a former colleague, "Then I could talk to my opposite number in Moscow!" This arose in connection with my emphasis in the introduction to this edition on diplomacy in reading, and coming to terms with, the adversary's procedures and aims. Admitting that we are a long way from such liaison, but asserting a CIA advantage in being less politically beholden to the Administration in power than is the Department of State, my friend inquired, "Why not direct exchange?" Some clear-headed observers who are also first-rate thinkers might usefully leave behind the scorn these ideas will surely provoke in our day, and play around with them a bit.

2. An unnamed British reviewer of this book, writing in *The Times Literary Supplement* in 1963, pointed out that the operation with the corpse clothed as a British officer—the reviewer specified as a "Marine"—was not connected with Overlord (1944), but with Husky (1943) and the invasion of Sicily.

CHAPTER IX

Political Operations

It is a misfortune that most of what has been written about secret operations is concerned almost exclusively with intelligence operations and their related functions. The result is a very misleading picture of the secret war—sometimes affecting even those actively engaged in it. For the central and decisive battles of the secret war are fought in the vast realm of covert political operations. One proof of this statement is that I must necessarily be somewhat less explicit in this than in preceding chapters.

Secret intelligence is essential, indispensable; it is also, as previously pointed out, inseparable from political operations. But it is not, and should not be allowed to become, an end in itself. The ultimate national aim in the secret war is not simply to know. It is to maintain or to expand national power and to contain or to reduce the enemy's power; it is the exercise of power, itself a dynamic not a static thing.

Intelligence gained by the Soviets about the atomic bomb would have been a pointless drill had they not had the intent, the technical knowledge, and the industrial capacity to create their own nuclear arsenal. In brief, they converted knowledge into power by means of action. Similarly, the most precise intelligence available to the United States about dissension within the satellite Communist Parties and unrest among the satellite masses is of only potential value until the moment when we can combine an intent to exploit that intelligence with effective forms of action in order to weaken Soviet power in the satellites.

The exercise of power, the transformation of intelligence and policy into power by means of action, takes place daily and visibly in strategic policy, economic policy, diplomacy, defense, propaganda—all the overt aspects of international relations. It also takes place daily, but invisibly, in the secret war in the form of covert political operations.

The range, both functional and geographical, of secret political operations is almost unlimited.

Geographically, secret political operations have marked human history in all lands. The only new feature produced by our own times is the universal extent—Antarctica excepted—of a single conflict, that between the Communist and non-Communist blocs. The human conflicts which employ secret political operations have always been limited geographically by the transport and communications technology of the age and by the power of other nations not involved in the conflict. Englishmen fought Spaniards simultaneously in the Netherlands and in the Caribbean; Frenchmen fought Englishmen in Flanders, North America, and India at one and the same time. Today, Communist and non-Communist maneuver in combat all over the globe—a measure not only of modern transport and communications, but also of the historically unprecedented emergence of but two great power centers whose preponderance relative to the rest of the world is such that, until other nations or combinations of states can achieve some parity with them, they inevitably tend to divide the world between them.[1]

The first great post-Second World War engagement between East and West in the sphere of covert political operations was the Italian national elections of April 1948. With all of Eastern Europe already in the Soviet grasp, with civil war raging in Greece, the West awoke to the fact that Italy could be lost to the Soviets by political action. Hastily improvised operations, a number of which could barely be dignified by the adjective covert—certainly the vigorous speaking tours of the American Ambassador to Italy were anything but covert—narrowly saved Italy for the West that year. (The elections of 1958 in Italy had, once again, a similar air of urgency, suggesting that not a great deal of progress had been made in ten years in cutting back the inroads previously made there by the Soviets.) After Italy, the lines were swiftly drawn on either side of the military division of Europe. From there the conflict spread to the Far East, to the Middle East, to Southeast Asia, to Latin America, to Africa. (The effort to keep the Cold War, in the sense of hostile blocs of nations aligned with East or West, out of Africa is a sound, even noble one; it does not and cannot eliminate the secret war, as a talk with any African trade union leader, from Morocco through Nigeria and Tanganyika to Madagascar will show.)[2] In all these areas the secret war is waged not by intelligence agents, but by agents whose function is, in the broadest sense of the word, political.

The functional range of covert political operations is so vast as to defy listing. It runs from the simple, obvious "spontaneous demonstration"—in Tokyo or Caracas, in New York or New Delhi—through the quarrels of an international labor organization, the speeches at an international conference of intellectuals, the resolutions of a congress of lawyers, the organizational maneuvers of churchmen, the patient and persistent pressures of exiles, and a staggering variety of publications, to the Viet Cong guerrilla hidden in the jungles of South Vietnam and a Cuban prisoner captured at the Bay of Pigs.

(Contrary to a widespread impression, there is a more or less tacit understanding between states today to refrain from including political assassination in political operations. Stalin used it, but only against those he considered renegades from his own authority, e.g., Trotsky, Krivitsky, et al. Alexander Foote has pointed out that Stalin could easily have had Hitler assassinated before the Russo-German Pact, but refrained. Smaller nations sometimes resort to it, as in Trujillo's attempt on the life of President Betancourt of Venezuela or the prewar assassination of King Alexander of Yugoslavia, the work of Croat terrorists who had Italian and Hungarian support, or the Puerto Rican attempt on President Truman's life and attack on the U.S. House of Representatives. It should, however, be clear to observers on both sides that the existing conflicts between the great powers can in no way be resolved by political assassinations—which is at least some advance toward civilization.)[3]

These varied activities have a common political objective: the organization, exploitation, and direction of existing human passions and purposes so that they contribute, no matter how indirectly, to the fortunes of one or the other side in conflict. It is the substance of power, wherever and in whatever form it may exist, which the political agent pursues, recognizing that all organized or social human activity has a political content and significance.

If this seems obscure it is because of general acceptance of a too narrow definition of what is "political." As used in covert political operations, "political" is not limited to the complex of activities surrounding the gaining and holding of public office, of the constitutionally designated seats of power. It refers instead to a much wider concept—to politics as the general and infinitely varied struggle for and the exercise of power in human society. Under this concept all organized or social human activity represents potential or actual power ultimately transformable into control of the state and the society.

To claim that the scholar, the artist, the philosopher are apolitical is to deny the interrelation between human thought and action; it is to regard the founders of the United States as illiterate but dexterous constitutional carpenters, the upheaval of the French Revolution as an outburst about bread, the conscious theoreticians of the Bolshevik seizure of power in Russia as unlettered bombers who had never read a book, and the Chinese Communists as merely envious of Chiang Kai-shek and the Kuomintang. By the same token, the allegation that the businessman with foreign investments is apolitical because he "doesn't mix in politics" is naïve and implies two things which are patently untrue: that national wealth is not a part of national power, and that the businessman will under no circumstances seek his government's protection for his business.

The narrow definition of "political" can have serious consequences in international affairs. In the overt domain it can lead to the false and vulnerable position of appearing to back corrupt, tottering, or tyrannical regimes, as with the United States in South Korea and in South Vietnam (see also Latin America until very recently), or to the waste of vast amounts of economic aid aimed at reinforcing the viability of the regime, as in Laos and Iran. In the covert domain it can lead to futile involvement in mere palace intrigues (and to the even more grave error which I call the "our boy" theory— "Look, let's just put our boy in there and he'll run this show for us"—of which more below). The inherent limitations of palace intrigue, that is to say, exclusive involvement with the official center of power, are no modern development. In the sixteenth century, Don Bernardino de Mendoza, Spanish Ambassador to Henry III of France, was fully aware of these limitations in the operation which he conducted and which successfully immobilized France while Spain prepared to attack England. Mendoza was fully active at court; indeed, his intrigue in support of the Duc de Guise against the King and his bribery of Catherine de Medici were essential elements in his scheme. Nevertheless, he spent almost as much time and money on petty nobles, merchants, and, almost as importantly, on the organizers and instigators of the

Parisian anti-Protestant mobs, who were to defeat the King where court intrigue could not.

The sixteenth century, so akin to our own, also gave us another of history's finest recorded examples of a sustained covert political operation in the Jesuit underground in England. Over more than five decades the Jesuits sent covert missionaries to England to perform rites for the Catholic families, to make converts, and to recruit additional agents for training in the English College at Rome. Their story is a textbook of covert and clandestine techniques; hunted men, they were experts at disguise, cover, escape, secret inks, safe houses, hiding places, and all the paraphernalia and tricks essential to their mission. When caught they gladly suffered the penalty of death, regarding it as enviable martyrdom. But the ultimate purpose of the Church of Rome in mounting this covert operation was political: it was to return the rebellious Church of England to the authority of Rome. The fact that the issue was religious authority does not alter the fact that the purpose was the enhancement or recovery of power, meaning that the operation was political.

That even the Christian churches have not forgotten their ancient heritage of secret operations was illustrated by a bizarre incident which occurred in 1950. There was living in Paris at that time the Metropolitan Vissarion of the Rumanian Orthodox Church. This elderly prelate had two distinctions: one was that he had been at the Tiflis Theological Seminary with Stalin; the other was that he was the senior Orthodox hierarch in exile from the lands under Soviet control. It was the latter which aroused the interest of the Churches of Rome and of England. At stake was the Roman aim to draw the Orthodox Churches even closer to recognizing the authority of the Pope, and the aim of the Anglican Church to align the Orthodox Churches firmly with Protestantism against Rome.

The Metropolitan was quite content to remain in Paris, where gradually, under the guise of brotherly assistance, he was being persuaded to accept Catholic offers of priests to minister to the exiled Orthodox who suffered from a shortage of priests. (The schism between the Orthodox and Catholic Churches is many centuries older than that between Rome and Canterbury, but in certain sacramental respects much less profound.) There then appeared in Paris one day an Englishman who presented himself to the Metropolitan, showing credentials as an emissary of the Church of England. He extended to the Metropolitan an official

invitation to come to England to live, as a guest of the English
Church. For days the Metropolitan vacillated, and finally agreed to
leave. When the time came, however, he had once more changed
his mind. This was apparently too much for the British agent,
whose instructions one can only surmise must have been quite
categorical. For at this point he proceeded to kidnap the Metropolitan, bodily spiriting him away to a house outside of Paris prepara-
tory to transferring him to England. Probably fortunately for everyone concerned, several Rumanian Orthodox communicants
became suspicious, with the result that the French police, after
several days, found the Metropolitan and his abductor.

Notwithstanding this misfire, the Church of England succeeded
in its aim: the Orthodox Churches, including finally in 1961 the
Russian Orthodox Church itself, became members of the Protestant World Council of Churches. Rome's position in any eventual
negotiations for the reconciliation of the Christian churches is obviously thereby weakened; a unified opposition is much more for-
midable than a number of separate adversaries—provided, of
course, that the opposition is genuinely unified.

It is this political—in the broad sense of power—characteristic
of all organized and social human activity which imposes the extraordinary variety of secret political operations. My own diverse
but not unusual experience in this field has run the gamut from
organizing a literary evening in New York to directing the operation of a clandestine radio transmitter; from providing speakers for
five different groups in the same national election to arranging for a
gift to an important tribal leader; from organizing a political committee of exiles for the infiltration and invasion of their native land
to reorganizing the same group some years later to eliminate their
military activities; from supervising a dozen publications in half a
dozen languages to rewriting a manifesto; from persuading twelve
men representing as many different nationalities to agree on a single point to working a resolution through a congress of three hundred men representing thirty-five different nations; from subsi-
dizing summer camps for children to running an escape chain out
of Soviet-occupied territory. This partial list is not intended to
demonstrate virtuosity on my part, but the ubiquitous quality of
the political element in human affairs.

(That by and large the West recognizes this quality only to the
extent of covert political operations, rather than openly proclaiming it as a justification for subjecting all organized human activity

to the direction of the state, as in totalitarian systems, is a tribute to the steadfastness of purpose of democratic leaders and the resiliency and resourcefulness of our societies.)

The relevance of some of this variety to the secret war is not always evident at first glance. Those summer camps for children, for example, seem a far cry from political conflict. And yet they were the answer to a situation in which a Communist state arranged for summer vacations in their native land for children of exiles at less than a quarter of the cost of similar vacations in their adopted land. The fact that the parents were voters in a country in which there existed a strong Communist Party and in a district in which they had, until the advent of the Communist offer, constituted an important non-Communist force seemed to justify the subsidy of local camps, precisely as it had moved the Communists to their original plan. That in present conditions of greater prosperity in their adopted land, and of greater American public awareness of the importance of these problems, genuinely private assistance could probably be forthcoming does not alter the conditions as they existed at that time—which were that timely and adequate assistance had to be, if it was to be at all, in the form of a covert governmental subsidy for a definite political purpose.

The foregoing illustrates a point about covert political operations which distinguishes them sharply from secret intelligence operations. In the vast majority of political operations the true function of the operation itself is overt and acknowledged. This does not necessarily mean that it is publicized, but it is at least not hidden. If, for example, it is decided to strengthen a political party in a neutralist country which is wavering in the face of Communist subversion, the reinforced efforts of the party are not and cannot be hidden or disguised, nor is it even desirable to do so. What is covert is foreign government involvement in the process, whether it be in the form of subsidies or advice—and the two are rarely separated in practice. Since cover is limited to but one essential point—relationship to government—it is obvious that the choice of cover, the choice of agent, the forms of communication, and the nature of the case officer-agent relationship are all affected. Generally speaking, the cover possibilities in political operations are more flexible than in secret intelligence, the choice of agent is more difficult, the forms of communication are equally restricted, and the case officer-agent relationship is less prone to duplicity.

A clear understanding of the simultaneous unity of purpose and variety of forms of secret political operations is frequently obstructed by loose and conflicting terminology. Much is spoken and written, for example, about political warfare, psychological warfare, guerrilla and unconventional warfare, as though these were all separate and arcane fields of action.

Political warfare is a term sanctioned by frequent official usage. It embraces the same field of activities as the term political operations, but my own feeling is that it has a narrower connotation. Its inevitable emphasis is on war rather than on politics. It suggests a state of war and the existence of a specific enemy, but does not convey the full scope of activities or the existence of multiple rivalries as does political operations. I doubt, for example, that assistance to non-Communist parties in the 1948 Italian elections could be considered political warfare—although the signs posted in Rome in 1961 after the Twenty-second Congress of the Soviet Communist Party falsely summoning Italian Party members for a full discussion of Stalinism might be so considered. In any case, official labels cannot be taken too seriously. During the Second World War what were in fact deception operations and even mere publicity gimmicks were labeled political warfare, and what was a genuine case of political warfare—Allied involvement in the bomb plot against Hitler—came under the heading of intelligence.

Psychological warfare is another wartime term which has spread confusion. It has been widely used to signify political operations, but it hardly does justice to their real content. The blunt realities of a political operation aimed at the overthrow of a government can hardly be called psychological warfare. There is, however, a wartime operation which is highly useful and which is properly termed psychological warfare. It embraces a host of actions, from leaflets dropped to enemy troops, through broadcasts to the enemy, to the manufacture and spread of demoralizing rumors in enemy territory, and its sole aim is to weaken the enemy's will to resist. What is called psychological strategy, that is, the co-ordination and exploitation of a government's actions for maximum political effect, is, obviously, a political function, covering a government's overt as well as covert operations.

Guerrilla warfare has lately been the object of considerable attention. As guerrilla tactics themselves are as much a part of open war as of the secret war, the term unconventional warfare has been coined to describe the peacetime use of guerrilla tactics—among many other techniques—in bringing about the overthrow of a government and the capture of territory and populations. Taken as a whole, unconventional warfare is a political operation, initially covert, then clandestine, and finally overt.

The Communists successfully utilized this technique in French Indochina and continue it today in Laos and South Vietnam. The Soviets have made sporadic efforts to use it in Iran and Iraq, without success, and they have failed in its use in Greece, Malaya, and the Philippines. The F.L.N. mastered it successfully, and indigenously, in Algeria, as did Castro in Cuba.

Very briefly, the technique involves infiltration, agitation, recruitment, harassment of the civil and military power, and, finally, open assault. From the first day to the last, however, the entire structure rests on ever-widening control of the local population. Territory is a secondary and only ultimate consideration. But it is the population which provides food, recruits, and intelligence. (Experts estimate that a successful guerrilla force requires from at least five to ten or more times its own numbers as an intelligence screen, that is, sympathizers or agents in the local population who will provide reliable information on government troop movements.) This control of the local population is achieved by persuasion, by indoctrination, and by terror, i.e., reprisals and the threat of reprisals against those who will not co-operate. Thus the vital element on which the success of unconventional warfare rests is a political one.

Authorities on unconventional warfare without exception recognize its political character. In his *Problems in the Guerrilla War of Resistance Against Japan,* Mao Tse-tung wrote:

> There are often military elements who "care for only military affairs but not politics." Such one-track minded military officers, ignoring the interconnection between political and military affairs, must be made to understand the correct relationship between the two. All military actions are means to achieve certain political objectives, while military action itself is a manifested form of politics.

(An interesting contrast to General Marshall's letter to Eisenhower concerning the British proposal to press eastward in Germany and take Berlin if possible: "Personally," wrote the U.S. Chief of Staff, "I would be loath to hazard American lives for purely political purposes.") Mao continues:

There are, of course, differences between political and military affairs, each with its special characteristics, but the one should not be disconnected and isolated from the other. . . . Only those who misinterpret the significance of guerrilla warfare would consider that "Guerrilla warfare is not a political problem, but one purely military in nature." This type of simple military viewpoint causes the loss of the political objectives of guerrilla warfare and must inevitably lead to the abandonment of political work, the dissolution of popular support, and the eventual defeat of guerrilla warfare. . . . If guerrilla warfare is without a political objective, it must fail; but if it maintains a political objective which is incompatible with the political objectives of the people, failing to receive their support, participation, assistance and active cooperation, then this too must fail. . . . This is because guerrilla warfare is basically organized and maintained by the masses, and once it is deprived of these masses, or fails to enlist their participation and cooperation, its survival and development is not possible. . . . There are those who cannot imagine how guerrillas could survive for long in the rear of the enemy. But they do not understand the relationship between the people and the [guerrilla] army. The people are like water and the [guerrilla] army is like fish. How can it be difficult for fish to survive if they immerse themselves within the mass of water? But if the water is taken away or dries up, the fish must also die and pass away.

Franklin A. Lindsay, an American expert who learned his basic lessons with Tito's Partisans in Yugoslavia during World War II, writing—somewhat less picturesquely, but just as realistically as Mao—in *Foreign Affairs* on "Unconventional Warfare" has the following to say:

Where the effective political control of the country has passed to the Communists, it will not be enough to conduct long-distance propaganda activities or to make plans on the assumption that the very real and very considerable dissatisfactions with the Communist regime will automatically result in a popular uprising as soon as the guerrilla forces appear. Clandestine support of at least a part of the villages and the countryside is an absolute prerequisite to the employment of guerrilla forces, for they must have local intelligence support and supplies if they are to survive in areas in which superior enemy forces are openly in control. In Jugoslavia, for example, in World War II, the Communist partisans had in many ways as favorable a situation for guerrilla warfare as might be expected anywhere. The main German forces were engaged by powerful allies on other fronts. Tito's partisan forces had as overt allies not only the Soviet Union but the United States and Great Britain. And from the latter two they received massive air support. In Slovenia, where there were no Cêtnik forces of Mihailovich to contend with, the political commissars of the Communist-established National Liberation Front could represent themselves to the people as the only force fighting the invader, and as having the complete support of all the major powers fighting the Germans. Yet they still found it necessary, in the words of one commissar, to "prepare the area intensively by the introduction of clandestine political organizers for a period of several months before we dared to introduce guerrilla forces."

Lindsay makes the point even more precisely:

> The first step in mobilizing a civilian population against Communist subversion and guerrilla attack is to establish a set of political goals in terms that the average person can understand. They must be goals that strike a sympathetic response and that aim to remove the inequities in the existing society and the grievances which they have caused. Through mass communications these reform programs must be communicated effectively, and repeatedly, to the population. . . . But this is only the beginning of the task. Political organizers must be recruited and trained in sufficient numbers to reach by direct contact nearly every family in the land. They must be as thorough as the best of ward or district leaders in American politics.

In this light, the suggestion, heard after the Cuban debacle, that American responsibility for unconventional warfare—or paramilitary operations—should be vested in the Pentagon is revealed as something less than logical—or politic.

As a matter of record, in the general proposition—however crude it may sound—of overwhelming governments by remote control, the United States has had about the same proportion of successes as the Soviet Union. However, this is not a statistically measurable subject. Where the Soviets have failed it has been at an enormous cost to us in the application of overwhelming military might, as in Greece—and even there the Tito-Cominform dispute played a large role in stopping the conflict. On the other hand, where we have failed it has been because of too great a reliance on military force and too little attention, if any, to the vital political elements. Our only real success in this ultimate field of covert political operations was Guatemala—and there we displayed our customary tendency to get things over with in a hurry and to substitute might for politics.[4]

Guns, however, at best only act as a temporary substitute for sound and patient political preparation. In one American operation other than Cuba which failed, political preparation was, to put it mildly, hastily improvised. In another our impatience was such that when the operation did not immediately succeed in the military sphere, we abruptly switched sides. (This at least earned us the gratitude of the Head of State whom we were trying to overthrow.)

Since political operations are concerned with human beings, they have an organic development of their own: for real rather than merely apparent results, their timetable can at most be hastened, but it cannot be artificially imposed from without. Notwithstanding the rapid changes which mark our epoch, the long view of history is still the key to international politics in our time.

Secret political operations are based upon three major characteristics which dictate the potentialities, the timing, and the working relationships of such operations.

The first is that any political operation must be based on something real, something which in fact exists. Secret political operations are neither skulduggery nor legerdemain. It would be, for example, the height of futility to undertake an operation in Switzerland to bring about the abandonment of Swiss neutrality in order that Switzerland should join NATO. There would simply be nothing effective to work with, even if the idea were sound. One of the greatest wastes of American time and money I ever encountered was the success of a Hungarian Catholic in persuading the appropriate authorities to send him to London to agitate against the decision—already made—of the Anglican Church to sponsor the invitation to the Russian Orthodox Church to join the World Council of Churches. The decision having been made in the highest councils of the English Church, after full deliberation, and having been duly accepted by British opinion, this agent's mission was largely an exercise in talking to himself.

For a thing to be real it need not be organized or even coherent, but it must exist. A sentiment, an opinion, a movement can be exploited, developed, organized, even astutely exaggerated, but it cannot be created out of thin air. The Communist Peace Campaign was a masterpiece of organization and exploitation of an unorganized sentiment. Again, in 1954, the Soviets organized in East Berlin a cover organization called the Mikhailov Committee—named after the Russian general who headed it. The announced purpose of this Committee was to assist the return to their homelands of Russian and Eastern European political exiles. The formation of this group was greeted with hoots of derision in the West, since a more unlikely undertaking seemed inconceivable. Nevertheless, a certain success—rapidly capitalized upon by the Soviets—accompanied the Committee's efforts, for what they were able to exploit to a considerable degree was simple nostalgia and the economic suffering of many refugees in the West.

The Mikhailov Committee illustrates a corollary to the rule that an operation must be founded on a reality, however tenuous. It is the corollary that is, in fact, the foundation of all political operations. It is simply that in human affairs there is no such thing as a monolith. There may be repression, there may be terror, but there is no uniformity. Ingenuity in political operations consists in recognizing dissent, however hidden, and then in devising ways to exploit it. Viewing the Communist Empire in 1947, for example, a serious observer was entitled to weigh the measurable dissension in Eastern Europe and assume that Yugoslavia would be the most loyal of the satellites. History records, of course, that it was the first—and so far only—Eastern European satellite successfully to declare its independence of Moscow's domination. It was a fundamental Leninist doctrine—in his application of military doctrine to politics—to insist on the "monolithic unity" of the Communist Party. But what has happened? Today there are three major brands of Communism within the Communist bloc—the Soviet, the Chinese, and the Yugoslav. In this sense, of course, Chou En-lai was right when he spoke at the Twenty-second Congress of the Soviet Communist Party and asked that the differences between the parties not be made public, to be exploited by the enemies of Communism. And Khrushchev knew it as well as he. But the pressure of dissension in human affairs will prevail, and Khrushchev's only choice was to jettison—without openly acknowledging it, of course —the myth of monolith.

This does not mean that any and all dissension is directly exploitable. The West cannot at this stage persuade any of the Communist dissidents into alliance against one or both of the other two. But political operations are, in most cases, infinitely more subtle than that. To exploit a disagreement between Mao and Khrushchev it is no more necessary—or possible—to enter into direct contact with Khrushchev on the subject than it is for him to capitalize on differences between American Democrats and Republicans by secretly offering financial aid to the Democrats. Khrushchev does not have to enter into alliance with the German industrialists who think enviously of the Eastern markets in order to exploit their impatience with the inflexibly pro-NATO and pro-European stand of Adenauer. Nor does the West have to make agents of the Eastern European intellectuals in order for their discontent with rigid Soviet control to create real problems for Khrushchev and some easing, however slight, of the satellites' plight. In both cases it suffices to recognize the dissension and then, by ingenuity and indirection, to nourish it.

The second basic characteristic of secret political operations is that they must be performed by others. Obvious as this sounds, it is all too often overlooked in the directions given to political agents. If the objective is to have the Socialist International take a particular stand, to have a neutralist conference adopt a certain policy, to have the Liberal Party of country X support a given step, or to have the progressive opposition seize power from a tottering, corrupt regime, then for the desired action to be valid it must be the Socialists, the neutralists, the Liberals of X nationality, or the members of the opposition who themselves take the desired action. This obviously puts the highest premium on the arts of persuasion and indirection and on individual qualities of personal influence, tact, comprehension, forcefulness when necessary, and resourcefulness.

These necessities have direct implications for the case officer-agent relationship in political operations. While discipline must still be present, there cannot be the ambiguity of purpose and motive which most often characterizes intelligence operations. In a political operation the case officer must have arrived at a clear and workable accommodation of interests with the agent. Control by the case officer there must be, but not duplicity. The purposes of case officer and agent must have been presented with the maximum permissible clarity, and then a reconciliation of conflicts and limitations negotiated. In brief, the outstanding characteristic of the political case officer-agent relationship is that it must be an alliance, not a utilization of the agent by the case officer, as often occurs in intelligence.

In politics a "no" is acceptable, and even defeat is understandable. Highhandedness, particularly on the part of a great power, must often be swallowed; but irresponsibility carries with it its own destruction, however long the process may take. Irresponsibility in political operations is a readily identifiable fault: it can be measured against the cardinal rule of such operations—do not make unnecessary promises or promises you have neither the ability nor intention to keep. Once a promise is given, an agreement made, it must be kept to the best of one's ability. In the jungle of international politics this is the equivalent of "honor among thieves." The Middle East, whatever its complications, is a monument to British understanding and observance of this classic rule. In the First World War Lawrence, with full authority, extended solemn promises to the Hashemite dynasty of the Hejaz, in return for the help of the Bedouins against the Turks. The British could not, after that war, save the Kingdom of the Hejaz from Ibn Saud of Arabia. But today the Hashemite great-grandson of the last King of the Hejaz sits on the throne of Jordan as witness to a kept promise. The same promises were made in World War II to Idris el Senussi, in return for his help against the Italians and Germans. Today, King Idris I of an independent—even if economically unviable—Senussi Libya bears witness to another kept promise. The result is that even with all the vicissitudes of history, and the fulminations of Nasser, the British position in the Middle East today remains more solid and effective than the history of the last fifteen years would otherwise warrant.[5]

There is yet another implication of this second fundamental characteristic of secret political operations which may possibly be disturbing to Americans. It is the clear inference which can be drawn of a client-patron, an almost feudal relationship between lesser states and the great powers. This is a fact of international life which has always existed and continues to exist, but it is one for which the United States, by virtue of its isolation, was ill prepared when it almost overnight emerged into the world as a great power. It is a fact contrary to our understanding of independence, to our proclaimed ideals, and, we sense, to our own history. But our own history was a very special case. Washington in his Farewell Address warned not only against entangling alliances, but against the meddling of great powers in our internal and factional affairs. The United States grew to maturity free of this external meddling not because of innate American qualities, but because of a combination of historical, geographical, and technological accidents—and for many years behind the protective shield of British policy. New nations today are not so lucky.

However, the hegemony or domination of the great powers is not without its cost. The influence and power which the great powers exercise in the affairs of the smaller states work both ways. There is a permanent tendency for the lesser powers to factionalize the great powers. A prize example of this was Yugoslavia during the Second World War, which for a period was a source of acute friction between Great Britain and the United States, the British supporting Tito, the Americans favoring General Mihailovich. Similarly, in the Congo the British, for both European and African reasons, maneuver behind Tshombe and Katanga, and the United States, with an eye on what it feels are larger issues, maneuvers behind Adoula and the Leopoldville Government. An adept politician in a small country need not necessarily fear his own weakness; a political operation works two ways, and in return for accepting influence he finds he can also exert it.

The third fundamental characteristic of secret political operations is that it matters less what you do than how you do it. The wrong thing done well is always preferable to the right thing done badly. The principal British criticism of the American operation in Cuba which came to my attention, for example, was summed up in the observation of one Britisher: "Good Lord, man," he said, "if you're going to do things like that, then for Heaven's sake do them. Hard, and with everything you've got. No halfway measures in that sort of thing." It is a fact, however lamentable, that the Soviets were aware of this in Hungary in 1956. It is also a relevant fact that the Head of State whom we tried to overthrow—and failed, switching our support after the fact—is today, not many years later, one of the leading purveyors of enthusiastic statements about the greatness of the United States—which serves to show that bruises for doing the wrong thing heal quickly in the international arena. But ineptitude, which fosters loss of confidence, is not so quickly forgotten. One of the principal problems of international

relations—including secret political operations—is simple communication across the barriers of linguistic, historical, and cultural
differences. In international politics the *lingua franca* is the language of power. Talking with a nation which follows a bad policy,
but executes it reasonably adeptly, at least permits communication
if not liking (South Africa comes to mind.) But communicating
with a nation which is inept in the execution of its policy is like
talking with a man with an insurmountable stammer—you don't
know whether what he is saying is good or bad.

Americans are deeply concerned about the rightness of their
national policies. This is healthy and useful. But too often the
assumption is made that if the policy is right, its proper execution
follows automatically. Vast improvements have been made in se-
lecting and supporting the best-suited personnel for secret political
operations in recent years, but there is still insufficient understanding of the fact that what is the American's meat may well be the
foreigner's poison. I recall with a shudder the remark of an American responsible for a highly important Eastern European operation. "What I don't like about X," he said, seriously referring to a
leading Czechoslovak politician, "is that he has none of that good
old American get-up-and-go." The rejoinder is obvious: if he had it
he wouldn't have been a leading Czechoslovak politician. (This
same American, left inexplicably in his post for two years, was
able, at the end of that time, to shock a Pole into disbelief with his
remark that Poland had every right to all lands up to the Oder-
Neisse line because, "After all, they were always Polish territory
until the Germans took them away." The Pole was embarrassed,
but he was a forthright man. "I am very grateful for your sympathy for our cause," he answered, "but, please, I beg of you, do not
let it be known that you base it on that reason. I am obliged to
inform you that historically it is simply not true.")

These things still happen, but the United States owes a not inconsiderable debt of gratitude in this connection to Allen Dulles
for two reasons: first, he maintained, during his stewardship of the
Central Intelligence Agency, and against strong and persistent
pressures, the vital principle of civilian control of this powerful
organization; and second, he instilled and developed, as rapidly as
possible in the circumstances, precisely that sense of professional-
ism essential to the best conduct of secret operations. But the full
process is a long one.

In the present transitional stage, the principal handicaps to

American secret political operations stem from the imposition on such operations of purely American standards which are laudable at home and inappropriate when exported. One such, for example, is haste. The result is what has been referred to, in some anguish, as the doctrine of immediate results immediately arrived at. In a field where quiet patience, the long view, and sustained effort are prime qualities the American bureaucracy is constantly pressed for demonstrable results to justify action. I recall spending two years creating a political organization whose ultimate purpose was the penetration of an already existing European institution. At the conclusion of the first meeting of the organization it was no closer in fact to its ultimate aim than at the outset. But it had at least been put into position to accomplish its mission. To my surprise I received high praise at this premature stage because, of all irrelevant reasons, two New York newspapers had published accounts of the meeting, and these clippings could be exhibited as proof of success. This impatience for quick and visible results leads also to what is generally interpreted by other nations as an American lack of tenacity. If results from a political operation are not almost immediately evident, the Americans will tend to lose interest, abandon the operation, or turn its personnel to other, frequently inappropriate uses.

The most common European charge against our operations, for example, that they are "not serious," stems from this same haste and its concomitant satisfaction with artificial results. As a Frenchman said to me in some disillusionment after watching the sudden turnabout of a highly complicated operation to a wholly new "priority" target, "The trouble with you people is that you only want to look good; you don't care about really being good."

This criticism also stems from promises too easily broken, almost always on the justification that high policy demands it or that overriding domestic American considerations require it. Under full authority I once made a careful agreement with a Western European political party which required guaranteed American participation for eighteen months. Five months later the American participation was canceled and the European personnel let go onto the street. In due course I found out that as a compromise in an American budget argument, this operation had been traded away for some funds for something else that now seemed more attractive. I had also to experience the quiet comment of a European Senator: "We shall never make the mistake of working with your organization again." The only saving point for the United States in this case was that he was speaking of a cover organization.

In a policy sense our operations also suffer from the application of purely American prejudices to situations where they are not applicable. The high Presidential adviser who once started to say that my residence abroad had made me "un-American," but who had the grace to pause and amend his sentence if not his thought, was exercised at the time over my proposal to bring an extremely well-known European Socialist into a European organization. "I don't understand why we can't just go along with our own people whom we've always worked with," he said. "You just don't understand that Socialism is a dirty word in this country." His observation about Socialism was no doubt true—notwithstanding the fact that it was by and large Socialist Governments in Western Europe which created NATO with us—but it was irrelevant to the fact that the organization we were discussing was formed to be effective in Europe, not in the United States.

(The bias is at least not one-sided. When on another occasion I proposed limited aid to an exiled monarch who had genuine popularity in his native land, the refusal was accompanied by the remark, "Surprised you'd even suggest it. What if Congress found out we were tied up with a *king*?")

The Presidential adviser's viewpoint was, of course, a close cousin of the "our boy" theory of political operations. I so label it because in a Western European country, functioning under a coalition of two dominant and independent parties—which meant greater effort on our part to maintain and develop our influence in this particular country—a neo-Fascist party was formed only a few years after the war. To my astonishment I encountered a serious proposal to back the neo-Fascist party with all our resources. The proponent of this plan ascribed my astonishment to ignorance. "Don't you see?" he said. "The leader of this party needs support; once he gets it we'll keep building him up until he throws out the coalition. Then we'll have our boy in there, and none of these headaches." Quite apart from the lack of political wisdom involved in this particular case, the "our boy" theory substitutes puppets for allies, corruption for viability, our prejudices for local reality. Syngman Rhee was "our boy," as were several others, now forgotten, in Laos.

In the purely technical aspects, our political operations suffer from an excessive prejudice in favor of intelligence objectives and procedures. When the inevitable conflict between intelligence and political objectives arises, the decision is too often in favor of the intelligence objectives. Similarly, the case officer-agent relationship in political operations is too often clouded by the duplicity and the type of rigid control characterizing intelligence operations. This prejudice arises from misunderstandings in Government departments other than the CIA of the value of political operations, with a consequent stressing of intelligence requirements, and from the fact that the great majority of CIA personnel are the products of training in intelligence rather than political techniques.

The heart of the secret war in our time, however, lies in the political conflict. Intelligence is essential and cannot for a moment be neglected. But we advance or we retreat, we make gains or suffer losses in proportion to our mastery of the details of the political struggle—meaning the living characteristics of men, the ever-changing human relationships within and among societies, from which flow the tides of power.

1. While the conflict "between the Communist and non-Communist blocs" continues, the world is no longer governed exclusively by this "single conflict." The "two great power centers" are no longer in a position to dictate unilaterally within their own spheres without recourse to force (which increasingly involves greater risks). Neither is even in a position in today's world to solve its own domestic problems with purely domestic solutions. (Note the Soviet Union's difficulties with productivity, and the United States' transformation in three years in the early 1980s from the world's greatest creditor nation to the world's greatest debtor nation.) No "other nations or combinations of states" have yet achieved "some parity with them" in terms of power, but the West European GNP now exceeds that of the United States—which has long exceeded that of the Soviet Union. While both superpowers meddle in the Middle Eastern conflicts, they certainly cannot now "divide" that "world between them," and the major shifts in the balance of power now originate in East Asia.

2. We can perhaps still agree that the "effort to keep the Cold War, in the sense of hostile blocs of nations aligned with East or West, out of Africa is a sound, even noble one," but the effort has neither succeeded (cf. Ethiopia, Angola, and Chad) nor failed. Where it has not failed much is due to the Africans' own rejection of bloc alignments. But, as the text states, this "does not and cannot eliminate the secret war" from Africa.

3. This was written before the revelations in the mid-1970s of the singular efforts to assassinate Fidel Castro. When the Office of Policy Coordination was established in 1948 the question of assassination arose, and was

promptly dismissed—one participant in the meeting observing, "Let's not get into that. They're so much better at it than we could ever be." This paragraph was written in 1962 with that in mind, and plainly in ignorance. I was therefore stunned (and appalled) at the 1970s revelations: Obviously my hailing of "some advance toward civilization" was premature. That "advance" then had to be legislated by the Congress. Still an "advance," of course, but not as much as would have been a voluntary decision within the Executive Branch.

4. Essentially the same can be said of the failure in Vietnam (which was only a cloud on the horizon when this was written).

5. Much has since transpired in this part of the world—including Qaddafi's overthrow of King Idris and, of course, the British withdrawal from the area. The basic point remains valid, however; note that the British still exercise important if inconspicuous (perhaps important because inconspicuous) influence in the Persian Gulf.

PART 2

Fundamentals and Forms in Action: The Seventy-Fifth Passenger

The reader who has come thus far probably feels that he has earned a story. It was my intention, in the account which now follows of an operation which I conducted in Soviet-occupied Hungary in 1946 and 1947, to provide him with a case history. But in setting down the case history, it turned into a story. A true story, but still a story.

The difference between the two is mainly an emotional one. Despite the intervening years, I found myself, in writing this account, immersed again in the sights and sounds, in the sensations and impressions, in my own emotions of the time—outrage, anger, worry, fear, suspicion, curiosity, pride, sympathy, hope, frustration, satisfaction, brief triumphs, occasional humor, and final sadness—all of which were as much a part of the reality of the operation as the events and actions themselves. As I said at the outset of this book, secret agents are not necessarily coldly unemotional. Thus this story may be a more accurate case history than a case history would have been.

Its accuracy depends in part, however, on the reader, on his willingness to view this account critically in the light of the principles described in Part I. For one of the strongest emotions experienced by any secret agent, both at the time of action and in retrospect, is, of course, the very human desire for self-justification. It is not absent from this account.

Nor is the reader spared the intrusions of my personal cast of mind. When, for example, in discussing courses of political action open to me at a critical point in 1947, I reject a particular course as "tantamount to buying an effort," on the basis of which, I state, "no long-term policy can be constructed," the reader will recognize that this viewpoint is at least historically debatable.

With the drawbacks of these personal desires and intrusions in *mind, I have appended at the end of this account a brief, general critique of the operation. I still advise the reader, however, to follow the story without suspending his own critical judgment.*

CHAPTER I

Budapest 1946

My emotional involvement, my shock, on the night of November 4, 1956, as Soviet troops assaulted Budapest, had their roots in a fight I had waged in that same city, in the same cause, ten years before. That fight too had been lost to the Soviet steamroller, but we who lost had emerged not entirely without honor.

I first saw Budapest in the summer of 1946. I came as a covert agent, member of an American intelligence organization—there then being no CIA—which has since ceased to exist.[1] I had been offered the mission because I spoke Russian and was primarily interested in Eastern European affairs. And Budapest in 1946 was as much a Russian as a Hungarian problem.

In the winter of 1944–45 three Russian armies had swept into the country from Yugoslavia, to the south, from Rumania, to the southeast, and over the Carpathian Mountains from Ruthenia, to the east. The Russians came, and were by and large awaited, as liberators. Nevertheless, the memory still lingered in Hungary of the last Russian invasion, ninety-seven years before, when, at the invitation of the Austrian Emperor, they had come to drown a revolt in blood, to maintain ideological purity, and to keep the virus of political liberty away from the borders of their empire—exactly as they were to do again only twelve years from this winter of 1944–45.

Remembering 1848, remembering Bela Kun's Communist regime of 1919, the Hungarian Government in 1943 and 1944 had established contact with the Allies in neutral capitals in the hopes of bringing about an Anglo-American invasion which would forestall first, a German occupation, and second, an exclusively Soviet occupation. A British colonel, in hiding in Budapest but in touch with both London and the Hungarian Government, had been secretly flown down to Allied Headquarters at Caserta. The Hungarian proposals were not acceptable to the Allies, who, in accordance with decisions taken at the Tehran Conference, told the Hungarians to approach the Russians. The military aspects of the proposals were in any case regarded as unfeasible in view of the planned Normandy invasion.

Knowledge of these maneuvers had been but one item in the German decision to occupy Hungary in March of 1944. A further effort in October by Horthy to surrender to the Russians had led to the arrest and kidnaping of Horthy—another successful operation by Otto Skorzeny, the Nazis' secret operations expert—and the installation in Budapest of the Szalasi Nazi puppet regime.

Less than a year after their seizure of the country, the Germans in Hungary were faced with the driving Russian armies, now broken out of the confinement of the mountains ringing the *puszta*—the Great Hungarian Plain. Here, a thousand years before, the Magyar chieftain Arpad had decided to settle his people, to cease their nomadic wanderings and plundering forays which had terrorized Christian Europe. As the Russian armies followed in the paths of the earlier Huns and nomad Magyars, their front-line Central Asian troops, with their rape and rapine, struck a special terror into the civilian population. (There was an atavistic ring to all this: Hungarians, with a thousand years behind them of Christian civilization in a beautiful and fruitful land, are sometimes wont to forget their own Asian origins.)

The Russians quickly cleared southern and eastern Hungary of the Germans, but it became clear that Budapest could not be bypassed: all the rail lines in the country passed through the capital. The Russians encircled the city on Christmas Eve, 1944, and attacked from the direction of Vienna, striking first into Buda, the more residential half of the city, lying on the western right bank of the Danube. The siege lasted fifty-nine days before the last Germans, holding out in the Var—Castle Hill—ancient seat of the Hungarian Kings and site of the Royal Palace and Coronation Church, and on St. Margit's Island, a wooded pleasure area slightly upstream, were finally slaughtered.

Their communications secured, the Russians went on to the west, to take Vienna on April 13, 1945, and to confront the Americans, at war's end less than a month later, at Linz in Upper Austria. Austria, while permitted a Government, was divided into four zones of occupation—with a fifth International Zone in the heart of Vienna—and the Soviet Zone was interposed between Hungary and the Western zones of Austria. Then the Hungarian drama, which the Hungarians hoped was ended, began.

The Yalta agreements had specified that Bulgaria, Rumania, and Hungary, although at war with the Allied Powers, were to be treated as "liberated" countries. Accordingly, as soon as Debrecen, the major Hungarian city in the eastern part of the country, had been taken from the Germans, the Hungarians had been permitted to form a Provisional Government there. An Allied Control Commission had earlier been established, chaired by none other than Marshal Voroshilov, and with American and British representation in the form of Major-Generals. The Russian Kommandaturas throughout Hungary operated in the name of the Allied Control Commission, which was run entirely by the Russian Chairman. At Potsdam the United States had proffered a set of proposed regulations for the Control Commissions, which the Russians, in one of their time-honored gambits, had accepted as a "basis for discussion." When some highhanded Soviet action in the name of the Control Commission provoked a British or American reference to the regulations, the Russian Chairman's reply was simply that they were merely a "basis for discussion" and that, in view of more urgent business, the chair would not entertain any discussion on that subject. When Budapest was freed, this comedy, along with the Hungarian Provisional Government, moved to Budapest, in the spring of 1945.

However, the Provisional Government was not a comedy, either from a political or an intelligence point of view. It was a coalition government, made up of the four political parties authorized by the Allied Control Commission: the Smallholders, the Social-Democrats, the National Peasants, and the Communists. A fifth party, predominantly Catholic, had been authorized in principle, but due to some dissension within the Church itself, did not succeed in organizing until late in 1947—which was, as we shall see, too late. Another minor group, the Civic Democratic Party, was authorized, but was not part of the coalition.

The Smallholders Party was a prewar opposition group which

sought agricultural reform in favor of small land holdings by the peasantry, but which also had some appeal among the small merchants and artisans of the cities and towns. It had a good resistance record and was conceded to be the majority party. The Social-Democrats, tolerated by prewar governments, were primarily a trade-union Socialist party; there was no Hungarian Socialist equivalent of the British Fabian Society or of the German theoretical Marxists. The National Peasants were more an idea than a party; the brainchild of a group of writers and intellectuals who sought to base Hungarian political life on the traditional values and preponderant numbers of the Hungarian peasantry, this was, in effect, the Hungarian version of the Fabian Society—romanticizing the tillers of the soil rather than the workers in the factories. The Communists—at least the presidium of the Party—arrived in the baggage of the Red Army, removed their Soviet uniforms, and set to work. Some 500 Hungarian Communists returned with the Russians. They didn't have much to work with: various agents who had been parachuted in during the fighting, and between 1,000 and 1,500 underground Communists who had managed to survive police nets over the years. The parties which had held power in the country during the previous quarter-century were abolished as responsible, in greater or lesser degree, for Hungary's Axis role.

By the time the curtain rose on the Hungarian drama, the same play, with the same producer, had already been on the boards for a brief time in Poland, Rumania, and Bulgaria. The plot had unfolded sufficiently in those countries so that the only question was whether the producer, a talented but mono- and megalomaniac Georgian, was going to open with the same show in Budapest. The David Merrick of his day, he knew that it was bad box office for the audience to leave in the middle of the first act. He was therefore reluctant to announce the name of the play—there were already faint stirrings among the critics—and it was plain that we would get nothing out of the producer's assistants—the Russians in Hungary. We therefore turned to the cast—the Hungarian Government—in the hopes that as the play progressed, they might slip us the title. In brief, we had to learn about what the Russians were doing in Hungary from the Hungarians. This was one part of the intelligence significance of the Hungarian Government.

The other part was the Government itself. If Stalin was putting on the same old show, it was the Hungarians about whom we would have to know in the future: the factions in the country, the trends of opinion, the personalities, who was prepared to oppose and who not, why, and what for, which people could work together and which not, the talents and motives of various leaders, actual and potential, who were Soviet collaborators and why, the resources and capacities of the country—the interminable and inexhaustible range of questions which go into assessing an entire nation.

Further, the Hungarian Government's interest to us was not only as a source of intelligence. The United States' interest in Hungary was a part of our objective of a stable peace in Eastern Europe, so long—and still—a major temptation and battleground for the Great Powers. With this end in view we would obviously seek to develop and maintain influence in the councils of the Hungarian Government. Also, if Russian intentions turned out to be of the worst—of which there was little doubt among experienced observers of the Russian performance—there would then arise the question of whether the American Government would oppose this development, and if so, how and to what extent. These were questions as yet undecided. But whichever way they would be decided, it was clear we would want the Hungarians on our side. The most direct, though not sole, instrument to achieve this was their own Government. Thus this hodgepodge Government, existing on sufferance of the occupiers, had a considerable political significance of its own in the international scene.

Insofar as the purely Hungarian elements in the immediate postwar scene were concerned, there was much on our side. To understate the case, the Russians were cordially disliked by the overwhelming majority of the population. All political leaders with any genuine following in the nation were oriented to the West; indeed, their major aspiration was to avoid being swallowed up in the Soviet Empire. While there was strong sentiment for political and economic reform, there was no class or group in the country interested as such in applying Communist solutions to their problems; the bitter taste of the short-lived Hungarian Communist regime of 1919 lingered. The American position was particularly strong: there were certain historical associations—Kossuth, among others; Hungarians of all classes were quick to recognize that the United States was now the leader of the Western world; and there were the innumerable ties resulting from the large Hungarian population in the United States.

Ranged against this was the presence of the Red Army. Its effectiveness was doubled by the fear it inspired. Its menace was reinforced by the hard fact that, except for the Allied Sectors in Vienna, the nearest Western outposts lay almost four hundred miles to the west of Budapest. To the north Czechoslovakia lay close, but the Czechoslovaks were hostile and had strong claims against the Hungarian state.

The Hungarian Communists, then, had little on their side, but what they had was implicitly effective—the Red Army had to intervene openly only once to assist the Communist take-over of the country—and decisive. Among their Hungarian opponents they had two allies: personal ambitions and dissension.

In November of 1945 Hungary's first postwar elections were held. They were free and unrigged, the sole such instance in Soviet-occupied territory and Soviet history. The results were striking: the Smallholders Party—which had interestingly enough also won a majority immediately following the collapse of the Hungarian Soviet Republic in 1919—received 57 per cent of the votes. The Socialists won 18 per cent, the Communists 17 per cent, and the National Peasant Party 8 per cent.

There has been much debate over the reasons for Soviet acquiescence in holding these elections. One theory is that they were misled by exaggeratedly optimistic claims of the Hungarian Communists. Another is that the decision was the result of factional quarrels among the Russian and Hungarian Communists—each Hungarian Communist leader had his own patron in the Soviet Politburo. Some students of the matter feel that the Russians desired to delude the Western powers as to their ultimate intentions while consolidating their hold on all of Eastern Europe. Matyas Rakosi, who directed the Communist seizure of power in Hungary and became dictator until his final fall from power in 1956, has stated, but without reference to the elections as such, only that the period from April 1945 to the end of 1948—distinguished for his famous "salami" tactics, or gradual take-over—was necessary to bring the majority of the workers and peasants to support the Communist Party, in accordance, so he claimed, with Lenin's teachings.

Whatever the reason for these unusual elections, the Communist 17 per cent was fully as striking as the Smallholders' absolute 57-per-cent majority. The fact is that a party comprised of no more than 2,000 members at the outset had, seven months later, at the time of the elections, 700,000 members. A minority of this number was obtained from peasants who had benefited from the land reform, for which the Communist Party took credit, and from workers, particularly miners. The great majority was taken from the so-called "small Nazis," that is, the rank and file of the Hungarian Nazi Party which, in 1944, had numbered a million members. These people were by definition subject to reprisals; their easy way out and their safety were gained by joining the Communist Party, which, by its control of the Political Police, could decide who would be prosecuted and who not.

On the basis of these elections, a Government was formed which was quickly granted full recognition by all the major powers—with the exception of France, which chose to delay, ostensibly until the settlement of certain property questions, but in fact as part of characteristically De Gaullian maneuvers to assert the voice of France. The leader of the Smallholders Party, Zoltan Tildy, was elected President of Hungary—the second in its history, Count Mihaly Karolyi having held the post in his short-lived republic at the end of the First World War. The Prime Ministry devolved upon another Smallholder leader, Ferenc Nagy (no relation to the Communist Imre Nagy who was to become Prime Minister eight years later and then again during the 1956 Revolution). The Government was a coalition of the four parties which had participated in the elections, notwithstanding the Smallholders' absolute majority, since a majority Government would have excluded the Communists from power—a solution the Russians were not prepared to accept. Accordingly, Arpad Szakasits for the Socialists and Matyas Rakosi for the Communists were each made Deputy Prime Minister. The various ministries were then apportioned out on the same principle; of the key ministries the Smallholders received Foreign Affairs and Finance, the Socialists the Justice Ministry, and, on standard Communist insistence supported by the Russians, the Communists—in the person of Imre Nagy and later Laszlo Rajk—received the Interior Ministry, meaning, in Hungary as in the rest of Europe, the police power. Within each ministry, in turn, each of the coalition parties had its own representatives (although in the case of the Communist ministries this participation was purely nominal). In those days Hungary was so much a coalition that it was scarcely possible to summon a plumber or have lunch except on a coalition basis. The American Minister to Hungary at the time gave it as his opinion that not even France, with its traditional individuality and multi-party system, could compare for sheer complexity of partisan politics with postwar Hungary.

This ferment was not solely a political phenomenon, but was a reflection of the whole Magyar temperament. While it is true that Hungarians are given to streaks of melancholy, and even that Budapest had one of the world's highest prewar suicide rates, it is also a fact that as a people the Magyars are vivacious and resilient. The theater is probably their best art form; and the coffeehouse—kavehaz—astir with gossip, intrigue, and, above all, a flourishing and irreverent sense of humor, is the national institution. Their forthright, tolerant, highly appreciative, and continuous, but withal balanced, regard for the joys of the relations between the sexes causes even the most repressed Anglo-Saxon or dour puritan characters to realize almost exuberantly that life is much richer than they feared. The Hungarians are susceptible to a streak of self-pity, but they are also capable of laughing at themselves, and they combine with this a simultaneous streak of rashness often emerging as bravery. They are cynical of slogans, but they are beguiled by living.

The vitality of the Hungarians was nowhere more evident in the summer of 1946, when I arrived, than in the comparison between Vienna and Budapest. In Vienna, prostrate under four occupation armies, life just barely dragged along: there was no black market, the currency was stable, food was rationed and scarce, and people trudged through the streets, silent, gray, drab. In Budapest, which had suffered a degree of destruction comparable only to the major German cities and which lay at the not so tender mercies of the Red Army, there was whipped cream for the numerous daily coffees—and milk for the babies; reconstruction went on energetically —immediately following the siege the people of Budapest had voluntarily restored the famous and favorite Coronation Church on the Var, in Buda; the theater flourished wherever a stage could be found, and the night clubs were legendary in Europe for the period —one of the best being ultimately purchased with the profits of their loot by a consortium of nine Soviet officers; the currency entered upon the fastest and farthest inflation ever seen—rising in eighteen months from some 50 pengös to the dollar to a final quotation of 11,000,000,000,000,000,000,000,000,000 (27 zeros) to the dollar; and stimulating it all was one of Europe's liveliest black markets in which, of course, theft and hijacking played no small part.

The flavor of the Hungarian black market was well illustrated at the time by a statistic and a joke: statistically it was a fact that the number of automobiles in Hungary—without an automobile industry—increased tremendously in the first year after the war, while Austria, with several plants, experienced a sharp decline—to the point where the American Army in Austria would send a mission to Hungary from time to time to look for their missing cars. This was also the period when the coffee-house wags, seeing a friend in a new suit, would remark that he was "a Hungarian by day and a Russian by night." (These stories do not, however, do justice to the full range and flavor of the Hungarian genius: the story is often recounted of the meeting in Washington in the early fifties of the Scientific Advisory Board of the U.S. Atomic Energy Commission. When a count of the members showed a minority absent, but still a quorum, another count enabled the Chairman to say to his colleagues, in his faultless and native Hungarian, "Shall we conduct the meeting in the mother tongue?" Agreed and done.)

Notwithstanding all this variety and activity, the problem of my cover posed some special difficulties. The Russians controlled all entry into and exit from Hungary, and were most strict on this score. Entry was permitted only for members of official missions—and even they often had to wait a considerable period; for some correspondents—with similar delays; and a very few businessmen who had to be representatives of already existing American properties in Hungary. As the American companies with interests in Hungary—principally the manufacture of electrical equipment and the oil industry—needed whatever entry permits were available for their own people, and since it was a matter of policy to avoid jeopardizing either the American investments in Eastern Europe or the access of bona fide correspondents to Soviet-controlled territory, there was no possibility of a private cover which would give me residence privileges. It was therefore decided that official cover was the only possibility. This gave a choice of either the U.S. Legation in Budapest or the U.S. Military Mission, which was the American Representation on the Allied Control Commission for Hungary. As my functions involved some risk, it was, as is customary, decided to avoid any possibility of embarrassment for the Legation, our permanent diplomatic mission, and to attach me to the Military Mission.

The Military Mission was, of course, a temporary institution. It was not known how long such a mission would be maintained, for it was American policy to seek the departure of foreign troops from all occupied European countries except Germany at the earliest possible moment—which meant in practice, of course, U.S., British, and French departure from Italy; U.S., British, French, and Soviet departure from Austria; Soviet departure from Hungary, Rumania, and Bulgaria; and a limitation of the Red Army in Poland to supply and communications lines to Germany. (This was the effort and hope at the time, due to be blocked by the Soviet refusal to sign a State Treaty with Austria for many years, thereby giving them the pretext for continued stationing of troops—as supply lines to Austria—in Hungary and Rumania.) In support of this aim the Paris Peace Conference had already been convoked for the autumn of 1946, and it was thus hoped to be only a matter of time before the U.S. Military Mission in Hungary, like those in Rumania and Bulgaria, would be withdrawn.

With this time limit in mind, and with the enormous bureaucratic obstacles to transforming me into an Army officer at a time when our Army was to a large extent being disbanded, I was designated as an Adviser to the Military Mission, acting as a civilian. This cover not only gave me greater flexibility than if I had been in uniform, but it offered the possibility that, if circumstances turned out propitiously, I might, with the ultimate departure of the Military Mission, be readily able to transfer to some form of private cover. Alternatively, one of my tasks was to explore the ground and arrange or recommend a suitable cover for a successor if it should prove impossible for me to stay.

To explain to the Russians the somewhat unusual presence of a civilian adviser on the staff of the Military Mission, advantage was taken of the functions of the Allied Control Commission itself. There was at the time, in the U.S. Government, an operation known as "Safehaven," the purpose of which was to uncover hidden Nazi personnel and assets in areas outside of Germany. At the same time, one of the principal agreed functions of the Allied Control Commissions was to eliminate the last vestiges of Nazism in the countries where they operated. It was therefore explained to the Soviets that the tracing of refugee Nazi personnel and assets outside of Germany was a civilian function under our arrangements, and that, in effect, I would be at their disposition for whatever co-operative activity in this field they might find useful. It was thus hoped not only to explain my civilian status, but to give me a special access to the Russians themselves from which something of value might emerge. This manner of presenting things also served to provide a valid explanation for my command of the Russian language.

Communications were somewhat easier. I was instructed to enter into friendly personal relations with "Mark," a high official of the American Legation, who would, without knowledge of their contents, handle my communications. (The code names used throughout this account are obviously not those really used in the operation. Furthermore, none of the personnel of the network knew the code name by which I referred to them in my communications, although they had, whenever necessary, different code names for operational use among ourselves.) I would give Mark a sealed envelope addressed with only a code word for my organization, inside of which was another envelope with a code name for my case officer in Washington. He would forward all this by regular diplomatic courier in another envelope addressed to a cover office in Washington. Incoming mail arrived addressed in an outer envelope to him, which was the only one he opened; he then gave to me an inner envelope with the code word for the organization, which contained a final envelope addressed with only my code name. Telegraphic communications I simply gave to him already encoded in my own cipher. It was then encoded again in the Legation and transmitted to Washington. Messages for me came to the Legation, were decoded, and—since the Legation's decoded version ended up still encoded, but now in my cipher—then given to Mark, who would pass the message to me.

My instructions were specific and strict: I was forbidden to disclose to Mark any details of the network I was operating, nor could I reveal to him in any way actual operations in which I was engaged. I was to take political guidance from him as to U.S. Government policy; and, while I was not to withhold information from him of direct value to the Legation, I was to limit it insofar as possible to matters of urgency or of physical safety of the Legation itself, and then without revealing the sources. This was sound practice: the procedure may seem roundabout, but in fact all the information which I obtained, and which was considered to be essential to the Legation's functions, was in due course transmitted to the Legation in general or special Government reports and intelligence analyses. What was omitted, and thus protected, was the source. Thus the network and the agent were protected, the organization was shielded, the information which the network obtained was subject to the necessary control of who should benefit from it, and the U.S. diplomatic establishment was not unduly compromised.

For full efficacy, such arrangements always depend upon the human relationships involved; in this case, the key relationship was that between Mark and myself. To everyone's good fortune it turned out to be very nearly ideal: a genuine meeting of the minds, as the lawyers say, and a due respect for the value of each other's functions led to a most effective working relationship.[2]

In addition to these regular arrangements, I was also given a connection with another agent residing in Switzerland. Facilities were established whereby I could contact him directly in case of emergency; in such cases I was entitled to take his word, if he gave it, as equivalent to full authority from headquarters. This agent, known as "Peter," traveled widely and often throughout all of Europe. I was therefore authorized to discuss with him the details of my work whenever a meeting rendered that possible. As important, it was also his function to provide me with funds. In the Hungary of the period, this meant transfer by hand to me of cash sums, either in Swiss francs—preferred—or American dollars. This money I then cashed, either myself or through cut-outs, on the Hungarian black market, which continued to flourish well after the replacement in August 1946 of the pengö by the new, stabilized forint, or, if my recipients so preferred, I simply disbursed to them in the original currency. (In view of the nation's acute shortage of foreign exchange, both non-Communist and later Communist Governments were happy to blink at illegal transactions which continued for long to bring in hard currencies. Thus my transactions aroused no suspicion. Even after the black market was later severely reduced in scope, remittances via banks and such organizations as CARE from exiles and emigrants to their relatives, no matter what the source, were—and are to this day—encouraged by all the Soviet satellite regimes as a valuable source of foreign exchange.) Peter, in Switzerland, was the only other agent in Europe —outside of my own network in Hungary, of course—with whom I was in touch. While I could reasonably assume that there were other networks operating in the various countries neighboring on Hungary, I obviously never inquired about them—until an emergency did one day arise.

With cover, communications, and funds arranged, my headquarters had done all it could do. The rest could only be worked out on the spot in response to what were bound to be rapidly changing circumstances. What I didn't know, as I arrived in Budapest in late June 1946 and remarked, in the hot and lazy summer sunshine, the contrast between the pretty and chic Hungarian girls and the sullen and soiled Russian soldiery, was how fast and how far all would change.[3]

1. "Brigadier, U.S. Army, retired January of this year, sir, after some 35 years' service, 20 of which have been devoted to intelligence in various places; during the early days of the war, Deputy G-2 of the War Department, and Chief of the Military Intelligence Service. . . . About April, I believe, sir, of 1942 . . . it was decided . . . that the more active operational side of intelligence should go to . . . Coordinated Information [sic], that is, you know, the office that preceded the OSS, and that the regular intelligence services should proceed from there with their own intelligence activities. This gave the official approval for me to organize and set on foot the secret intelligence service.

"By December of that year this directive was expanded, perhaps it was October, was expanded to instruct me, which I in turn instructed my predecessor at this hearing [Col. John V. Grombach], that he would not only institute a secret intelligence service, looking to the needs of the current war effort, but that he would lay the foundation for a perpetual, a far-seeing, a far-distant, continuing secret intelligence service . . ." (Testimony of Brigadier-General Hayes Kroner, before the Committee on Expenditures in the Executive Departments of the House of Representatives, on H. R. 2319, National Security Act of 1947, June 27, 1947. *Hearing,* pp. 53–54.)

The crux of this Hearing was the question of whether to limit the collection of secret foreign intelligence to the Central Intelligence Agency in the new legislation creating the CIA, or to allow the Army, Navy, State, and others to engage in these operations as well, with the CIA as the central coordinating, evaluating, and disseminating authority. There were six witnesses before the Committee: Lt.-Gen. Hoyt S. Vandenberg, Director of the Central Intelligence Group; Allen W. Dulles (speaking as a civilian); Peter Vischer, former Secretary, Joint Intelligence Commttee of the Joint Chiefs of Staff, and author of a 1946 study on intelligence for the Military Affairs Committee of the House of Representatives; Brig.-Gen. Hayes Kroner, former Deputy G-2 of the War Department and Chief of the Military Intelligence Service; Col. John V. Grombach, Director, Secret Intelligence Branch of the War Department General Staff; and Rear-Adm. Thomas Inglis, Chief of Naval Intelligence. Vandenberg and Dulles spoke forcefully for a CIA monopoly of collection; Inglis was prepared to give the organized role to the CIA, with bits and pieces left for the services on an ad hoc basis; Vischer was opposed to a CIA monopoly role in collection, and for the rest wanted to maintain the Presidential directive of February 5, 1946, giving limited authority to the CIG; Hayes and Grombach had no objection to a CIA monopoly on coordination, evaluation, and dissemination of intelligence, but wanted to preserve independent secret collection operations and to exclude the CIA from collection. Although the final 1947 legislation went with Vandenberg and Dulles, other departments continued collection operations. (The 1947 Hearing was in executive session, and only one transcript was made. It was loaned to the CIA, where it was copied, and the original returned to the House Committee. In 1950 the Committee Chairman ordered the destruction of the original. The CIA copy was discovered during a House Intelligence Committee review, in 1981 or 1982, of CIA records [although it had been provided by the CIA in 1975, without House permission, to the Senate Committee known as the "Church Committee."] The House Intelligence Committee asked for its declassification in 1982, and the CIA concurred. Hence the thirty-five years between the Hearing and publication of its transcript.)

"The U.S. Secret Intelligence Branch . . . was organized just before the U.S. became involved in the war or a short time thereafter, but certainly long before the OSS. In fact, it began operating officially and actively under covers toward the end of 1941 and certainly by early January 1942 . . . I owe a great deal of credit to . . . members of the Secret Intelligence Branch, which I directed from January 2, 1942, to January 1, 1955, for the War and State Departments. . . . Credit is also due . . . for legal advice to me as director of the S. I. Branch in its friendly termination in preference to its being taken over and integrated into the CIA in 1955 . . ." (John V. Grombach, *The Great Liquidator,* Doubleday, New York, 1980, pp. 112, xi, xii.)

In late 1981, a year before his death, Col. Grombach was inverviewed by Professor Charles Gati, of Union College and Columbia University. In the course of the interview Col. Grombach gave to Professor Gati a memorandum which, though undated, contained internal references placing it in late 1954. Mainly devoted to Grombach's multiple grievances against the CIA, the memorandum does contain a brief section on the history of his "S.I. Branch," which states, *inter alia* [emphasis added], "This organization, tied in with the State Department for communication and necessary cooperation . . . scored many intelligence successes during the war. . . . In 1947, the newly created CIA, after first trying to take over and absorb the organization, forced the War Department to drop it . . . as part of a high level jurisdictional struggle for control and absorption of all . . . secret intelligence collecting agencies. This organization could not accept absorption by CIA. . . . *From 1947 to 1951, the State Department . . . secretly continued it* unknown to CIA *'as an adjunct to the Foreign Service.'* In late 1950 or early 1951 the State Department, against advice of the organization, revealed its continued existence to CIA. . . ."

2. I do not recall now what impelled me to describe this relationship as

"very nearly ideal." The adverbs were superfluous, since "Mark," at the time a career Foreign Service Officer, Second Secretary and Chief of the Political Section of the Legation, was James McCargar. (cf. Charles Gati, *Hungary and the Soviet Bloc,* Durham, Duke University Press, 1986, pp. 9 and 23; and *Foreign Relations of the United States, 1947,* Vol. IV, Washington, Government Printing Office, 1972, p. 398.)

   3. April, not June. Should thus read, "bright spring sunshine."

CHAPTER II

The Network

Whatever my difficulties would be, I had one great initial advantage. I did not have to start absolutely from scratch, since I had a predecessor already in Budapest who had an established and functioning network. As his cover was considerably different from my own, I saw him only rarely and then always clandestinely. When we met in public we were, as two Americans in a foreign land, friendly and polite, but gave no visible sign that we saw each other apart from such chance encounters. Furthermore, his departure, which was a result of the need for arranging well in advance of future changes the possibility of a more permanent cover for either myself or my successor, was postponed for some four months after my arrival in order that no one should be able to draw any correlation between the two.

   In this interval I settled in, so to speak, concentrated on establishing my cover, and began to move in as many different circles as possible. This is, of course, classical procedure. No agent—and least of all one with as broad an assignment as mine—is really of use until he is securely oriented in his surroundings. This involves a thorough absorption in the local habits, customs, traditions, and personal traits. Until this is achieved, any agent is ill advised to operate in any but the most limited or routine way. The alternative is to risk early exposure through simple faults of detail—such as, for example, a clandestine meeting place badly chosen for want of knowledge of local police habits—or a successful opposition penetration for want of insufficient familiarity with local personalities.

I was early able to find a small flat on the Var. This was probably the most destroyed area of the city, but that in itself gave certain advantages. The Var is a kind of bluff, with very steep sides, rising some 200 or more feet and running northwest from the Danube's right bank. It was in ancient times a fortified citadel, dominates the old city of Buda spread out around it, and overlooks the city of Pest across the river. The Royal Palace was on the Var, and most of the old city of Buda and its modern suburbs were residential areas, running up the flanks of the great wooded hills which here mark the west bank of the river. On the east bank stood the Houses of Parliament, somewhat similar in location and conception to those in London, although unique in style, and behind spread the city of Pest, on a great flat area signaling the start of the Great Hungarian Plain. In Pest was concentrated most of the city's business life, theaters, and, after the war, the Government.

My flat, on the northern edge of the Var, looked up the river, to the far mountains of Slovakia, and east onto the Houses of Parliament.[1] It also commanded a view of the single Danube bridge available to automobile traffic when I first arrived, as well as of one of the only two approaches up the Var itself. Nearby were the crenelated battlements and the winding terraces of the Coronation Church. The streets of the Var were obstacle courses of rubble piles, built up from the ruins of palaces and houses behind. To enter my own miraculously intact two rooms, it was necessary to traverse three tunnels dug through rubble, a series of confusing passageways, and then a small staircase leading only to my apartment. All of this added up to an area favorable to clandestine meetings, and reduced to a minimum the danger that one could be followed without it being known, for which I was later to be grateful.

In gradual stages my predecessor handed over to me the network which was already operating. It consisted at that time of eight persons.

"Leo" was a member of a noble family who had had an outstanding record in the Resistance. He had successfully avoided arrest by the Germans during the occupation, and following the liberation had entered into political life. He was a Smallholder Member of Parliament, and in numerous articles which he wrote for various papers he established himself as one of the younger spokesmen of a liberal group within the party who stood for various needed reforms, but who also sought to avoid Hungary's disappearance into the Soviet orbit. He provided steady and valuable information on the intrigues within the Smallholders Party itself and on the real policies of various party leaders as they reacted to the various Communist encroachments on the party's dominant position.

"Eugene" was likewise of a noble family, but without personal political ambitions. A man of conservative views and of eminently decent instincts, he had become mixed up during the war in a series of anti-German actions, including the saving of Jews, the operations of the Polish Underground through Hungary, and the abortive effort to surrender to the Western Allies in Italy. He had been arrested and deported to the Mauthausen concentration camp, which he managed to survive only through the intercession with the Germans of certain very highly placed neutrals. He had long represented a number of foreign firms, including American, in Hungary, and had resumed these connections after the war. He was able to provide valuable information due to his Resistance connections, with many of whom he did not share domestic political views but with whom he had shared the experience of a concentration camp, and he was also in a position to furnish useful information on developments in the business world.

"Paul" was a very high member of the Government, a Smallholder. A lawyer by profession, he also had an excellent wartime record of resistance. Besides his inside information on the high councils of the Hungarian Government, he also provided a transcript of all Cabinet meetings. (Since this was a coalition Government, and a growingly uneasy coalition, Cabinet meetings were inclined to be either a kind of formal battleground or a place for the final enactment of compromises already agreed upon outside in more informal, acrimonious interparty meetings. Even so, this material was obviously of very high value.)

"Simon" was a brilliant young economist. A non-party man, he was employed in the National Bank. As a Jew he had been lucky to escape with his life during the German occupation, and he was also vigorously anti-Communist. A gentle, scholarly man, he provided reams of detailed data on the Soviet plunder of the entire Hungarian economy, and valuable analyses of the means by which the Communists were gradually bringing the nation's financial institutions under their control.

"Jane" was a cousin of "Simon" and a close friend of "Paul." Although she worked in a Government housing office, she was herself a scholar. Her connections were due to her personal friendships in intellectual circles and not to her work. She functioned as a cut-out to both Simon and Paul, whom I rarely saw, which arrangement was facilitated by the fact that she lived not far from me. (Her role of cut-out was dictated by prudence concerning Simon and Paul, of course, and not by any need to protect identities.) It was also her function to provide likely recruits for the network.

"George" was a career Hungarian diplomat. While he had successfully undergone the "denazification" procedures for Government officials and employees, his position in the Foreign Office was not a senior one. Nevertheless, he retained the confidence and friendship of many of the higher career diplomatic officials and was thus initially able to provide useful information about Hungarian foreign relations, including notably those with the Soviet Legation in Budapest, and advance information on the planned assignments of Hungarian diplomats abroad. As time went on, however, he found himself more and more cut off from information, and eventually himself took a minor assignment abroad, from which he went into exile.

"Henry" was another aristocrat, a man of ebullient nature and many accomplishments. He had been a leading member of the Hungarian Upper House and active in Hungarian society, and his information, while never dramatic, reflected a wide range of interests and sources. In addition, he had had a bizarre experience at the end of the war. In hiding from the Germans, he had emerged when the Russians arrived, only to be arrested immediately by them and put in a Soviet concentration camp near the Austrian border, which was maintained by the Russians for Hungarians against whom they had no charges, but whose leadership potential was such that it was desired to keep them out of circulation until the postwar political structure had taken on the desired form. He was there for many months, and then, on his release, was required to walk the streets of Budapest, followed at a distance by Soviet agents, greeting anyone he knew and thus in effect providing the Russians with a quick file on all his numerous friends and acquaintances in all walks of Hungarian life. It was our hope that the

Russians might at some point try to use him again in more serious work, which would, of course, have provided us with a line into Soviet operations. In this we were disappointed—but Henry, understandably, was not.

"Louis" was a distinguished scholar. Although his field of study enabled him to provide useful works which bore to some extent on the general Hungarian economic situation, it was in fact neither that nor his status as an aristocrat which were of primary interest. Louis was the scion of a family which had for centuries occupied a decisive position in Hungarian history, and because of the role his family had played as recently as the past thirty years he was a figure of great prestige in the nation. He had been instrumental in bringing about the surrender to the Russians, and had himself played a part in the formation of the Provisional Government. He was not old enough to be an "elder statesman," but his prestige, his somewhat aloof, nonpartisan attitude, and his unquestioned patriotism put him in an analogous position. Furthermore, the Russians were not only cognizant of his prestige, but were also appreciative of his part in the surrender. They accordingly deferred to him to a certain degree—at least for a while—and even held what might be considered for the Russians as confidential conversations with him occasionally. These were clearly of interest.

Of these eight persons, none knew of my connection to a specific intelligence organization. However, Eugene, Paul, Simon, Jane, and Louis knew that they were connected through me to "American intelligence" in general. Leo, George, and Henry, although they must certainly have surmised the facts, were willing to look at the situation simply as being in touch with "the Americans." Of the eight, only Jane knew the identity of any other agent, and she knew, of course, in her role as cut-out, of only Simon and Paul. This arrangement meant that I had to hold most of the meetings with agents myself; this added risk was offset, however, by the greater security of confining knowledge of agents' identities to an absolute minimum—worthwhile in a city rife with personal intrigues and political gossip.

Not one of these agents received any kind of salary, and only Jane had need for expense money. I occasionally did personal favors for some—my predecessor was able to save a valuable library for Louis, and I would transmit gifts between some of the agents and their friends in the West, as my cover enabled me to do without risk—but these favors were never asked or performed as a form of compensation. Jane and Simon both had personal ties in America which gave them particular reason to assist the United States; the rest acted purely as Hungarian patriots in the framework of what each had personally concluded would best help to avoid the catastrophe of Soviet domination, if at all possible. In brief, political support was the motive of all of the agents in the network.

This network had certain obvious limitations—which was no reflection whatsoever on my predecessor, who had organized the group in a very limited time with what was readily available. It was outstandingly useful with respect to the Cabinet, the majority Smallholders Party, and Soviet seizures of property. It was satisfactory with respect to the Foreign Office, the economy in general, and informed opinion among center and conservative leaders. It had potentialities with respect to some Soviet activities, but not enough. On the debit side it was much too heavily weighted in favor of the former, ruling upper class. It was either weak or non-existent so far as very important areas of Hungarian life were concerned: the other political parties, especially the Communists; organized labor; the Communist-controlled Interior Ministry, and in particular the Political Police, destined to become the organ of Communist terror; the military; and the Roman Catholic Church. (There is a sizable Protestant minority in Hungary, and a tragically reduced but still important Jewish population; but the Roman Church was of capital importance. Rome had granted Hungary the title of Apostolic Kingdom and its senior Catholic Bishop, the Archbishop of Esztergom, who in 1946 was already Cardinal Mindszenty, was also by law the Prince Primate, the country's chief personage after the Head of State. The Church's importance had in fact been recognized by the Allied Control Commission in its grant in 1945 of authority for the formation of a Catholic political party.) These limitations meant not only that the range of the network's intelligence was too narrow, but also that the intelligence was susceptible to a too uniform slant.

Notwithstanding the limitations of this network in terms of specific targets—and of partisan prejudice—the problem in Budapest was never, during this period, a lack of information. On the contrary, by the simple process of allowing others to do the talking, one lived in a veritable deluge of rumors. The daily crop of these rumors invariably contained some interesting kernels of truth, and the winnowing of the wheat from the chaff was a full-time process, involving innumerable conversations, checking, confirming, far into the night—a process made somewhat easier by the nocturnal habits of politicians in general, and Russians and Hungarians in particular. In addition, there was always the stray nugget of information that one stumbled upon by accident. (Later, toward the end of 1947, I found myself having a coffee one day with an American Government architect who was in town to discuss technical details with Hungarian architects about certain buildings purchased by the American Government. An excellent and thoroughly apolitical technician, he was discussing with me his impression of Hungarian baroque architecture. Offhandedly I remarked that the Government seemed to have plentiful resources for the atrocious Stalin Monument, but was averse to restoring the Royal Palace, even as a museum. "Oh, no," he said. "They're going to restore it. In fact, soon. The architect I saw in the Government Building Office today showed me the plans." I perked up and asked what it was going to be. "It's to be the headquarters of the Danube Federation," he answered. "Tito has already given the plans his approval." This chance remark led eventually, in conjunction with other items from elsewhere in the Balkans, to advance information on the Tito-Cominform dispute, which featured as one of its early phases an argument between Tito and George Dimitrov of Bulgaria, supported by Stalin, over whether a Danubian Federation should be based on the four states of Yugoslavia, Bulgaria, Hungary, and Rumania or—as Tito obviously desired—it should be composed of nine states: Hungary, Rumania, Bulgaria, and the six member states of the Yugoslav Federation.) Nevertheless, one could not rely on the stray nugget or on a spate of rumors. What was needed was reliable, steady information, keyed to all of the vital centers of power where the Hungarian fate was being worked out. To expand the network thus became one of my principal tasks.

During the autumn of 1946 I moved slowly, becoming thoroughly familiar with the city and the surrounding countryside, establishing contacts with foreign and Hungarian newspapermen, diplomats, politicians, always aiming, without notable success, at the targets I had set for penetration. My headquarters continued to be satisfied with the flow of intelligence and counseled caution in my efforts to expand the network.

But events were moving rapidly. In the city one could sense the steady pressure of the Communists, supported by their Russian backers. In October the peace treaty negotiations in Paris began. (These negotiations, in which the United States was obliged to assume a role, not entirely successful, of protecting Hungary from the maximum demands of its Czechoslovak, Rumanian, and Yugoslav neighbors, all egged on and supported by the Soviets, had at least one light moment. It seems the Hungarian Delegation, led by the Prime Minister, were holding highly secret discussions one evening in their hotel, when the door giving onto the balcony of the room they were using opened softly, and a strange man entered. Without a word he crossed the room and opened the door leading to the hallway. As the Hungarians sat thunderstruck, wondering what nationality of agent this eavesdropper was, the man paused in the doorway before disappearing. "Excuse me, gentlemen," he said, "but Monsieur returned unexpectedly.")

Meanwhile, in Budapest, there were enough light moments, but they were set to a counterpoint of people who simply disappeared one day or night, arrested by the Russians or the Hungarian Political Police, never to reappear; of trigger-happy and acquisitive Red Army patrols at night—shooting incidents between Russian and the few American soldiers in Budapest were not uncommon; of growing unease among even the smallest property owners; and of a general realization that the Soviet objective was to install the Hungarian Communists in full power. In September the Political Police were changed from being simply a branch of the National Police, which was directed by General Balassa, a Socialist, to an autonomous agency called the AVO—the Hungarian initials for State Security Agency—the head of which, Gabor Peter, reported directly to the Communist Minister of the Interior, Laszlo Rajk. The realization spread that a race was on: if the Communists could be prevented from seizing power in the period before the Peace Treaty took effect, that is, during the time when they would still have maximum support from the Red Army, then Hungary might be saved. This meant, for all practical purposes, that the coming year of 1947 would be decisive.

In these days I made the acquaintance of "Guy," the holder of an important post in the National—not Political—Police. As all responsible official positions required membership in one of the coalition political parties, Guy, on being offered his post in the Police as a reward for his Resistance record, had joined the Peasant Party. A city man, a prewar owner of houses and real estate in Budapest, his status as a "peasant," even a purely political one, was a perfect example of the fortuitous meeting of a wholly artificial system and an utterly cynical man. I liked Guy for his wit and intelligence, and he seemed to me at first glance to offer some professional interest. However, his work was exclusively preoccupied with criminal matters, and he spoke very little of it. By listening I gathered that he had spent much time in England, and I also noted that he seemed somehow apart from the people making up the circles in which he moved socially—circles which seemed more the natural result of the associations of his extraordinarily beautiful, aristocratic mistress than of his own. I realized eventually, however, that Guy was trying harder to learn what he could from and about me than I was about or from him. It did not seem plausible to me that he was a Communist agent; what struck me as more likely was a pressing need for money, to gain which I had the impression he was not likely to be too scrupulous. Despite my enjoyment of Guy's company, caution seemed indicated; it did not appear at all likely that this man would eventually be my most valuable agent in Hungary.

At this same time, I was still hoping for some more productive link to the Russians themselves. On my arrival, the Russians had indicated that a Colonel Tyushin was the appropriate officer for me to see if I had business to transact. Apart from an initial courtesy call shortly after my arrival I had barely seen Tyushin, who certainly seemed to have no business to transact with me. On our rare encounters, however, he was exceedingly affable; a stocky, barrel-chested man, he had an ease of manner and equanimity with foreigners unusual for a Russian official, suggesting either that he held high authority or had been much abroad. Whether the former was true or not was inascertainable, although he was popularly rumored really to be a Lieutenant-General in the N.K.V.D.—the equivalent, for sheer power in Stalin's and Beria's Russia, of a Field Marshal in anybody's army. As for his travels, he had been, he said, on numerous "trade missions" all over the world. It was Tyushin himself who suggested I see more of him.

In the late autumn of 1946, the Hungarian Government resurrected the annual Tokay Wine Festival, and at the invitation of the Prime Minister, practically everyone, Hungarian or foreign, with even the remotest connection to the Government, journeyed to the village of Tokay for a day of wine-tasting, sight-seeing, and speeches, to be followed by an official dinner at the college in the nearby town of Sarospatak. Tokay itself is an extraordinary sight: a lone, conical mountain, in shape something like a very large, man-made pile of dirt, rises from the plain. At its foot is the village of

Tokay; on its slopes is grown all of this magnificent wine, a little sweet for my taste, but so long famous in Eastern Europe that for centuries no King of neighboring Poland could be crowned without three bottles of Tokay at the ceremony.

Inside the mountain are long tunnels and caves where the wine is aged and stored. This year, however, they were empty. With Russians about, the villagers would describe how the Germans had looted the caves; when the Russians strolled on, the villagers would curse and say that the German looting was nothing compared to the thoroughgoing Russian job which followed it. There was, of course, the current harvest. This had not yet matured to wine, but was in the stage which the Hungarians call "must" (pronounced "moosht"), when the taste is somewhat sour, but an expert—and any villager—can already tell the quality of the vintage. ("Put this on your 'must' list," wrote one American on a postcard to a friend who had for years irritated him with cards from faraway places.) Once drunk, it continues to ferment, now more rapidly, in the stomach, and then packs a neat wallop—as a highly confused assemblage for the dinner at Sarospatak testified. It was in this melee that Tyushin sought me out to say that I should call him when we returned to Budapest; he would like to talk with me.

My headquarters viewed this invitation as a logical outcome of my cover arrangements and instructed me to pursue it. As it happened, the "must" at Tokay had so inspired one American Army officer that he had lost his way en route to Sarospatak. In this northeastern part of Hungary, as a result of the war and the generosity of the Beneš Government in giving up the entire easternmost province of Czechoslovakia to the Soviet Union, the Soviet border was now across the Carpathian Mountains and onto the edge of the Hungarian Plain. The American officer was last seen heading in that direction. Accordingly, I persuaded the Military Mission not to take the matter up officially, and I went to see Tyushin. He deplored the officer's carelessness and regaled me with long stories of the ferocity and what he characterized as the bureaucratic stupidity of the Soviet border guards. Five days later, however, the officer reappeared in Budapest, no worse off for a week in a Soviet jail. This was an auspicious start.

I next saw Tyushin at a large American reception for the Hungarian Prime Minister. Any social function in Budapest, no matter how labeled, which started after 6 o'clock in the evening went on until the last guest had departed, which was invariably some time well after midnight. In the far reaches of this particular evening, when the guests had dwindled to perhaps a dozen, I saw a remarkable tableau. In one corner of a large room Tyushin was reclining on the floor, his head in the lap of an American girl, remarking to no one in particular on how excellent a solution this was to international problems, while in the opposite corner an American colonel, shortly to become a general, was being restrained by several others as he shouted, "Let me at him! We'll atom-bomb the bastards off the face of the earth!" I interposed myself between Tyushin and his view of the American colonel—Tyushin only looked bemused and asked, "What is he shouting about?"—and suggested we leave together. He accepted the suggestion, but, as we were about to get into my car, his driver came over and in effect ordered Tyushin into his own car. Tyushin reluctantly went with him, but turned as he got into his car and, pointing to his driver, said in heavily accented English, but with the lordly manner of an ancient boyar, "I shall have him horsewhipped." Not a very auspicious second round.

The third round was totally unproductive and went to Tyushin, as these things will. I encountered him at the November 7 Soviet celebration of the twenty-ninth anniversary of the Bolshevik Revolution. The Russian generals in their rich green tunics, gold belts, gold epaulets, barrel chests covered with medals, and scarlet-striped trousers were a reminder, if none other was needed, that those who ruled in Russia were determined to profit to the maximum from their victory in war. Tyushin, surrounded by his colleagues, was still affable but more formal, and in effect I found myself in a drinking bout with a coterie of Russian officers whose intent was unmistakable. I regret to say that I went down in just under an hour; I was then escorted, almost tenderly, to a waiting Red Army staff car outside, and the driver ordered to take me home.

At the foot of the steep, narrow road up to the Var, we were stopped by a Soviet patrol. They had been celebrating too and demanded that the driver surrender the car to them. He refused, saying he had an American general with him. I accepted my promotion without protest. The patrol insisted, and suddenly my driver cursed, slammed the car into gear, and we shot up the hill. He wasn't even in second gear before the patrol opened fire, the submachine gun among them sounding as though I were standing right next to the muzzle. The car was struck a number of times, but miraculously we reached the top of the hill and I was deposited at my door, intact and stone-cold sober.

I returned to the fray by calling Tyushin in a few days and accusing him of plotting my murder. He thought it a great joke. We agreed to lunch several days later—at the Russian hour of 5 o'clock. To my surprise, Tyushin suggested a popular, crowded political café right in the center of town. When we met, he started things off right away by ordering a bottle of cognac. I had learned long before, notwithstanding my lamentable November 7 performance, that a strong determination not to succumb plays a large role in this matter of liquor in such encounters; and I was fully determined on this occasion.

We talked for almost seven hours. My recollection is that we went through three full bottles of cognac in this time, and that we at some point lunched. But it was the talk which dominated. It was all political, and it ranged over the entire spectrum of the Soviet occupation of Hungary and the personalities, Russian, Hungarian, and Western, who were involved. Tyushin did not speak by any means as a disaffected Soviet citizen. When, for example, I raised the question of the Soviet plunder of Hungarian industry, he forthrightly proclaimed their right to restore Soviet industry and territory, utterly devastated when occupied by the Germans and their then Hungarian allies. When I observed that this surely did not include stripping the peasants' homes of furniture right down to mattresses and pillows, he said quite simply, "If the Russian peasant had only half of what the Hungarian peasant has I would be satisfied."

From the range and forcefulness of Tyushin's remarks it became clear to me that he played a much more important role than was indicated by his ostensible rank of Red Army colonel. Remembering the rumors which placed him as a high N.K.V.D. officer, I probed this by steering the subject around to arrests, concentration camps, and forced labor. He inquired as to my estimate of how many Soviet citizens were in concentration or forced labor camps. When I answered ten million, he smiled, paused for a moment, and then said, "Look, I know something about this subject. I have seen most of the camps. I can assure you, their population is not more than a million. One half of one per cent of our total population." While I had the impression that he wished this were so, more than he really believed it to be so, the important point was that he freely admitted special knowledge of the subject. Even more importantly, however, he admitted knowledge on a more immediately Hungarian aspect of the subject. It was common knowledge that, quite apart from the depredations of the Hungarian AVO, the Russians themselves were still occasionally arresting Hungarians. They repeatedly denied this and declared themselves innocent of all interference in Hungarian domestic affairs.

Only a few months before this, a notable case had occurred in which Count Geza Palffy, a very well-known Hungarian aristocrat, himself not active in politics, had been abducted by Soviet officers before numerous witnesses in broad daylight, on a crowded city street. I mentioned to Tyushin what was—in those pre-Khrushchev days—the unofficial loyal Communist explanation of the excesses of the Soviet purges of the late Thirties, namely, that Yagoda and Yezhov, Beria's predecessors as head of the N.K.V.D., had misled and betrayed Stalin, and suggested that perhaps the disappearance of Count Palffy was an indication that Yagoda and Yezhov's methods were being exported to Hungary. Tyushin did not deny Soviet involvement in the affair; instead, he reflected quite long and seriously, and then said, "That is a very serious case." I had the impression here of a distinct ambiguity in his answer; that is, that the seriousness of the case might be due to factors other than some act of Palffy's. Tyushin's manner and phraseology seemed to suggest that Palffy was not himself guilty of anything in particular, but that this was not the point or significance of the case.

Most importantly, the sense of Tyushin's comments and observations over several hours began to add up to a strong inference of disagreement among the Soviets themselves as to how to proceed in Hungary. Of all the personalities discussed in that long conversation the names of Georgi Pushkin—then Soviet Minister to Hungary, later Ambassador to East Germany, then Deputy Foreign Minister, and most recently Soviet co-Chairman of the Geneva Conference on Laos—and of General Sviridov—then Soviet Chairman of the Allied Control Commission in succession to Marshal Voroshilov, later Soviet Representative on the Allied Control Commission for Austria—were never mentioned by Tyushin. He was courteous and complimentary in his remarks about the American personalities in Hungary. He spoke very highly of the Yugoslavs, he having arrived in Hungary with the armies which came from the south. He exhibited marked impatience with Matyas Rakosi, the Hungarian Communist leader: "If you think he's one hundred per cent our man, you're mistaken," he said. (History proved him Stalin's man; the question was who was meant by Tyushin's "our.") Instead, he spoke more warmly of Rajk, Kadar, and Losonczy—Hungarian Communists who each had his own following in the Party, but whose common characteristic was that none of them was a "Muscovite," that is, a Moscow-trained Communist who returned to Hungary with the Red Army, as did Rakosi, Gero, Revai, Imre Nagy, and most of the Party leadership. (Ten years is a long time in a man's life: in 1956 it would be Imre Nagy, the loyal "Muscovite," who would lead the revolt against Moscow, and Kadar, the "Titoist," who, having suffered imprisonment and torture, would betray that revolt back into the hands of Moscow.)

I left Tyushin that night aware not from any single remark, but from the total impression of hours of talk that there was disagreement among the Soviets. I did not think then, nor do I now, that this disagreement was over objectives. I believed then, and do now, that it was over tactics and methods: how far to go and how fast, it being recognized that the tactics of maximum speed would be bound to provoke opposition from the West. It was also clear to me that Tyushin, whatever his importance, was not a decisive element in resolving this dispute. But there were bound to be those behind him, in more decisive positions, whose views he shared or reflected. The difficulty was that I had no way of knowing, even with the frankness of much of Tyushin's talk, and even by the most correct deductions from his comments, what exactly were the alternative courses being weighed by the Soviets. Tyushin had given me some vague ideas of who the clashing personalities might be, but this, in the dark labyrinth of Kremlin politics, was far from enough to deduce the issues. In short, I felt I had recognized the hidden dissent, but I was at a loss how to exploit it.

The following day—fortified with aspirin—I dispatched a long report to my headquarters, recounting the conversation in factual detail. I added my personal impressions—labeled as such—and then decided to check with Louis. Without giving him the entire substance of my conversation with Tyushin, I explored with him the possibilities of strong policy divergencies among the Soviets about the Hungarian situation. My impressions turned out to be similar to his. For one thing, he recounted his experiences with the Soviets in the matter of the Armistice, when he said it was apparent to him that every Red Army Commander had a patron in the

Politburo, that every political commissar at army or corps level
also had a patron in the Politburo—usually a different one from
the Army Commander—that the same was certainly true of the
diplomatic representatives, and that all this rivalry and dissension
was deliberately encouraged by Stalin, who thus played all his subordinates and any possible rivals off against each other. For another, he had had similar indications in a series of conversations
with various Soviet officials prior to the Paris Peace Conference,
when it was his impression that they were undecided how far to go
in supporting neighboring states' claims against Hungary. Louis
took the Soviet stalling on an Austrian Treaty as a very serious
sign, possibly negating any benefits from the Hungarian Peace
Treaty, and pointed out that the strategic advantages to the Soviets
of their continued occupation of Austria gave them time to resolve
any differences over how to handle the Hungarian situation. He
had no more concrete ideas than I had of exactly what alternative
courses the Soviets might be weighing, or of the personal roles
being played. "Anyway," he commented dourly, "by the time you
figure all that out, and before you can exploit your information,
they will have resolved their differences, most probably by force,
and will run over us all with a steamroller."

Within three weeks Louis was proved right in this prediction.
The first thing that happened was that Tyushin disappeared. On
calling his office I was repeatedly told that he was out; the last time
I called a brusque voice said that he had returned suddenly to
Moscow. At a reception some days later I was standing with General Sviridov, Pushkin, the Soviet Minister, and others, when
someone in the circle mentioned that he had not seen Tyushin for
some time. Pushkin said quickly, "He returned suddenly to Moscow," and then added, with what I thought was singular casual-
ness, "A death in the family, I think." As Tyushin has never since
shown up on the international scene, so far as I know, one can only
assume whose death it was. (The then Prime Minister, Ferenc
Nagy, has remarked in his memoirs that he noted a distinct shift in
the relative importance of the principal Soviet officials in Hungary
at just this time.)

The second thing was that during December rumors began to
spread around Budapest of important arrests made by the Hungarian Military Political Section—a Communist-controlled unit
within the Army established at the same time as the civilian Political Police, and still theoretically separate from the AVO. Between

Christmas and New Year's, Leo gave me a partial list of those arrested, and next day Jane brought from Paul a complete list, which included the name of a Hungarian correspondent for a Western newspaper who had attempted to file the story. According to both Leo and Paul, those arrested were being subjected to torture, and the charges were of a "conspiracy" to restore the Horthy Government—about as harebrained a thought as could be mustered in Hungary at the time. Henry, who knew a number of those arrested, said the charges were pure fabrications.

The press, including the Communists, was still silent on the matter, and I thus at first took the "conspiracy" as just more terrorism by the Communist police. I was wrong. The Soviets had indeed reached a decision—with Tyushin most probably on the losing side —and the steamroller was getting under way.

1. Southern side of the Var. Quite different view than described—but pleasant. My occupation of this flat, which was actually my fourth and last residence in Budapest, coincided with the last and most active phase of my mission there.

CHAPTER III

Conspiracy

In early January Eugene reported a singular incident. In the early evening, in a crowded section of the city, there had been some shots fired in a nearby darkened street, and shortly afterward a Hungarian officer, wounded and bleeding, stumbled out onto the main avenue and managed to board a streetcar. Some fellow passengers helped him off, called an ambulance, and then stood about to protect him until it arrived. When it did, he was, at his own insistence, taken to the British Military Mission.

A casual comment to the man I had every reason to believe was my British opposite number produced only a very stiff upper lip. It took some time to find the answer to this mystery, but when uncovered it provided one key to the problem of the "conspiracy."

The Government was also, quite naturally, apprised of the arrests, and, after due consultation, the Defense Minister summoned General Palfi-Oesterreicher, Communist head of the Military Political Section, for an explanation. (The Defense Minister was a highly respected General, Albert Bartha, who had been recalled from retirement to reorganize the Army. Bartha had been with Kitchener at Khartoum, and still held, as he once told me with obvious pleasure, the rank of Lieutenant in the British Army.) Palfi-Oesterreicher at first refused any information, and then made allegations about a "conspiracy" against the "democratic regime." This being a political question, the matter was taken up with the Prime Minister, who ordered Palfi-Oesterreicher to make the prisoners available to General Bartha for questioning. At first Palfi-Oesterreicher agreed, but when Bartha showed up at the prison he was refused access to the prisoners on the grounds that the Soviets had forbidden it. The Prime Minister approached General Sviridov, who denied any such order. Accordingly, disciplinary action was instituted against Palfi-Oesterreicher. But the very same day this step was taken, General Kondratov, head of the Military Section of the Allied Control Commission, called on the Prime Minister and told him in no uncertain terms that if the proceedings against Palfi-Oesterreicher were not dropped immediately, the Soviet High Command would take the matter of the "conspiracy" into their own hands.

The proceedings were quashed, but in the meantime, in his rage at Palfi-Oesterreicher's insubordination, General Bartha had let drop the fact that his source of information about the arrests was the Socialist deputy head of the Military Political Section, a Colonel Viktor Kruchina. Some days after Kondratov's ultimatum, Kruchina was invited to tea by the Smallholder deputy head of the AVO, one Janos Gyurics. On emerging from Gyurics's apartment Kruchina was attacked by an AVO squad. Kruchina had been active in the Resistance against the Germans and the Hungarian Nazis, and had been in contact with the British during the war. He was thus experienced in these matters, and had gone to tea armed with two pistols—in some circles a more vital question than how many lumps of sugar. He fought his way out of the trap, was wounded, but escaped.

It was thus, by working through from an isolated if dramatic street incident, that we became aware of the extent of Soviet backing of the Communists' "conspiracy" maneuver. (The answer as to why the Government didn't tell us officially is simple: the Soviet Chairman of the Allied Control Commission had at the outset forbidden the Hungarian Government to communicate with the American and British Representatives on the Commission, and vice versa, except through the Chairman. To have told us unofficially would not have provided a basis for any American or British action—of the possibilities for which, in any event, the Government was, correctly, doubtful.)

Shortly thereafter, Rajk, the Communist Minister of the Interior, announced the "conspiracy" to the press. The Communist papers took up the cry. They thundered against "the fascists still in our midst." The Communist Party, in its press, in Parliament, in public speeches, had for some time been pursuing the line that the Smallholder majority in the 1945 elections was simply due to the fact that former Nazis had taken refuge in the party, and they had steadily been pressing for the expulsion of various Smallholder deputies from the Parliament and of certain Smallholder officials from the Government. They now shouted that the "conspiracy" at last uncovered was proof of what they had been saying for months.

All through the first weeks of 1947 the Communist press and speakers kept up a steady campaign against the Smallholders Party on the basis of the alleged "conspiracy." There was in fact no "conspiracy." There were discussions among everyone—including the Communists themselves, quite naturally—as to the situation which might exist in Hungary when the Peace Treaty went into effect. Such discussions among non-Communists—the great majority of the population, the Parliament, and the Government—were simply a meeting of the minds to the effect that the Communists should not succeed in gaining absolute power by the time the Occupation was legally terminated. (The opposite conclusion, basic to Communist discussions of the situation among themselves, was naturally not characterized as "conspiracy.") The question was how to avoid a Communist take-over, but no responsible Hungarian politician was under any illusions that the Western Powers would ever intervene by force to block such a seizure. They were, moreover, under no illusions about the neighboring and immediate power of the Soviet Union and the necessity to accommodate their foreign relations to the Soviet demands for security on their western borders; indeed, one of those initially arrested in the "conspiracy" was one of the three original signers of the Armistice with the Soviets. The outstanding fact, and the one which was ineradicably graven in my mind, was that among those arrested, and later among the hundreds accused, were almost all those who had distinguished themselves by active resistance to the Germans and to the Hungarian Nazis.

Nevertheless, the Communists, supplied by their police cohorts, continued to announce "confessions." These "confessions" were regularly alleged to have implicated more and more persons; these were in turn arrested, and then alleged to have themselves "confessed" and implicated still further persons. And so the pool widened, the rising waters claiming more and more victims; with each new victim, the hopes and future of those still on shore were also drowned.

The "confessions" were the result of interrogation methods which have since become well known. Notwithstanding the strict security surrounding the arrested, word began to come out of the prisons of these methods. Paul obtained a smuggled letter, signed by one of the accused, which warned that the "confessions" were false but were unavoidable in the face of the methods being used, and that the questioning was seeking to implicate the entire leadership of the majority party. (It was at this time that rumors first began to circulate of the use of drugs in interrogation. As I later learned, a Red Army medical major named Istvan Balint had come to the AVO at the end of 1946; he began using actedron, pentothal, scopalomine, and morphine on the political prisoners.) I informed Mark of these developments, about which I had a growing feeling of urgency and alarm. He shared these feelings, and shortly took the opportunity, while seeing the Prime Minister on other business, to express concern over the potential danger to the Government. Nagy answered that he and his colleagues were aware of the danger, but retained the hope that they could manage to keep the matter under control. What this diplomatic exchange really conveyed was the Prime Minister's knowledge of the Soviet willingness to support the Communists actively in the "conspiracy" affair, and his conclusion that, unless the Western Powers indicated that they would, and could, intervene effectively to offset Soviet pressure, he had no choice except to try by his own resources to minimize the damage.

In late January the Communist charges, which had already engulfed one Smallholder Minister and six of the most capable members of Parliament, spread out to include Bela Kovacs, the Secretary-General of the Smallholders Party. Kovacs, a peasant, a long-time associate of the Prime Minister, and a gifted organizer of enormous popularity, was the crucial support upon which the whole majority edifice rested. The charges against him were tantamount to accusing him of conspiring against himself. Nevertheless, they were pressed with all the vigor the Communists could muster —and with behind-the-scenes pressure from the Soviets.

This was the critical moment for postwar Hungary. The Parliamentary majority sensed this. Leo took the lead with several of his Smallholder colleagues in declaring that the affair had gone far enough. Independent of the leadership they introduced a motion for the creation of a Parliamentary committee to investigate the "conspiracy." The Communists raged and threatened to withdraw from the coalition if the measure passed the Parliament—a serious menace in view of Soviet insistence on their presence in the Government. The non-Communist Government leaders, who were aware, as the rank and file were not, of the Soviet presence behind the Communist pressure, sought to find a compromise which would save Kovacs—and with him Hungarian independence—and at the same time provide an effective sop to the Soviets.

On February 10 the Peace Treaty was signed—to come into effect ninety days after ratification. The hopes this aroused were used by the Smallholder leaders to calm the deputies. At the insistence of President Tildy, the Parliamentary investigating commission motion was withheld from debate and efforts were continued to negotiate with the Communists. These efforts were doomed to failure: the essence of the Hungarian position was lack of power; without it the concept of compromise is unknown to the Soviet vocabulary. Apparently the efforts dragged on too long.

On the night of February 25, 1947, Jane telephoned for an urgent meeting. We met—as prearranged for such emergencies—by the Coronation Church, from where I could see if she was being followed. She was not, but she was accompanied by Paul—agitated as I had never seen him. Earlier in the evening he had been on his way to see Bela Kovacs. Arriving at the block in Pest where Kovacs lived, he found the area sealed off by several companies of

Soviet troops. As he waited, he saw some Soviet officers emerge from Kovacs's apartment house. Kovacs was between them. He was shoved into a Soviet staff car and taken away. It was as simple as that—with the added benefit for the Soviets of a show of force to intimidate the Government majority.

I enciphered a message to headquarters, including my comments on the significance of the open Soviet intervention, and then telephoned Mark. We met in one of the city's livelier night clubs—it fitted well with the Communists' preconceptions of what Americans might be doing on a politically eventful night—and discussed the possibilities for the future. He knew as well as I that in one night all the implications and complications inherent in an intelligence network based on political motives had materialized. Political support as a motive naturally involves some reciprocity on the part of the nation benefiting from the intelligence. Whether Washington liked it or not, the Soviet challenge was political and strategic, and thus directly affected the intelligence potential of the network—as the questions of each member of the network in the next few days showed. What support will the United States give us to fight back now? To be able to assist the Hungarians effectively would require more than an attitude of disapproval by Washington toward the Soviet actions in Hungary. Similarly, expressions of sympathy to men whose lives or freedom were immediately endangered would be tantamount to refusal of assistance—with the consequent deterioration not only of an intelligence network, but also of American strategic and political interests in the area. For Leo and Paul, with the duties and possibilities of public office, these questions were urgent. But such questions can seldom be answered forthrightly in international politics.

In early March the American and British Governments sent notes to the Soviet Government protesting the Soviet unilateral interference in Hungarian affairs and the conduct of the Hungarian Communist Party. The notes called for a joint Soviet, American, British, and Hungarian investigation of the so-called "conspiracy" and of the role of Bela Kovacs. The anticipated Soviet rejection was followed by further American and British notes, without effect.

Prior to Kovacs's arrest, the United States had granted a $15,000,000 credit to Hungary for the purchase of surplus materials. On March 12, President Truman asked Congress for an appropriation of $400,000,000 for economic and military aid to Greece and Turkey. The accompanying statement, which proclaimed the United States' intention to aid peoples everywhere in resisting Communist aggression and was immediately labeled the Truman Doctrine, caused Americans in Budapest, increasingly somber these days, to walk in the streets with their heads held high.

These various moves were sufficient to restore some measure of courage among the Hungarians. Although Paul was more cautious, Leo felt that the American response now made it incumbent upon the Hungarians to move in their own defense. He felt that, at the minimum, they should make the position of the Hungarian majority clear, and that they should avoid any possible inference being drawn from their conduct that they had been supine before Communist and Soviet pressure and force. He resurrected, with the support of a numerous, rebellious faction among the Smallholder deputies, the proposal for a Parliamentary investigation of the "conspiracy." The leadership of the party was less sanguine about the possibilities for maneuver, and in mid-March the struggle came to a head. President Tildy summoned the dissidents to the Presidential Palace. There he cajoled, threatened, pleaded, blustered, and eventually succeeded in persuading the majority of the rebels to support the Government's policy. The motion for a Parliamentary investigation was abandoned. Leo was in tears as he told me of the session with Tildy and its outcome. It was indeed a turning point. When Seymour Freidin, then Eastern European correspondent of the New York *Herald Tribune* and an experienced observer of the westbound Soviet steamroller in Poland, Rumania, and Bulgaria, heard the news, he said, "That does it. At this rate I'll be filing my next dispatches from Hoboken—if I can make it to the ferry."

(In 1955 Bela Kovacs was released by the Soviets and returned to Hungary, his health broken. In the 1956 Revolution he reappeared as leader of the resurrected Smallholders Party in the coalition established by Imre Nagy. The contrast between the America of 1946 and of 1956 was most marked on the night of November 4, 1956. As the Red Army assaulted Budapest Kovacs appeared at the American Legation to ask asylum. On direct instructions from the State Department in Washington, which at the same time granted asylum to Cardinal Mindszenty, Kovacs was refused. There followed alternating periods of prison, hospital, house arrest, and limited detention, until his death in 1959.)

A lull now followed in Hungary. The Smallholders had been

forced to expel a number of their deputies and officials, and the party was demoralized. Most important, it was now clear that no one was immune from the "conspiracy" danger. Trials of a number of the accused were held, at which, as confession and self-denunciation poured forth from the defendants, the efficacy of the Communists' methods became apparent. (Retractions in open court—as occurred in the case of Balint Arany, a principal defendant—were followed by immediate adjournment of the case, to be resumed only when the defendant reappeared in court to retract his retraction.)

The trials, under the jurisdiction of the Justice Ministry, supplied a key to the critical question of why the other two non-Communist parties in the coalition collaborated with the Communist campaign of destruction of the majority party. Istvan Riesz, the Minister of Justice, was a Socialist—but this did nothing to protect the administration of justice from the Communist juggernaut. Furthermore, the Socialist Party, as well as the Peasant Party, throughout the whole course of the "conspiracy," had vigorously supported the Communist attacks. The answers to this suicidal policy were both overt and covert. The overt answer lay in a statement of Rajk, the Interior Minister: "Learn from Lenin," he said. "If you have five enemies, you should ally yourselves with them; arrange to incite four of them against the fifth, then three against the fourth, and so on, until you have only one enemy left in the alliance; you can then liquidate him yourself and kick him out of the alliance." But these tactics would not have worked alone; they were supplemented, as I was to learn in detail, by the covert answer: penetration, intimidation, and subversion on an enormous scale.

The Socialists, the second largest party in the coalition and with considerable strength in the trade-union movement, obviously could, if they so chose, act as an effective brake on the Communists. They were also in a position to know much about Communist plans and actions.

The deficiencies of my network which I had earlier remarked were by now becoming apparent. In the constant reshuffling of the Government Paul, himself long under attack by the Russians, had been removed from his post—although not from his seat in Parliament; Leo was becoming increasingly isolated after his defeat in the Parliamentary investigation question; Henry became less and less active as the danger increased; and George was now almost useless in a Foreign Office housekeeping assignment. Eugene was still active, but his sources were not in vital positions. Simon continued to provide valuable economic information, and Louis was still consulted by politicians of all parties, and by the Russians. Jane, of course, continued to operate effectively as a cut-out, but not as a source of important information. The situation was far from satisfactory and promised to deteriorate unless I could broaden the area of my work. However, the same events which had made my position more difficult had also gravely alarmed others; as I was looking for them, so they were looking for me.

In April a Hungarian newspaperman in whom I had full confidence, and who had been most helpful in arranging for me to meet persons in whom I was interested, came to me and said that certain important Socialists would like to talk secretly to an American. I arrived at the rendezvous given, which was simply a certain floor of an apartment house. There I was met by a young man who was intensely serious, but possessed of a sense of humor withal. He led me up one floor, around to the service staircase, into what I took to be an unused storage closet— "Sorry about the back entrance," he said—and there, hidden behind a curtain, was a door leading into the building next door, which fronted on another street. Unlocking the door, he explained that it had been cut between the buildings during the German occupation to assist the escape of Jews, including himself, and that now that the building was once again under surveillance it came in very handy. He led me into a comfortable apartment, where I found five other people. One of the group I recognized as Karoly Peyer, for many years leader of the Hungarian Social-Democratic Party, until his incarceration in Mauthausen by the Germans in 1944.

Peyer looked exactly as one would expect a Viennese tavern-keeper of the old Empire to look. Short, round, with shaved head, he sported magnificent handlebar mustaches, and his eyes frequently lit up with an irrepressible twinkle. He was shrewd, but there was no mistaking his ingrained decency. Peyer had been in the Socialist and trade-union movements ever since the beginning of the century. Under his leadership the party had managed to survive increasingly rightist regimes in Hungary, and for the average Hungarian worker the trade-union movement meant Peyer. On his imprisonment, one of his assistants, Arpad Szakasits, succeeded to the party leadership in his absence. By the time Peyer was liberated from Mauthausen by the American Army and had made his way back to Hungary, Szakasits had already entered into a close compact with the Communists. He relegated Peyer to a minor position in the party, which Peyer, for the sake of the party and notwithstanding his enormous popularity, accepted quietly. However, Szakasits's control was based on nothing less than bribery and corruption—a trip Szakasits himself had made to Western Europe at the end of 1945 in a private railroad car had been a scandal throughout the Continent—and Peyer, fighting all the way, had more and more come into active opposition while still within his party.

Peyer now saw the direction in which Socialist co-operation with the Communists was leading the country. His talk with me, although it took several hours, had basically but two questions: what is the attitude of the United States Government? And: what will the United States Government do in support of its attitude? Peyer was considering an attempt to reassert his leadership of the Socialist Party. His object was to deny Socialist support, automatically given by Szakasits, to the Communists, and thus block a Communist seizure of power before the effective date of the Peace Treaty; he was also anxious to save his party from the forced merger with the Communists which he foresaw in the Communist plan. But he was reluctant to expose his followers to Communist police reprisals and Soviet terrorism and abduction; against these only the West could provide a defense.

Now it was abundantly clear that the inexorable pressure of events, the effects of Soviet moves and the implications of American responses, were transforming my mission into a political operation. I had no aversion to such a development; on the contrary. I was personally enthusiastic, but I was nonetheless skeptical of what the United States was really prepared to do at this early juncture. Peyer had phrased his remarks with circumspection, but their burden was clear. I told him that the American attitude was summed up in the notes delivered to Moscow on the occasion of the Soviet arrest of Bela Kovacs, and I reminded him of the Truman Doctrine. For the rest, I said that I was not in a position to know what further steps the United States would now take in the case of Hungary, although I would see that his intentions and problems were made known in the proper quarters. I observed that questions such as his were not ordinarily susceptible to direct answers. To this he smiled and said, "Usually not soon enough."

On leaving, my guide— "Sam"—asked if I would mind coming

back in a few days: he and another young man— "Edmund"—who had been present but had remained silent most of the time, wished to talk to me about other problems. I returned on the agreed day, and what I heard was a considerable step toward answering my own problems. Sam and Edmund had both been active against the Germans and Hungarian Nazis: Sam had operated a clandestine radio station during the German Occupation; Edmund had been an Army officer and a member of the Hungarian Front, the clandestine organization of the Smallholders, Social-Democrats, and Communists, and had time and again risked his life saving Jews. Both had escaped imprisonment, Edmund on one occasion by shooting his way out of a police ambush. Sam was now an official in the Trade Union Council—a Communist-run organization used chiefly to dominate the individual unions and to organize "spontaneous demonstrations" for Communist political demands. Edmund, to my astonishment, revealed himself as an officer of the AVO—pointing out gravely that any carelessness on my part with this information would mean his instant death. He was one of the few Socialists permitted in the organization as a theoretical sop to "coalition."

Both were absolutely loyal to Peyer. However, as Sam pointed out, Peyer was working at the political level, in the situation as it was. He and Edmund, on the other hand, while they would work as hard as possible to help their party leadership, were convinced that the handwriting was on the wall. They believed it would not be too long before they would once again be forced underground by a totally Communist regime, and they wanted to prepare now for that eventuality. They emphasized that an underground network prepared now would have infinitely better chances of survival than one hastily assembled at the last moment. One purpose of such a network, as they conceived it, was to maintain contact with the West, and to this end Sam asked for the supply of radio sets. In the course of the afternoon they gave me vital details of the Communist and Soviet violence, blackmail, and intimidation behind the recent political developments, including the "conspiracy," and promised more.

I was curious as to why this approach had come to me. "Look," Edmund said, and mentioned the name of the newspaperman who had brought us together, "he vouched for you, as did several of the American correspondents he knows." I reflected that my hours spent with the journalistic fraternity had not been merely time pleasantly spent after all. "Furthermore," Edmund went on, "if you are not the man with whom we should speak of these matters, we can only trust you to put us in touch with the right man. It is in your interest as well." I did not acknowledge whether I was or was not the "right man."

I did ask a further question which puzzled me. "Why not the British?" I inquired. "Surely you have close fraternal ties with the Labour Government in England?" Sam laughed. "First of all, we don't trust the British because of their support for Tito," he answered. "Secondly, they seem to have no realistic conception of Soviet aims, and therefore they take Szakasits and his stooges as genuine Socialists, instead of the Communist tools they are. Thirdly, we suspect that the British, Socialist or not, don't really object to Soviet control over Eastern Europe—look at what they forced on Mikolajczyk and the Poles. Fourthly, America tried to help Hungary with the Peace Treaty; Britain couldn't have cared less." I remarked that I was glad the word had gotten around at least about American efforts. "Lastly," concluded Sam, "it is America that leads today." I thought it a quite complete answer. I looked at Edmund. "Quite a risk you're running." He shrugged.

I cabled my headquarters for a check on both Sam and Edmund. They had no information. Without telling her anything of my conversation, I asked Jane to make a few discreet inquiries. She came back with exactly the stories given me by Sam and Edmund of themselves, plus the fact that Paul had known Edmund in the wartime Hungarian Front and thought very highly of him.

At just this time, George decided to take advantage of the possibilities of a foreign diplomatic assignment. He went abroad, and in a few months resigned and stayed on in exile. But before leaving, he brought to me a woman whom I listed as "Sara." She had worked in the same administrative section with George, but was shortly due for transfer, because of a nominal Peasant Party membership, to the Political Section of the Foreign Office, where she was to have a position giving her access to all of that section's most confidential correspondence. Sara was forthright: she was convinced that the Communists would soon seize power; she was determined to do what she could to obstruct that, and when she could do no more, she planned to leave the country for a Western capital where her fiance resided—a fact unknown to the Communists, she pointed out.

I now had three potential new agents, with easy access to highly valuable material, all of whom were motivated by political support. Furthermore, the initiative had come in all three cases—although less in the case of Sara—from the prospective agents themselves, which was not undesirable in my role, vis-à-vis them, of case officer. I began to feel somewhat encouraged as to my ability to ride through the changes which were bound to come in the succeeding months with a minimum of damage to the work and with some hopes for a future for the network.

While I was in this frame of mind, Guy came to see me one evening at my apartment. He did not seem personally concerned about the political situation, but told me, quite casually, that he had resigned from the Police. He made no comment about this, but proceeded to a proposition he wanted to put to me. It was astoundingly simple. If I would make available to him an American Army truck for two afternoons a week—a thing I had only to lift up the telephone to do—he would guarantee me $12,000 per month payable in any currency and in any bank anywhere in the world that I wished. I was stunned.

My first reaction was to throw him out of the house. I realized that this would accomplish nothing, however, so I asked him for further information. I could get nothing from him, except that the trucks would be used to cross into Slovakia, to the north, and his insistence that there was no danger. I finally gave up probing and told him simply that I was not in a position to help him. He seemed offended and deeply disappointed.

The next day I told Jane I wanted to see Simon. When we met, I told him of the offer I had received, but without saying who had made it. He laughed uproariously. Finally recovering himself, he said, "That would be the perfect deal. You working for the Communists. Take it. You'll be rich." Again he was overcome with laughter, but I finally got the explanation from him. The Communist Party had, the previous year, as one of the brainchildren of Zoltan Vas, the Communist economic wizard, formed something called the West Orient Corporation. It was, quite simply, an enormous and privileged black-market outfit. They stole cars in Austria and sold them in Hungary; they imported scarce goods from the West and sold them at enormous profits in Hungary; and they capitalized on Hungary's few products of export value by means of the Party machinery throughout Europe. The traffic to Czechoslovakia was simply the smuggling of Hungarian tobacco and cigarettes. At a time when cigarettes were still a medium of exchange everywhere in Europe, the income from this traffic swelled the Communist Party's coffers. Obviously they had been having trouble of late with the Czechoslovak border guards, not yet Communist, and an American Army truck was the ideal solution. I had to laugh myself. They could well afford the $12,000 monthly.

The implications were less worrisome than they looked. If the Communists had suggested me to Guy, it was a good sign that they took me for just another American profiteer—a not entirely unique specimen in Europe at the time. If Guy had come to me on his own, simply because I was the only American he knew who could help him, then there was also no danger. But I decided to keep Guy at arm's length.

For some time past I had been communicating to my headquarters the increasing and unavoidable political implications of my operations in Hungary. No guidance had been forthcoming. Now the Communists had begun to agitate for new elections, which could only intensify the pressures on me. My inability to take a line one way or another in the circumstances would sooner or later jeopardize my usefulness, even for intelligence work, let alone its effect on the willingness of Hungarians to continue to resist. I therefore asked for permission to meet Peter in Switzerland, under the guise of a holiday in Italy, to discuss these problems urgently. In reply, I was told to let it be known that I was going to Italy on vacation, but to come to Washington instead. I accordingly set out by car for Italy, driving to the southwest toward the British Zone of Austria. Apart from being arrested in Veszprem by a Russian sentry who, speaking mostly Ukrainian himself, took my imperfect Russian as proof that I was a Russian deserter, I arrived safely in British-occupied Graz, continued on over the Grossgluckner— then Europe's highest road, where I encountered more Russians, but this time former Russian prisoners who refused to return to the Soviet Union—and went on down to Salzburg in the American Zone, where I took a plane to Paris and thence to Washington.

Washington seemed unreal and excessively comfortable. In just under a year I had become accustomed to the ruins and rubble of Budapest and to the sense of danger in the air. Washington was alive with movement and confusion, but the sense of danger was noticeably absent; the general atmosphere was still that of victory in the war, and there was seemingly no public awareness of the erosion of that victory being so harshly pursued in Eastern Europe.

I went over every detail of my operations with my chief and his

assistants. My use of Sam and Edmund and of Sara was authorized, although without any intimation to them of the organization
for which I worked. There was an obvious CE interest in Edmund,
but I pointed out that, as a Socialist, his position in the AVO was
too much on sufferance to offer any opportunities for operations
more complex than secret intelligence. Sam's request for radio sets
was turned down cold as too dangerous at this stage. I was instructed to continue to seek out new agents in the areas not covered. They themselves, presumably working through the Hungarian Legation in Washington, gave me the name of an agent,
Anna, who would satisfy my requirements concerning Church affairs.

On the matter of political action, I presented my ideas for covert
support of a wide range of Hungarian non-Communist groups.
Here I encountered sympathy, but I sensed that I was considered
to be somewhat alarmist, and in any event this was not a matter for
decision by my organization. There seemed to be a general feeling
that such techniques were wartime measures only and inappropriate to the postwar period. It was assumed that the results to be
achieved by such action could be more properly obtained by direct
negotiation with the Soviets. It would take another year, the fall of
Czechoslovakia, the Tito-Cominform break, and the narrow victory of the Italian elections of 1948 before the United States Government realized the need for a political arm in the Soviet war.

I was, however, permitted to state my case to a high official, a
Presidential adviser. He agreed with my analysis of Soviet intentions in Hungary, but, he said, the American people were in no
mood to take serious steps to stop them. "The American people
have just finished a war," he said, "and they will not stand for us
taking action which seems likely to provoke hostilities with the
Russians." I pointed out that the net result of this was not simply
Soviet domination of Hungary, but a slaughter of the nation's entire leadership—beginning first and foremost with those who had
resisted the Germans. This would mean, I said, that if the Soviets
were allowed to pursue their course unhindered, they would have
in their hands a nation without leadership, from which in the far
future we could expect nothing except support of Soviet aims.
"You are too pessimistic," he answered. "You should read the reports on the popular initial reaction of the Russian people to the
German invasion. After almost a quarter century of terror, they
still rose up to welcome the Germans in the naïve belief that they

were being liberated. Even the Jews of Moscow, kept in the dark by Stalin as to Hitler's anti-Semitism, rioted in the streets as the Germans approached—convinced that they were to be liberated. These Russian reactions were pathetic, and when they found out the truth, the people fought for Russia. But their initial reaction is proof that people do not forget freedom as easily as you fear." I had little faith in this view at the time, but history was to prove him right. The Hungarian Revolution, in which a whole generation raised on Communism were to fight Soviet domination, was just under ten years away.

"At least we can save some of the people," I argued. "We cannot just leave those whose principles and courage will be our assets and their doom to prison, torture, and death." He thought awhile. "And can you save some of them without embroiling us in a series of clumsy mishaps that will only worsen their fate?" he asked. My answer, "Yes," may have been only bravado; it was still the only answer possible. "Well, we'll give that one some thought," he said, rising to signal the end of our talk. Before returning to Europe I drew up and presented a plan to my headquarters for a series of escape operations, designed to save political leaders whose resistance to the Soviets put their lives or freedom in danger, but with sufficient leeway to allow the inclusion of some persons who may not have been politically active, but who nonetheless merited our help. My headquarters received this without comment.

However, my chief had comments on another score which amused and at the same time irritated me for what it revealed of our confidence in our own agents. A large man of imposing appearance, quite the general he was, he took me to lunch just before my departure. Over the coffee I noticed that he was talking on at great length, seemingly without saying anything. I paid closer attention and finally realized what he was trying to say, with almost embarrassing discretion and a show of great personal interest in me. He was obviously well informed that in Budapest I saw a great deal of a particular Hungarian lady. I was embarrassed for him, but also annoyed. "You are afraid I will give something away to her?" I asked. "No, of course not," he demurred. "But you know how it is —blackmail and all that sort of thing." I felt genuine pleasure at what I knew I could answer. "You should have consulted the FBI," I said. "You will find that the Russians tried to blackmail me and failed. Where they failed their Hungarian stooges aren't going to succeed." He looked surprised. "I didn't know that," he said.

He appeared somewhat mollified, but still not completely happy. I gave him the rest. "What your informant was unable to tell you," I went on, "is highly relevant, however. It is true that I see a great deal of the Hungarian lady, but what your man apparently doesn't know, and the lady does, is that I am planning to marry someone completely different—a Frenchwoman, as it happens." His discomfort vanished in a flash. "Wonderful," he cried, and we parted in backslapping mutual confidence. What I had not done was to find out who was watching me in Budapest: whether I was the incidental object of some CE operation, the deliberate subject of a security surveillance, or merely an item of gossip.

I flew back to Europe. As I arrived in Paris I was met by the news that the Hungarian Prime Minister, Ferenc Nagy, on vacation in Switzerland, had been implicated in the "conspiracy." It seems that he had, with the agreement of his Cabinet, including Rakosi, requested the Soviets to turn Bela Kovacs over to the Hungarian authorities—obviously in the thought that even that was a lesser evil than imprisonment and possible death at the hands of the Soviets. General Sviridov had replied—in Nagy's absence Rakosi was acting Prime Minister—that the Soviets were unable to surrender Bela Kovacs, but included with his reply a copy of Bela Kovacs's "confession," which he noted showed that the Prime Minister was also a "conspirator." I hastened to Salzburg and drove on to Budapest. The day I arrived the Prime Minister's four-year-old son, left behind in Hungary during his parents' vacation, was handed into his father's arms at the Swiss-Austrian border by a Communist functionary in direct exchange for the Prime Minister's resignation.

CHAPTER IV

The Opposition

The Soviets and the Hungarian Communists had made their point: no one was immune from the "conspiracy." To eliminate anyone who opposed them the Communists had merely to announce in their press that he had been implicated in some "confession"—imprisonment, torture, death, or at best exile were the rapid consequences. For the sake of temporary appearances, the Communists found men in the other parties who were either utterly intimidated or of limited attainments and ridiculous ambition who would serve them as figureheads. In this way, they replaced Ferenc Nagy with another Smallholder Prime Minister who was but a puppet. The Smallholder President of the Parliament, Monsignor Bela Varga, surely the next on the list for elimination, disappeared—we learned only weeks later that he had escaped to Austria. He was replaced by Imre Nagy, a Communist, since the battleground now shifted from the Cabinet and Government to the Parliament, where opposition still existed.

Shortly after my return I met with Sam and told him that for the time being I would have no radios for him. I still had hopes that my headquarters would shortly see things in a different light. He was disappointed, but urged me to press the matter. He then told me that Edmund was working on a series of reports for me about the AVO, but it being too dangerous to meet with me, they would be passed to me through Sam. I received the first of the series that day. In due course I had the complete report; it came to several hundred pages, setting forth in detail the brutality, treachery, and corruption which was the Soviet version of "liberation." I confess it made me feel neither confident nor comfortable.

In January of 1945, while Budapest was still under siege, Gabor Peter, a Hungarian who had been a Soviet agent working with the

Red Army during the war, established the Budapest headquarters of the Political Police—a branch of the newly reorganized National Police. Peter's liaison to the Soviets was a man named Janos Kovacs, a Hungarian major and simultaneously a Soviet colonel. The ostensible purpose of this organization, proposed by the Communists and agreed to by the other parties of the Hungarian Front, was to uncover and bring to prosecution the Hungarian Nazis. About one month after getting into operation, Peter and his men in Budapest caught one Janos Kessmenn, head of the Hungarian Nazi organization charged with exterminating the Jews. (Even during the siege of Budapest, when it was no longer possible to ship them to Germany for extermination, the Hungarian Nazis continued to round up Jews: they were lined up on the quays of the Danube by the hundreds and shot, their bodies falling into the river.) The Political Police promised Kessmenn not only his life, but freedom from prosecution if he would show them the hidden cache of property confiscated from the Jews. Kessmenn produced about $90,000 in foreign exchange, some 1,500 carats of diamonds, and more than 10,000 different gold pieces. This became the Political Police secret fund. All during 1945 the Political Police added to this by simple robbery, theft, and extortion—mostly from small shopkeepers. They did not hesitate to murder, and countless innocent persons disappeared during this period. In the confusion of the time it was impossible to tell whether a person who had disappeared was a victim of Russian looting, Russian deportations for forced labor, the settlement of grudges, or the Hungarian Political Police. Nonetheless, Edmund's report contained quite a list of those known to have fallen into the latter category.

During 1946 the Political Police worked closely with the Soviet MVD; as often as not someone arrested by the Hungarians was turned over to the Soviets for interrogation. In such cases it was rarely that he was ever seen again. In 1946 it would appear that the Soviets concluded their tutelage had produced satisfactory results; in September the Political Police were reorganized out from under the National Police and established as the State Security Authority —AVO—with Gabor Peter responsible in theory to the Minister of the Interior. The AVO was, of course, directly responsible to the authority of the senior Hungarian Communists; but, as elsewhere in Eastern Europe, it became an integral part of the Soviet secret operations apparatus. It was a specially qualified local arm.

In the new AVO the coalition received lip service in the form of a

Smallholder deputy to Gabor Peter, one Aladar Gyuris, and a
Socialist deputy, Istvan Bittmann. Neither of these two deputies
exercised any authority whatsoever. Of the fourteen, later nineteen,
Budapest districts, only three were under the command of Socialist
AVO officers—and their authority was purely nominal. Of the seventeen divisions which comprised the AVO organization, only one
was headed by a Socialist.

The structure of the AVO, quite apart from the vicious brutality
which was its chief characteristic, was an interesting example of a
painstakingly conceived and executed broad secret political operation. Against such a comprehensive and realistic—and ruthless—
machine, ordinary political and diplomatic maneuver and negotiation—the mainstays of American policy at the time—stood not a
chance. A study of this structure showed a notable disregard for
administrative balance. From the point of view of American professional administrators such a structure would appear disperse,
unwieldy, even sloppy; it would be difficult to reduce to the charts
and graphs favored by Business Administration schools and Government bureaucracy. In fact, however, it was designed to perform
with maximum effectiveness a special and precise function; to this
end the factors of administrative balance and of theoretical organization were completely subordinated to the specific requirements
of the mission. It was "bad administration," but it was a flexible
and effective organization—even without rapine and murder.

As established in September 1946 the AVO had seventeen divisions, each with a special function to perform within the national
life. Of these seventeen, the existence of only three was publicly
acknowledged. The divisional functions were described and designated on the basis of what actually confronted the Communists,
not on the basis of what they wished Hungarian national life to be.
That came later, and only when it was achieved in fact. It should
be borne in mind that beyond this AVO structure there also existed
the overt political entity of the Communist Party—likewise politically trained—and, of course, behind both the menace of the Red
Army.

The task of Division One was to infiltrate and ultimately to
dominate Hungarian political life. Its director, Sandor Horvath,
was a Moscow-trained Communist. Infiltration was accomplished
in two ways—each for a different purpose. The first was the
recruiting of informers in all the non-Communist political parties
and their related organizations. Bribery was sometimes used—a

principal Smallholder speechwriter who had a single session at AVO headquarters and thereafter submitted daily reports was one such case—but the favorite method was simply intimidation. Taken from their beds in the middle of the night, maltreated, threatened with a worse fate, then released on the condition of reporting, with the express threat of instant punishment for any disclosure, most people did as directed—suicide seemed the only available alternative for many, and such cases were not unknown.

The other form of infiltration was the introduction into the other parties of active agents. In the case of secret Communists no lure was needed; for the rest, entire "left-wings" of the Smallholders, Socialist, and Peasant Parties were made up of men who, as political opportunists, as victims of blackmail, or as recipients of various forms of bribery, deliberately worked under Communist instructions. At the highest level, two of them—Istvan Dobi of the Smallholders and Szakasits of the Socialists—were ultimately rewarded in a fully Communist Hungary with the Presidency of the Republic, Dobi first from 1952 and then again under the post-1956 Kadar regime.

As a part of its political responsibilities, elections in Hungary also fell within the competence of Division One—with final disastrous consequences for Hungary in 1947.

Division Two of the AVO was charged with infiltrating all foreign missions in Hungary—the Soviets obviously excepted. I noted one day to Mark that the receptionist at the American Legation seemed upset and on the verge of tears. "She's picked up every night after midnight and is interrogated until the morning," he said. "She's exhausted from lack of sleep and plain terror, but they won't let her quit her job here, and for us to dismiss her would only make them suspect her of a doublecross."

The target of Division Three was the churches. One of the traditional church activities in Hungary had been the support and direction of youth organizations, both Catholic and Protestant. These organizations were of considerable social significance, and were a prime obstacle to Communist aims for weakening church influence and dominating the youth. In the summer of 1946 two Russian soldiers, engaged in a gun battle between themselves on a main street of Budapest, were killed. Within twenty-four hours the AVO—still then the Political Police—fabricated a story that a young Catholic boy had done the shootings from a nearby rooftop. He was never seen again, and according to Edmund, his body was burned. Before his death, however, the name of a Catholic priest, Father Szalaz Kis, was extracted from him; Father Kis was killed in the 60 Andrassy ut headquarters of the AVO, and all the young Catholic men who were close to him were arrested and disappeared. (Among them was a Smallholders Party employee, which fact was used as an extra dividend to try to implicate the Smallholders as well.) On this basis, the Minister of the Interior banned and dissolved all religious youth organizations. Thereafter, the question of religious youth organizations came under Division Four, in charge of youth.

Division Three also pursued infiltration of the churches, and achieved some success in the Catholic Church because of differences within the Church itself. Cardinal Mindszenty, notwithstanding his merits as a churchman, was no politician—although he took an active interest in politics. His inflexible line had resulted in the failure in 1945 to form the authorized Catholic Party, and a temporary agreement had been reached whereby the Church would support the Smallholders, and the latter would represent Church interests in Parliament. As the Smallholders began to disintegrate, the disputes among Catholic politicians and within the Church began again; a group of Jesuits emerged in political opposition to the Cardinal and with a political program of their own. Division Three capitalized on this schism, and, obtaining, among other favors, a charter for a Catholic youth organization for the Jesuits, proceeded to infiltrate them.

Division Five, the only one commanded by a Socialist, had the duty of infiltrating the circles and activities of former aristocrats, Army officers, and politicians.

Division Six, using the same techniques as Division One, was charged with applying them to the Government and the entire apparatus of the state. They were singularly effective. The suicide of one young official in the Prime Ministry, who preferred death to becoming an informer, was one testimonial. Another was the reorganization under Communist dominance of the Defense Ministry, even in the presence of a Smallholder Defense Minister. In 1946 large-scale reductions in the Civil Service were undertaken for economy reasons. Those to be dismissed were put in category "B," so that the whole procedure became known as the "B" List. Making up the "B" List was obviously of great political importance to the parties. In each Ministry a commission composed of a representative of the Prime Ministry, a representative of the Minister involved, and a representative of the trade unions prepared the list. The trade-union man, being an appointee of the Trade Union Council and not of the individual unions, was always either a Communist or a complaisant Socialist. In the Defense Ministry, the Prime Minister sent a Smallholder deputy and the Minister delegated a trusted aide, a Colonel Daroczi, thus insuring a majority over the trade-union representative. Division Six, however, had reached Colonel Daroczi, and he voted all the way down the line with the Communists, thereby turning the Defense Ministry over to the Communists. Another notable success was achieved by Division Six with Jozsef Bognar, former Smallholder Party Secretary for Budapest. Even while Minister of Information, Bognar was secretly arrested by Division Six, shortly after the arrest of Bela Kovacs by the Soviets. Within a few hours Bognar went free, still a Minister, but now one of Division Six's chief informants.

Division Seven, headed by a former Hungarian Nazi, Gyula Princz, was charged with surveillance and kidnaping. Surveillance was of course a service function for the other AVO divisions. Kidnaping—as in the case of Laszlo Filler, a Smallholder member of Parliament, who was abducted and turned over to the Soviets, never to be seen again—was most often a service function for the Russians, to hide the Soviet hand or interest.

Division Eight was one of the publicly acknowledged activities of the AVO. Ostensibly its function was to track down remaining Hungarian Nazis; it was, in fact, a cover for the other activities of the AVO.

Division Nine was occupied with establishing and maintaining files on the entire population, for such later use as might become necessary. Under Soviet theory and practice, any information about anyone is of possible value. The result is history's most enormous dossier system (Division Nine was the Hungarian branch), which often turns out to be highly useful. One high Government official, for example, occupying a post which could effectively block Communist plans, was discovered by Division Nine to have been an illegal abortionist at one point in his early career; thereafter he was no obstacle to Communist aims. (The late John MacCormac of *The New York Times,* present in Budapest during the 1956 Revolution, claimed that one of the gravest errors of the Revolution was the failure of someone in authority, while the enraged populace was killing any AVO man caught in uniform, to destroy, systematically and thoroughly, the AVO files.) At least some reservoir of undischarged guilt feelings, no matter how sub-conscious, are acknowledged by psychological sciences as existing in almost all adults. The Communists recognize this too; they seek to know exactly what it is that every man is feeling guilty about and, when necessary, to what usable degree.

Division Nine also was charged with arranging false identities for AVO agents when necessary, and with the related function of forging documents. The microphone and wire-tapping services were also a part of this division. Mark told me later that an examination of his small office in the American Legation showed eight microphones in the walls and ceiling; but such installations were by no means confined to foreigners—they were everywhere. One of the more striking ironies of the situation was that this equipment in Hungary was all secretly manufactured by Communist workmen in the plant of the local subsidiary of the International Telephone and Telegraph Corporation—the same American company once lauded by *Fortune* magazine as an outstanding prewar model of successful American investment and operations abroad.

Division Ten was another overt group. It was charged with official documentation, including the issue of identity cards, and it maintained the legal personal files on the population, as distinct from the secret files in Division Nine.

Division Eleven was related to Division Eight. Its ostensible function was to assist in the prosecution of former Nazis before the courts. As such, it was located in special quarters at the Marko utca Prosecutor's Prison, but this was also a cover, since it insured continued AVO hold over prisoners who had been legally transferred from the AVO's custody. Division Eleven was also charged with the preparation and conduct of show trials.

Division Twelve was the AVO's own supply department. Apart from the usual supply functions, it was also charged with the raising—by any means available—and disbursement of secret funds. It also supplied apartments, furniture, clothing, cars, and luxury goods to the AVO high officials. The information thus obtained by this Division was later used by the AVO against its own officials when their liquidation became politically necessary.

Division Thirteen, also overt, was the Hungarian Passport Office. From the spring of 1947 it was directed by a Russian officer, Antal Weller. It provided a cover for the activities of other divisions.

The personnel department of the AVO was Division Fourteen.

This Division was also responsible for surveillance and security of
AVO personnel. The Division's standards of performance might be
described as utterly ruthless. Edmund emphasized to me the story
of AVO First Lieutenant Mihaly Kovacs, an aide to Horvath, Chief
of Division One. Kovacs was discovered to be working for the
British. Both he and his wife were arrested and subjected to torture
in the cellars of the AVO headquarters at 60 Andrassy ut. Ultimately, Kovacs was killed—with his wife forced to watch his murder. Only then was the hapless woman herself put to death.

Division Fifteen conducted surveillance of all high state officials.
To this end, they appeared most often in the guise of "bodyguards"
from the National Police.

Division Sixteen comprised the AVO sub-headquarters in the
districts of Budapest. Originally these district offices had the power
of arrest, but from 1946 on they were deprived of this and functioned as the eyes and ears of the Headquarters. The establishment
of informer networks was their responsibility, and on the basis of
the information thus obtained they were required to prepare black-
lists of anti-Communists and "dangerous or hostile elements."
These offices operated in the classical style and preferred a number
of single key informers, whose responsibility was then to create
their own larger networks of informers. In this manner they had,
by 1947, 1,500 informers at the Budapest industrial complex of
Csepel Island alone.

Division One-A performed the same function for the rest of
Hungary as Division Sixteen performed for Budapest. By the autumn of 1947 there were, throughout the entire country, some
70,000 to 80,000 informers—out of a population of nine million.

This, then, was the "opposition." The relentless effort and the
horrendous human cost which had gone into the AVO's organization showed this to be more than a mere cover to hide the Soviet
hand; what had been constructed was a major line of defense, so
that if the Peace Treaty, or if other diplomatic negotiations with
the West, forced a Soviet retirement from Hungary, the nation
would still be left, thanks to the AVO, firmly in Communist hands
and tied to Moscow.

Following the forced resignation of Ferenc Nagy, the fragmenta-
tion of the opposition to the Communists was pushed with fero-
cious haste. Leo came to see me one evening in June. He knew that
he was marked for arrest for his role in pressing the Parliamentary
investigation of the "conspiracy." He had decided to escape, with

his wife and two children. I was deeply concerned about the risk,
but he assured me he had arranged it satisfactorily. I was dubious
and told him I was merely awaiting authority to establish an escape operation. "No," he said. "I thank you, but now one can
escape, with a little care and ingenuity. But in a few more weeks, or
at most a month or two, it will become impossible. You will see. I
must go now, while we still can." He left me his political papers,
which I agreed to send on to him when he should let me know,
writing under a false name, where he was. Four weeks later I had
word from him giving a Paris address. In due course he received
his papers, but I felt shame that I could not have rendered more
vital help.

Shortly after Leo's departure, Mark was confronted one day in
his offices by a member of Parliament whose immunity had suddenly been lifted and who had taken refuge from the AVO in the
Legation. Mark told me the man was verging on hysteria—but
Mark was forbidden to give him asylum. He had been obliged to
turn him out into the street, with only the advice, which he had
heard from me, to seek refuge with the Dominican friars and at all
costs to avoid the Jesuits. (An exact reversal of the situation which
had prevailed during the German Occupation, when the Jesuits
had distinguished themselves in rescuing those in danger and the
Dominicans had often refused help.) The deputy had left, never to
be heard of again. Mark was sick at heart from this incident.

I remembered it ten years later as I watched, with bitterness and
sympathy, the rending strain undergone by one of my colleagues in
Vienna, whose orders and role required him to answer "No" to the
pleas of Hungarian Freedom Fighter delegations from Budapest
for bazookas and ammunition to fight the Russians.

The deputy refused refuge was a member of the Freedom Party,
an opposition party led by Dezso Sulyok which had received in late
1946 an authorization from the Soviets, largely at the instance of
Prime Minister Nagy, to form and engage in political activity.
Nagy's theory was that there ought to be an opposition in Parliament, and he probably hoped in this manner to ease some of the
Communist pressure on the Smallholders. In this he was not successful, and, as the Smallholders disintegrated, the Freedom Party
gained in strength. The party had even attempted to publish a
newspaper, but its instantaneous success had led to a refusal by the
printers to set type for it. (Sam had told me the story of how this
was achieved by the Trade Union Council. The Council had issued

the order to the printers, who, favoring the paper themselves, had refused. They were then threatened with expulsion from the union —meaning also their jobs—and that was that.) Now the Communists were pushing through Parliament a bill for new elections. With the Smallholders in disarray, strong opposition to features of the bill was coming from the Freedom Party. Its deputies were consequently under constant harassment. A few days after Mark had been visited by one such deputy, Sulyok announced the dissolution of his party. Edmund reported that the AVO had quite simply informed Sulyok that when Parliament was dissolved for the new elections, all of his Parliamentary members, then without immunity, would be arrested en masse. Rather than expose his followers to this danger, Sulyok had given in; shortly thereafter he left the country.

We were doing pretty poorly. Not only was I without any effective political line in the circumstances, but even my proposal for an escape operation was still unanswered. While terror had silenced many, there still remained a number of politicians and leaders who were determined to fight the Communists in the forthcoming elections. At least some of them were going to require our help—and to earn the right to it. I therefore arranged to see Peter in Vienna. Since my return I had visited Vienna regularly, always going by car, in order to familiarize myself with the roads, the countryside, and to have continually in my possession a valid Soviet pass, the eternal *propusk,* without which one could not get by the Red Army roadblocks between Budapest and Vienna.

Vienna was still grim and gray, but by now my feelings had changed noticeably from the contrast so favorable to Budapest I had noted a year earlier. Arrival in the Western sectors of the city invariably produced feelings of relief, relaxation, and security. In an office where I didn't have to worry about microphones, I told Peter how rapidly the situation in Budapest was deteriorating, and emphasized the fact, which I found shameful, that I had been unable to be of any real help to Leo. I asked Peter to press Washington for the authority I had asked for escapes and for a political decision on which I could base some activity during the election campaign—which I pointed out might still result in a clear rebuff to Communist pretensions that they were assuming power legally and on a popular basis. It was my belief that such a rebuff might, at best, slow down the Communist timetable; at worst, it would still make clear to the world by what methods the Communists had achieved power in Hungary, a point which could be of great political value in future years if dramatized now. To my satisfaction, I found Peter in full agreement with my arguments, and there followed one of those typical conversations in which those working in the field commiserate with each other on the stupidity and myopia of headquarters.

Encouraged, I asked Peter to give me temporary authority to arrange a minimum number of escapes pending word from Washington. He insisted on pinning me down to an exact figure. I finally asked for ten outstanding political leaders and fifteen others as necessary, the latter to include members of the network. Peter agreed to this. I then pointed out that, assuming I could get my escapees over the Hungarian border, I could do nothing from Budapest about getting them safely through the 40-odd miles from the border to Vienna, nor through the 125 miles from Vienna to the American Zone of Austria. I asked for assistance from my opposite number in Vienna. Peter again agreed, and shortly I found myself introduced to our Vienna agent who was operating under the guise of an Army Colonel. The Colonel appeared eager to help, even while obviously studying the problem coldly and objectively behind a front of affability.

The Colonel's problem, it turned out, was bureaucratic, and bureaucracy won the day. He could help escapees from the Austrian border to Vienna, but from Vienna to the American Zone the facilities were in the hands of the local representative of the CIG—Central Intelligence Group, successor to the OSS, and predecessor of the CIA. To split the operation this way would risk revealing to the CIG representative both that our own intelligence agency was operating in Austria and the identity of the Colonel. I was stunned at this hapless example of wartime interorganizational rivalries living on into another age—but the Colonel, supported by Peter, could not be moved. However, neither he nor Peter had any objection to my approaching the CIG man—Hugh—provided that I maintained my cover with him and did not reveal any member of the network to him as being such. In brief, I could appear to him as a lone official of the Government who wanted to help some people in danger—a friendly but completely private secret operation. I accepted this way of doing it, being reminded in so doing of the German gesture of scratching the left ear with the right hand reaching behind the head, intended to describe either a deliberately complex brain or bureaucratic red tape. It was, of course, precisely this kind of bureaucratic conflict and artificial obstacle—markedly different from the innate, organic conflicts of secret operations, described in Part I—which the later creation of the CIA was designed—successfully—to eliminate.

I decided to await approaching Hugh until I had something definite in mind, and returned to Budapest. It was fortunate that I did. A week later Mark handed me a slip of paper bearing a name and a number. A man who said his name was Janos Majoros had called to see Mark at his office and had given him this much-worn scrap of paper. Majoros explained that he was a flier, that it was he who had secretly flown Hungarian negotiators and the British Colonel to Italy in 1944, and that an OSS officer, whose name and number were on the paper, had told him to use it at the nearest American diplomatic office if ever he were in danger or needed help. Majoros said he was now in danger of arrest and needed funds to arrange his own escape. I told Mark I would look into the matter for him, and then checked with Henry. Henry confirmed that there was indeed a flier named Janos Majoros, a genuine hero, but this of course didn't insure that the man who had come to Mark's office was in fact Majoros.

This was my opportunity to contact Hugh. I went to Vienna and called on him in his office. An intelligent and decisive man, Hugh was fully co-operative, and went immediately to the core of any problem. He checked the Majoros story, found it correct, and gave me the requested funds. Then he settled back to ask me a favor.

The Navy was interested in six Hungarian scientists and had, many months before, secretly signed contracts with them in the course of a Navy officer's visit to Hungary. The Navy was now extremely worried about their departure, and the scientists and their families, twelve persons in all, needed money and some assistance. Would I disburse $5,000 to them and if necessary help to arrange their departure? I could have looked on this request as a suspect gambit by Hugh to recruit me; instead I chose to regard it as a heartening example of interorganizational co-operation within the U.S. Government. When I left, Hugh and I were in business together: I had funds to disburse for him, but I also had the names of contacts in three Austrian border towns who would convey escapees to Vienna, and an address in the American Sector in Vienna where they would be housed before being taken on to the West by air.

(Highly personable and sensitive, Hugh's later career took an unusual turn. For some years he rendered most competent and effective, even distinguished, service in secret operations, but suddenly, while still in his early forties, he became sated and disillusioned with the world of politics and power. Renouncing his past for what he intensely felt was a wider and more profound perspective, he spent a year in a Trappist monastery and then went to Italy where, in a small seaside village, he devotes himself exclusively to work in ceramics. This kind of reaction among intelligent and sensitive men to the intense pressures of secret operations after some years is not infrequent, but few carry it as far as Hugh. However, I visit him from time to time, and of the many real and enduring friendships which this strange work nonetheless brought me, I value his highly.)[1]

Majoros and his money turned out to be a lesson in patience and relative values. Mark gave him the money and he disappeared. We heard nothing further from or about him. Six months later I apologized to Hugh for the loss of the funds; he dismissed it as part of the cost of doing business. But five years later a Hungarian airliner suddenly appeared one day over the Munich airport, asking permission to land. When it did, some fourteen of the passengers aboard requested political asylum in the West. One of them was Janos Majoros; he and another flier had taken over the plane while it was en route to Prague and had flown it to Munich. When asked about his disappearance five years earlier, Majoros said he was then being too closely watched. "I had to revise my plans. They took longer than I expected," he said, but with the confident air of a man who has worked hard to achieve his goal.

My own goal was far from being achieved. No one in the network was in a position to operate the kind of sure escape chain I had in mind. They were all tied to the city of Budapest by their work, and they had no forms of transport. I thought of Edmund; an escape chain operated by the AVO itself would be the kind of *tour de force* to make any agent's mouth water, but I rejected it as being much too dangerous and too susceptible to penetration. Both Eugene and Louis had told me of cases where the Russians themselves had arranged escapes. However, these were for money—the price was steadily rising—and the Russians involved were black-marketeers who were always in danger of being caught by their own troops or betrayed by rival Russian profiteers. Furthermore, these Russians were happy to take money from "capitalists," but would fear involvement with escapes of hunted political leaders.

There was one escape chain already operating through Budapest and tolerated by the Soviet High Command. This was the Jewish underground originating in Rumania which ran through Hungary and then alternatively by Austria and Yugoslavia to Italy. From there refugees were loaded onto ships for transport to Palestine. This operation had the tacit blessing of the Soviets since it contributed to British discomfiture and general unrest in the Middle East. In Hungary the operation was run by the American Joint Distribution Committee, the American Jewish organization set up for welfare work among the European Jewish survivors of the German slaughter. They were efficient—at a later stage they were reportedly running seventy-five persons a day through Budapest—but they categorically refused any non-Jews. In addition, Simon had obtained for me some time before several sets of the AJDC confidential monthly accounts, which showed sizable donations to the Communist Party in several districts of Budapest. I sympathized with their operation and admired the single-mindedness with which it was conducted, but it offered no possibilities for me. Even if I could persuade the AJDC to take some non-Jews, which was highly doubtful, it was not likely that they would risk their own people for the sake of defying Soviet and Communist political objectives, and the tacit co-operation of the Soviet and Communist authorities meant too great a risk of penetration.

While I was mulling over these problems, I gradually accumulated, in an unused garage in my building on the Var, a number of packing cases obtained from the American Military Mission, together with several tarpaulins and large sheets of the waterproofed, insulated paper used for packing large overseas shipments. To ship people out in boxes in the American Army trucks which regularly ran between Budapest and Vienna with supplies was not my idea of a discreet or desirable operation; but an emergency might necessitate something like it. I little knew how right I was.

In early July I went to dine at Guy's. I had not dropped him since his unwelcome offer to make me rich; I enjoyed his company and his wit, but I maintained a certain alert when with him. This particular evening we dined on the balcony of his apartment, overlooking a small, tree-lined public square. The people walking in the square, the summer air, and the night hum of the city hid the struggle and anguish which marked the day's reality. Guy, for the first time, spoke much of himself; I noted that, apart from a few sallies for their own sakes, he had dropped his cynicism.

He told me how he had resigned from the Police. The increasing Communist control had made him decide to leave, he said, but he knew that if this were to be interpreted as a sign of dissidence, he would only be putting himself in danger. He had therefore told Rajk, the Interior Minister, that he had to find some work which would pay him better while he awaited the award, under the land reform, of the 200 acres to which his Resistance record entitled him from a larger estate he had previously held. According to Guy, Rajk had intimated that he should act for the Communists in the Peasant Party to which he belonged, to which Guy had responded with a criticism of the Peasant Party which sounded at the same time like a eulogy of the Communist Party. He finished by saying how much he looked forward to working his land—obtaining a little bit of capital for this being the purpose of his looking for better-paying work. He then parted in most friendly fashion from Rajk, who told him to drop in to see him from time to time.

Guy paused here. "He's a murderer, you know," he said. I nodded agreement. Edmund had told me through Sam only a few days before that he had gone to see Rajk personally, on the basis of their Resistance work together, to intervene for another wartime comrade who was being tortured by the AVO. Rajk was expansive and assured Edmund that he could speak freely, as an old companion. When Edmund explained the purpose of his visit, Rajk's manner turned cold. Edmund reminded him of the man's wartime services. Rajk merely glanced at Edmund and, turning back to his papers, said, "The situation has changed."

Guy went on. "I didn't want Rajk hostile, and he was not, but that alone would not save me." For the ensuing two weeks, therefore, Guy had inserted anonymous personal want ads in the main papers, asking on each occasion if anyone knew the whereabouts of some ten or a dozen people. All the names Guy used were those of persons kidnaped or killed in the course of Political Police looting and robbery during 1945. He had then put the complete lists of these names, together with the date and manner of their liquidation by the Political Police—information he had carefully gleaned during his two years in the National Police—in a safe hiding place. He then resigned. Guy's idea was that if arrested, he would simply state that the lists detailing the fate of these people would be published if he did not reappear within twenty-four hours—he having arranged this with a friend—and that his proof of his threat would be the want ads. I could only admire Guy's imagination and his careful execution of his plans.

"So what happened to you and the West Orient Corporation?" I asked him. Guy laughed. "They came to me about a month after my resignation," he answered. "I decided to accept the offer," he continued, "because I assumed Rajk was trying to be helpful—and to ensnare me, of course. But even a month or six weeks of that would have given me enough to leave the country and live abroad.

"But I may have been wrong," he added. "It was perhaps just as well for me that I couldn't persuade you to give me an American truck. That at least showed I wasn't all that close to the Americans. To be perfectly frank with you, though, I was disappointed at the time. I didn't really care about this country then. I wasn't going to join the Communists, by any means, but I was sure the Smallholders weren't going to save the country, so I just counted myself out."

"So you're off to your farm?" I inquired.

Again Guy laughed. "My farm," he answered, "happens to be a plot of 200 acres adjoining the Austrian border. It took me a lot of intrigue to get just those 200 acres and not some others. People do escape now, but within a very few months they're not going to be able to. So, one day, working my fields, I'll just stumble through a bush into Austria and that will be that."

I laughed with Guy, but I was seeing him in a new light. "How soon will that be?" I asked.

"As late as possible," he answered. "I like life abroad, but now I have no money for it, and"—he paused— "when you're leaving for probably the last time you keep putting it off."

All that night I went over Guy's story. If he was not a Communist plant, he was the man to run the escape chain—provided he was willing. He had imagination, daring, and a conspiratorial cast of mind. The next day I checked the newspapers for the period he had mentioned. There were the personals. I then checked them against Edmund's list of victims of the Political Police. All of Guy's names were on Edmund's list. I then sent off a cable to Headquarters, asking for a check on Guy and explaining the purpose for which I wanted to use him.

The answer was both startling and encouraging. "Guy former British agent," it read in effect. "You may use him for stated purpose only provided you maintain your cover with him and provided you're satisfied he's not working with British." This was unusually generous. It left the responsibility on me to be sure he was not still working with the British, but at least his former service for them was not to eliminate him from consideration.

In about a week I invited Guy to dinner. He was unchanged from our previous encounter: always amused at some bit of irony, but more equable in temper than in the previous months. Politics took over our conversation, and I steered the subject gradually away from Hungary itself to the world situation. Guy made a number of remarks critical of the British. I responded with a defense of the British, always implying that Guy didn't really know or understand them. At last he said, "Look here, I worked with the British before and during the war. I know what I'm talking about. And I refused to work with them afterward." He then detailed his reasons; except that he was no Socialist I would have thought that I was listening to Sam's reasons for disillusionment with postwar Britain. I took no ostensible notice of what Guy had said, but I had what I wanted. It could still theoretically be an effort to penetrate my operation, but I felt the odds were against it. The decision was mine, as was the risk. I decided in favor of Guy.

The rest came easily. In a discussion of what could be done, as a practical matter, about Hungary now, we arrived together at the conclusion that an escape operation was the most necessary item. Guy was much less sanguine than I about the possibilities of the forthcoming elections, but he was personally enthusiastic about the prospects of saving those who would show the courage to fight in them. We bargained somewhat on the terms (in the circumstances the initiative to recruit Guy was in fact mine, however much it may have accorded with his own wishes). He wanted a veto on who would be taken out, and he refused to provide the names of those who would help him. The latter was contrary to the basic rules of secret operations, but to have insisted would have risked his concluding that I was a professional agent rather than simply an American wanting to be helpful. I gave in on that, in exchange for my insistence that he agree to take whomever I sent to him. Since I agreed to cover the expenses of the operation—an arrangement so obviously necessary in the circumstances that it provoked no curiosity—Guy agreed to inform me in advance of the identity of anyone he wished to transport. Finally, we agreed on occasional meetings at the same rate as in the past, but to utilize a cut-out for communications in the intervals between such meetings. He suggested a girl—Helen—a former countess now working as a bar-

maid in a popular bar who was known to us both as reliable. When
we parted Guy's enthusiasm was unmistakable. It had much the
quality of an adolescent who has found the perfect way of getting
back at some hated authority. I realized that I had not seen Guy
before as a lifelong rebel, someone always at the edge of his society,
who welcomed an opportunity to flout that society in what had
now become a desirable cause. Not at all a bad quality for the
operation we had in mind. But I would be hard put even today to
define Guy's motives: political support, certainly; the need for
money (I realized Guy was making a small personal profit on each
escapee); personal rebellion—but even beyond these factors, an important element of human decency which circumstances would
bring ever more clearly into relief.

Thanks to Edmund, I knew the opposition we faced. Thanks to
Guy, maybe we would give them some opposition of their own.

1. This parenthetical paragraph is a substitution for what was originally
written. When the typescript of this book was submitted by the publishers
of the first edition to the CIA—at my direction—the first response was a
telephone call to the publishers from the Public Relations Officer of the
CIA ("An oxymoron?" queried one editor). The message was a stern warning against publishing as "contrary to the national interest." Relations between American publishers and the CIA being very different in 1962 from
what they are today, the affair then languished for months, as the CIA
refused even to specify whatever might be objectionable in the text.
"Hugh," who thought the CIA should try to obtain an Official Secrets Act
from the Congress, and if unable to do so, live with the consequences rather
than trying surreptitiously to threaten and harass publishers, at one point
found himself discussing the matter with the Public Relation Officer. "But
he's giving away all our trade secrets to the Russians!" the PRO protested.
"Oh, come on," "Hugh" answered, "it's the other way around. We learn
from them, not they from us." The PRO was quick with his rejoinder. "Yes,
I see you got a favorable notice in the book," he retorted. When, finally, the
CIA got around to specifying objectionable items in the book (having hurriedly put two new officers on the task over a weekend, was how I understood it was done), they produced a list of two dozen items. I rejected about
a half dozen, modified another half dozen, and accepted about a dozen. The
original paragraph concerning "Hugh" was objected to on the grounds that
he was too easily recognizable. That was true. So the present paragraph was
my amendment. When "Hugh," very much a worldly type, saw it, he

commented, "Never was a more untrue paragraph written." That may be. But part was and is true: the friendship does still endure, and I continue to value it highly.

CHAPTER V

Defeat, But Diluted

The same message which authorized me to recruit Guy also brought the instructions from Headquarters which I had awaited since my May visit to Washington. I was disappointed, and no little bit surprised, to see that I was given authority to organize an escape chain and disburse funds as necessary for a total of twenty-five persons, of whom ten were to be leading political figures and fifteen at my discretion, including members of the network itself. These were, of course, the minimum figures I had set when seeking Peter's temporary authorization. The limitation seemed artificial and unnecessary to me, but I decided not to look a gift horse in the mouth. Take it and worry about the limitation later.

I was also specifically instructed to insure that Paul was among those taken out, and it was suggested that the sooner the better. Obviously Paul had friends in high places. As I had never had any intention of abandoning Paul I thought the instruction gratuitous, but to mention the fact would serve no purpose.

Most serious, however, the instructions contained not a word about what steps might be taken in political support of those Hungarians still fighting the Communist seizure of power. I must admit that I didn't really expect such instructions, but I had come to hope very strongly for them. The elections had now been announced for August 31, 1947, as Headquarters well knew, but so far as my instructions were concerned it was as though they didn't exist.

In the state of innocence then prevailing in the American Government about the possibilities, even necessity, of covert political operations, such an omission was not surprising. In the circumstances all that could be done was to read between the lines of my instructions and to do some careful guesswork on the basis of known official, diplomatic policy. So far as my instructions were concerned, it seemed clear that if I was authorized to arrange the escapes of political leaders whose safety was endangered by their courage and persistence in resisting the Communists, then by implication I could certainly tell them before they undertook such risks that they could at least count on this much. But was the latter truly a logical implication of the former? The answer is that it was a logical implication, but it was not a correct political implication, as will become clear.

So far as determining official policy was concerned, I had my own conversations in Washington, public American pronouncements—not the strongest of all reeds—and the guidance of Mark on which to rely. Without mentioning the details of my planned operations, I took up with Mark the political dilemma in which I found myself. I was authorized to save lives for political reasons, but without a word having been spoken as to the nature, purpose, definition, or substance of those political reasons. This gave me a very free hand—the dream of every secret agent. But it left unanswered the question of what I could do in prior support of those very political reasons which were admittedly the prerequisite justification for my saving lives—and for my guess as to the answer to this question I would ultimately be myself held answerable.

Mark agreed that we had very little to go on. My skepticism of Washington's mood, based on my conversations there and on the fact of the peculiar limitation on numbers of persons, made me unwilling to risk what I had already gained in the way of authority by seeking any clarification of it. I therefore insisted we work it out on the spot, and I further insisted to Mark that I would take sole and full responsibility for the execution of whatever line we adopted. There is bureaucratic sin involved here, of capital degree—but bureaucracy cannot function, any more than life itself, without sin. The sin, of course, is that of apparently excessive local initiative. Today, with a functioning secret political operations apparatus, such improvisations would—ideally—be neither necessary nor possible.

There was every official and publicly proclaimed support for the

basic thesis that the United States Government did not wish to see
Hungary become the victim of a Soviet-backed Communist seizure
of power. But it was also necessary to infer from the facts of American behavior that the United States Government was not willing
to take truly effective steps to block such a seizure—whatever may
have been the combination of domestic and strategic reasons for
that unwillingness. In brief, the United States wanted the maximum result possible for the minimum price. Mark's and my task
was to estimate what locally constituted the practicable maximum
result and the minimum price.

The practicable maximum was not too difficult to define. It was
any result in the elections which would either put an effective
brake on the Communist timetable or would alternatively force the
Communists to steps which would publicly demonstrate the falsity
of their claims to have come to power through popular support.
The former was doubtful, but the latter was possible. It was this
which set the price, for it was precisely the matter of those "steps"
the Communists would take which constituted the risk for those
fighting the elections. To have encouraged men to incur those risks
on even the implication that, if successful, the United States would
be able and willing to nullify those risks—when it was apparently
not—would have been political irresponsibility of the worst sort. It
would have boomeranged in bitterness and hatred against the
United States for years to come.

What we had in mind was the ability to offer to save the lives of
a relatively few leaders. But to offer this in advance to such leaders,
as a means of encouraging them to act, would have been a betrayal
of the masses who were expected to support their fight and for
whom no such rescue would be available. It would be tantamount
to buying an effort. No long-term policy can be constructed on
such a basis; in time its falsity and undependability will show, and
the cost of defeat multiplied a hundredfold. Mark and I therefore
agreed that I would refrain strictly from any such advance offers of
rescue for political purposes.

Members of the network were obviously not included in this
agreement. Furthermore, I was under specific instructions to inform Paul that he would be helped to escape—even though his role
in Hungary had now become predominantly political rather than
intelligence. I saw him, with Jane, to inform him of my instructions concerning him. He looked surprised. "No," he said, "that's

not the way it is. I'll tell *you.* " And then his politeness came to the fore, and he smiled. "But do thank them, of course."

Mark's and my decision naturally did not preclude political conversations in advance of the elections with those anti-Communist leaders who sought them; obviously they would be necessary. As a leak of such conversations could be seized on by the Communists as evidence of American intervention in Hungarian internal affairs, we decided that Mark would direct any initiative for such talks to me. This naturally would tend to draw some attention to me, but at the same time I was, by definition, expendable: I could be disowned by the American Government; Mark could not. My line with them —weak as it was—was simply to be that the United States Government would favor any purely Hungarian efforts to stop the Communist steamroller and that it would co-operate with any democratically elected non-Communist majority in the future (were such a miracle to happen). If this seemed weak to them, and insufficient assurance on which to risk their followers, then that could not be helped. That was the true situation. However, I also decided to argue that the future of Hungary merited their efforts, if they could accept the inevitable risks. Hungary had suffered after the war because of the policy of her leaders to accommodate themselves to the Germans; the same error should not now be committed in the face of Soviet aggression and expansion. A clear expression of Hungarian protest against Soviet aggression might not stop the juggernaut; but it would be historically valuable to Hungary at some future date. Or so I argued. As it happened, millions of Hungarians felt the same way then, and even more millions were to feel that way in 1956.

Mark also agreed to refer to me any political leaders who might come to him seeking escape. The first such, shortly after our conversation, was one of Hungary's most extraordinary political characters. Father Istvan Balogh had been the priest of a small rural parish and active as an independent in local politics. He appeared in the Debrecen Provisional Government as Undersecretary in the Prime Ministry. Not a very tall man, Balogh weighed some 270 pounds. He was a Rabelaisian type in his personal tastes: he relished eating and drinking, and all the material comforts and pleasures of life. Politically he was a Renaissance priest-politician; he was, I personally believe, the master practitioner of politics in Hungary during the period. Cunning, shrewd, intelligent, he was an invisible presence in every intrigue and political maneuver, advancing and retreating, exploiting and conceding. His policies were perhaps too personal, but no accretion of genuine political power exists without at least one such genius as Balogh pulling important strings in some nominally unimportant office. (A few days after the initial success of the Hungarian Revolution in 1956, a Hungarian politician came to me and, more in seriousness than in jest, said, "This Revolution cannot succeed." I asked why he was so sure. "I do not see Balogh anywhere on the scene," he replied.)

Balogh gave me lunch in his luxurious villa in Buda. After lunch we strolled in the garden. Very matter-of-factly he said, "I am threatened with arrest. I do not have much time to decide. Can you help me to escape?" This was typical Balogh. He considered it unnecessary, maladroit, and impolitic to make the full statement: "I am threatened with arrest if I do not co-operate with the Communists in some plan they have for me. I do not have much time to decide whether I can stay here, play their game, and ultimately outwit them. But there is nothing to decide, really, unless there is an alternative. The alternative, if it exists, is escape. Can you tell me if it does exist? If not, the decision is made for me. If it does, I will make the decision."

I replied that I was willing to arrange his escape—although I reminded him frankly that his easily recognizable bulk would make the matter more than usually difficult. Guy had told me that he would be ready to operate in about two weeks from our first talk. I therefore told Balogh that I could do nothing about actually removing him from the country for one week, but that I would undertake to hide him in the interim if he was in immediate danger. He listened, reflected a bit, and then said simply, "I will let you know my decision."

Balogh had not specified how he would let me know. I in fact learned his decision when it was announced about ten days later that he was forming a new political party for the elections and would publish a newspaper.

I didn't see Father Balogh again until the late autumn. He sent for me, and this time I found him in a palatial apartment in Pest. I wondered if he had now reversed his decision. Not at all. He explained to me at length how his party was keeping opposition to the Communists alive; because of this, he said, they were squeezing him on newsprint allocations for his paper. His proposition was simple: he wanted me to arrange for the shipment of newsprint to him from the American Zone of Germany. "And how can you get it into the country without the Communists confiscating it?" I asked, curious. Again, matter-of-factly, "I can arrange that." He continued, "You understand, I am not asking for financial help. I can pay for the newsprint, although not in foreign exchange. You have perhaps heard of my art collection?" Indeed I had. He pointed to a small table behind my chair. "That, for example, should be worth a fair amount." I picked up a small painting in a standing frame. It was a Renoir. "Turn it over," he said. The reverse framed a Degas. In a way I was sorry to have to turn him down.

Father Balogh's was not the only new party to emerge for the August 1947 elections. The Smallholders being completely fragmented, those who had composed its 1945 57-per-cent majority now undertook action in other parties. In place of the five parties which had contested the 1945 elections, ten appeared on the ballot in 1947. Sulyok's Freedom Party was by now forcibly disbanded, an example intended to be menacing to those who would attempt the same maneuver of rallying the broken majority into a cohesive unit. Nevertheless, the attempt was made. The problem revolved around the necessary authorization to form a political party. In addition to the four coalition parties, such authorizations were already held, since 1945, by the Catholics—the Democratic People's Party—and by a small, intellectual and liberal group called the Civic Democratic Party. The latter was composed of followers of Karoly Rassay, a perennial prewar oppositionist, a man of great personal influence, and probably Hungary's soundest politician, who had himself been inactive since the end of the war.

I arranged to have a talk with Rassay. His party was taking advantage of its authorization, but he himself was abstaining from the campaign. In the confused situation I feared too many splinter parties, and Rassay, so widely respected, offered a rallying point for a broad spectrum of non-Communist opinion. A man of great charm, he heard me out politely. Then he came to the point. "Very well. Let us suppose that I get out in the square on my soapbox. I even draw a good crowd. So much the worse for them. For what can you do when either the Russians or the AVO come and cart me off to prison? For that is surely what will happen. Would you be able to save me?"

I answered that that would depend entirely on the circumstances. Rassay laughed. "Even that is not the point," he said. "Let us suppose that the circumstances were such that you could save me personally. What could you do to save all those who had gathered in that good crowd to hear me on my soapbox? They are the ones who would need saving, more than just one man. And there, I fear, you would be quite unable to do anything." An irrefutable argument.

I knew that Rassay was neither a coward nor a defeatist, and certainly no fool. "I assume, however," I asked him, "that we are speaking of certain personal situations—that you do not mean to say that no one should contest this election?" He smiled for just a moment, then was silent. Finally, quietly, he said, "No, I do not mean to say that." We parted, I feeling certain that Rassay's inaction ever since the war was the result of Soviet fear of his potential popularity and a consequent direct order to him to retire.

I had, shortly after my return from Washington, contacted Anna, the agent whose name had been given to me by Headquarters as a reliable source on Church matters. (It should be clearly understood that my interest in Church matters had nothing to do with religious doctrine or sentiment; it was concerned solely with the existence in Hungary of a vital political issue of Church-State relations and with the Roman Church as a European political institution. The same applies to my comments on Church personalities and policies.) Anna was a woman of outstanding character and great decency; nevertheless, I found her a bit fanatic. She was a Monarchist—not surprising in a country which had, until only two years before, been a Catholic monarchy for 1,000 years. To her, her religion and the Hungarian State were both bound up in the person of Cardinal Mindszenty, Primate of Hungary. She was part of a group who, selflessly and in ancient loyalty, gave of themselves and their remaining property to support the Cardinal in his role of unyielding last line of resistance to change.

It does not diminish the Cardinal's stature as a religious symbol, or the tragedy of his fate as a victim of wanton violence, to state that as a political figure he was unfortunately inept. Once, during the Paris Peace Conference, when the United States was laboring with little support to soften the harsh terms being imposed on Hungary, the Cardinal made a very strong public speech denouncing all of the claims of Hungary's neighbors against her. Mark had occasion at the time to talk with the Cardinal. On instructions from our Delegation at Paris, he pointed out the practical difficulties confronting us in our efforts for Hungary and asked the Cardinal what, in his opinion, posed the greatest danger for Hungary's future welfare among three particularly severe demands being pressed at Paris. The eyes flashed, studiedly graceful and impressive hands swept in great arcs, as the oracular voice intoned the musical syllables. His priestly interpreter turned to Mark, speaking with utmost softness and respect: "His Eminence speaks with the moral authority and philosophy of the Holy Church. He says only a cheap politician can answer your question."

From Anna it became clear that the Cardinal was at odds with his own Bench of Bishops, who by and large in political matters sought a less provocative and more liberal position in Church-State relations. At the other end of the spectrum, the Jesuits pressed and maneuvered for a radical policy which would permit them to cooperate with the Communists. The issue at stake was which group would control the Democratic People's Party—the Roman Catholic political arm which sought nonetheless to include Protestants within its ranks, on the model of the predominantly but not exclusively Catholic Christian Democratic Parties of Western Europe.

In late July Mark suggested I talk with the Jesuits, who had approached him. The arrangements for the meeting suggested that I was dealing with an organization which knew my business better than I did. I was instructed to wait on a corner at a certain hour; a car passed, circled the block, and stopped to pick me up. The driver mentioned my name, motioned me into the car, and, without a further word, drove off by a circuitous route to a walled compound set in a forest in the hills of Buda. The security precautions were no less strict than those for the Vatican Secretariat of State itself—without the Swiss Guards, of course. The only trouble was that I knew from Edmund that this group was badly infiltrated by Division Three of the AVO. This sharply limited what I could say, but I was nonetheless curious to hear what would be said to me.

I was received by two Jesuit fathers, who were courteous but forceful in their discussion. (Hindsight touches this conversation with stark irony: one priest was to end up in the AVO prisons; the other—like Father Balogh—was to be defrocked and ultimately excommunicated. God and Caesar are not everywhere easily reconciled in our age.) They began by showing documents which they claimed were proof of Papal support of their work. They criticized all past non-Communist policy in Hungary and stated that their projects provided a realistic answer to the problem of Soviet occupation and Communist domination. They were two: the Democratic People's Party, and a broad and vigorous youth program. They emphasized the latter most strongly, pointing out that they had the Minister of the Interior's permission for their program. Then they stressed their need for funds—which they hoped the United States would provide. Their program was summed up in the phrase which both repeated to me at frequent intervals: "We can create and maintain a Christian society in a Communist state." (This idea is still not entirely dead in the political debates within the Society of Jesus and receives its strongest current support, in various versions, from French Jesuits and, astoundingly enough, Spanish Jesuits who are interested in avenues for the exercise of Spanish national influence in Europe.)

My hosts' sure conviction of their capabilities in this regard left no room whatsoever for argument. Since I could not be certain but what my remarks would be promptly available to the AVO and the Soviets I had no desire in any case to argue. I therefore said that it would be quite impossible for the United States Government to assist any political party, since this would constitute an impermissible interference in Hungarian affairs. To this they responded that they could probably manage so far as the party was concerned, and they appreciated my view. But the youth organizations, they stressed, were the heart of their program and, they believed, the real answer to the Hungarian future. I suggested that this was surely a matter for the Church itself to aid, and I mentioned their assurances of Papal support. "The demands on the Holy Father are great," answered one. I did not mention that I knew that their difficulties with the Cardinal were blocking financial aid for them from both Rome and the Hungarian Bishops. I instead assured them that I would certainly see that the appropriate authorities were informed of their views and work, but that they would surely understand that in the United States the separation of Church and State forbade Government support for the social or religious activities of any denomination. The atmosphere grew frigid, and I was escorted out.

Within a short period Istvan Barankovics emerged as the leader of the Democratic People's Party. He was grudgingly accepted by the Cardinal, more warmly viewed by the Jesuits. A vastly cultivated man, of philosophical bent, Barankovics was essentially a compromise solution, but in spirit he was closer to the Jesuits. Nonetheless, as the election approached even Anna waxed enthusiastic about him and the party.

What with political conversations, a continuing flow of reports, encoding and decoding, the mechanics of clandestine meetings—mostly at night—and endeavoring to spend the necessary time at the Military Mission in support of my cover, I was not blessed these days with much leisure. Guy was wasting no time either. About three weeks after our last talk he informed me he was ready to operate. From his Police days he had found three unmetered-taxi drivers in Budapest on whom he knew he could count. In towns near, but not on the border, and in the general region of his farm, he had found three more. At a point midway between Budapest and the border he had established a safe house—the property of a local priest. The Budapest cars would take our passengers to the priest's house. There they would be picked up by the local taxis and taken to Guy's farm. In this way the suspicion which would attach to a Budapest car wandering near the border was averted, and the rural cars were spared the long absences from their towns which might also have aroused comment. Furthermore, a reserve of three drivers at each end would avoid using the same car too often, plus insuring that one would be available when needed.

Ideally, the trip could be done in about five hours, allowing for back roads and with no delay at the midpoint. However, it was preferable to have a delay of maybe twelve hours at the midpoint to avoid suspiciously frequent traffic at the priest's house. There was also the problem of notifying the rural drivers. Guy declined to use the telephone and relied instead on the mails, using a set of prearranged phrases. It increased the travel time to as much as three days, but it was secure.

In addition, Guy would visit his farm regularly to obtain information in the neighborhood about the border patrols, their habits and general state of watchfulness. It was not necessary for Guy to be at the farm to assist those escaping; he had a caretaker at the farm in whom he had full confidence who would guide them to the crossing point at a safe time. However, Guy also planned to secure alternative crossing points; he had no desire for his farm to be under suspicion when it came time to use it himself. To avoid possible compromise of the facilities across the border, the names, addresses, and passwords of Hugh's agents in the Austrian border towns would be given by me, never in writing, to the refugees.

Guy beamed with genuine professional pleasure as he outlined all this to me. I felt a pleasurable excitement myself. We soon discovered, however, that we had overlooked one important item.

In the first two weeks we sent out eleven persons, made up of three deputies of the defunct Freedom Party, whose immunity had been canceled by the dissolution of Parliament in preparation for the new elections and who knew that arrest was a matter of days, their wives and children, plus a Rumanian girl, known to Mark, who had escaped from Bucharest on the Jewish underground, but had been discovered by the AJDC in Budapest to be non-Jewish and refused further help. In each case we came up against our oversight.

It was that we had no way of knowing whether the escape was successful until Guy made his next trip to his farm, or I made mine to Vienna. Hugh had no secure communications with me in Budapest, nor any right to communicate with Mark, and the Colonel in Vienna, who could have communicated with me via Peter in Switzerland—a roundabout procedure—had no contact with Hugh, who was the only one to know whether or not the refugees had arrived. Telephone calls between Vienna and Budapest, saying "The package has arrived," would be absurd. At the same time Guy wanted no communications from the rural drivers direct to him, either by mail or telephone, since it would link him to them in case of surveillance. Nor did he want his caretaker corresponding more than usually with him, and in any event that could involve as much as five or six days between the time a car left Budapest and the word was finally received by Guy. There was nothing for us to do but sweat the time out, Guy scanning the papers every day for the announcement of an arrest of persons trying to escape across the Austrian border. It was nerve-wracking; I became an almost daily visitor to the bar where Helen, the cut-out, worked, to reassure myself that there was no disastrous news.

The anti-Communist Socialists were having great difficulties in preparing for the elections. I had one further meeting with Karoly Peyer and the others in his group. They knew perfectly well that they were worse anathema to the Communists than Nazis or the most reactionary landowner. They were fully aware that the most violent means would be used against them. Nevertheless, they were willing to enter the fight. Their theory was that by forming an Independent Socialist Party they would, given half a fair chance in the elections, break the Communist grip on organized labor and destroy the fraudulent claim of the Communists and their Socialist sycophants to a monopoly in speaking for the workers. They also hoped that in so doing they would mitigate the American anti-

Socialist prejudice and convey an authoritative warning to the
Western European Socialist parties of the dangers of the Popular
Front tactic. They asked me for no help of any kind. Indeed, in
their difficulties I could have been of no help.

After breaking with the Szakasits leadership of the party, by
means of a manifesto, Peyer and his followers had been refused
authorization to form an Independent Socialist Party. Accordingly, Peyer had formed an alliance with Bela Zsolt, the leader of
the Civic Democratic Party which already had an authorization
since the days of Debrecen. They were now called the Radical
Party, and Peyer and other Socialist leaders were running on that
ticket, hoping that their personal popularity among the workers
would counterbalance the lack of a Socialist label. (The Hungarian
workers understood the maneuver; the slogan of "the solidarity of
the working class" continued, however, to bemuse Western Socialist theoreticians, and for years Peyer's action was the subject of
acrimonious disagreement in the Socialist International. Even
Anna Kethly, a latecomer to the Socialist fight against Communism, but for which she spent time in prison, came out to Vienna in
1956 as a Minister of State and emissary of the Imre Nagy Revolutionary Government, still denouncing Peyer's 1947 "betrayal of the
working class.")

It was only after the elections that Sam spoke to me on behalf of
the Independent Socialists' leadership. He said that they had decided it would eventually be necessary to send an emissary to the
West, and he asked if I could assist his escape. I assured him that I
would do so, and asked who it would be. "I don't know," he
answered. "They'll pick one from among themselves. The others
will stay." And so they did, at heavy cost.

Paul meanwhile had left the Smallholders Party and joined in
forming the Independent Party. This group was led by Zoltan
Pfeiffer, a lawyer, former Undersecretary in the Justice Ministry
and one of the principal Smallholder leaders in the anti-German
Resistance. Pfeiffer, a man of outstanding courage and toughness,
had acted as Bela Kovacs's lawyer up to the moment of his arrest
by the Russians. It was the hope of the Independence Party leaders
to re-create in effect the Smallholders Party and its majority, under
a new name—leaving the name of Smallholders to the now servile
group running that party. In an open political fight such hopes
would have been subject to serious discounting by the ability of
Father Balogh's, Barankovics's, and Zsolt's parties to appeal to the

same elements. This was, of course, a major element in the Communists' tolerance of Zsolt, their encouragement of Barankovics, and their pressure on Balogh.

But as if this were not enough, the Communist-drafted election law, rammed through Parliament by threats and bribery, provided that 3,000 signatures were required from each district in which a new party wanted to run a candidate. The four non-coalition parties were therefore forced to compete against each other not only in the elections themselves, but for even the number of constituencies in which they would stand. (There were two additional parties in this same position, other than the four mentioned here, but they were fractional and of no numerical importance.)

Notwithstanding these odds, the Independence Party fought on. Their success was such that the Communists began to resort to the strong-arm tactics they had used against the Freedom Party. In that case they had sent squads of thugs to break up the offices of the party—with the police standing by under orders to arrest, when the thugs had left, the surviving party officers and employees for riot and disturbance of the peace. With the Independence Party the warning was even more direct. Paul reached me through Jane one night in August, some ten days before the elections. We met by the Coronation Church. As we looked out over the lights of the city, with the smooth mass of the Danube flowing past, Paul's story turned the warm summer night into a shroud for evil.

Paul had been with Pfeiffer on a speaking tour along the left bank of the Danube in the villages to the south of Budapest. In one village Pfeiffer was addressing an orderly and attentive crowd when two truckloads of men drove into the square. The men clambered out and pushed through the crowd, shouting about "fascists," and then assaulted the platform. Pfeiffer had been beaten into unconsciousness with bicycle chains; Paul had a severe gash in his left cheek and was badly bruised and sprained; one man had several broken ribs. Paul recognized one of the leaders as an AVO agent. With the speakers silenced and the crowd dispersed, the thugs departed. Paul had brought Pfeiffer and the others back to Budapest—Pfeiffer's courageous wife insisting that he be kept in their apartment, which was also party headquarters, as being safer for him than a hospital.

As if all of this were not enough, the Communists had stacked the cards even more in their favor, leaving nothing to chance. Two days before the election Edmund sent me a report which events proved absolutely and unfortunately accurate.

As long before as October 1946, the AVO had received orders to prepare a list of potential opposition within the country. These were specified to be: former aristocrats, former politicians, former landowners, former Army officers, "B"-List personnel (those discharged from state employ in 1946 ostensibly for economy reasons), those who "spoke against democracy," "Right-wing" Socialists (i.e., followers of Peyer), "deviationist" Communists, former Nazis and members of the German Volksbund. (The last two were *pro forma:* former Nazis belonging to the Communist Party were excluded, and members of the Volksbund had already, on Soviet instructions, been ordered deported to Germany.) By the summer of 1947 this list contained 1,160,000 names.

At the same time, the new election law authorized the Minister of the Interior to draw up new election lists, specifying several indisputable categories for disfranchisement—such as former Nazis, persons deprived of civil rights for criminal reasons, etc. Rajk's list of 1,160,000 names was sent to all the Communist district headquarters in the country, with instructions to challenge any voter on election day whose name was on the list. Meanwhile, the Minister of the Interior's official new list of qualified voters was published. The list of those qualified to vote did not, of course, show how many were disfranchised. The number, however, was exactly 1,160,000—out of an electorate of 5,000,000. (Among these were 168,000 "Right-wing" Socialists and more than half a million persons who had voted for the Smallholders in 1945.)

Not content with this, the election law also provided for absentee voting in the sense that a voter was not required to cast his ballot in his own district. However, in order to vote outside of his district, an elector had to possess an authorizing certificate, known as a "blue card." The AVO itself printed these, in the number of 750,000. These were then secretly distributed to local Communist Party sections—minus 150,000 which were, by secret agreement, given to the National Peasant Party's pro-Communist leadership. Not many ordinary citizens required a "blue card"—the election was on a Sunday—but those who did, for legitimate reasons, found them difficult to obtain. The Communists, on the other hand, rallied all the transport at their command—not inconsiderable—and truck- and busloads of Party henchmen went around the country, voting not just twice, but again and again, mostly, of course, in Communist districts.

On Sunday, August 31, the farce was enacted. Mark told me that all morning the American Legation—which had sent teams around the entire country to observe the proceedings—was deluged with calls from protesting Hungarian citizens. He had just received a call from a well-known and rather reserved lawyer, who spluttered in outrage that he had been disfranchised for "prostitution," when several British diplomatic observers trooped in and announced that they had visited four or five polling places, and never had they seen a more "orderly, well-conducted, and honest election." The senior Britisher wanted the American Minister to report jointly with him in this vein. The American Minister calmly suggested they wait until the election was over.

The Government figures were, to put it mildly, interesting. The Communist Party emerged as the largest single party, with 22 per cent of the votes. The Socialists dropped from their 1945 18 per cent to 15 per cent. The Smallholders dropped from their 1945 57 per cent to 15 per cent. The National Peasants, with their share of the "blue cards," stood still at 8 per cent. Barankovics's Democratic People's Party—with Church backing—obtained 16 per cent. Pfeiffer and his Independence Party took 14 per cent. Father Balogh's party had 5 per cent and Zsolt's Radical Party, on which ticket Peyer ran, obtained 2 per cent. The splinter parties accounted for the remaining 3 per cent. Even these fraudulent official figures showed that 40 per cent of the country voted against the coalition; 63 per cent voted against the Communist-Socialist combination. But the figures are, of course, meaningless; to give them any validity it would be necessary to take account of over a million disfranchised voters and of 750,000 votes cast no one knows how many times over.

The only figure which was meaningful was the Communists' own secret official estimate of their real vote. Edmund reported it to me from a source in Division One of the AVO ten days after the election. It was 7 per cent.

We had suffered defeat, all right. But its bitterness was diluted with the honor and colored with the courage of several millions of Hungarians.

CHAPTER VI

The President's Decision

The results fraudulently produced by the Communists from the 1947 Hungarian elections were cleverly conceived and just as cleverly exploited. Stalin was temperamentally susceptible to one serious tactical error—as Lenin had long before noted: he was prone to violate the rule that it is not always advantageous to take immediately all that is within your potential grasp. He was to demonstrate this failing six months later in seizing Czechoslovakia, which finally stirred the West to some sense of danger. In Hungary, however, whether because they realized that the rebuff to the Soviets of the 1945 elections could not be erased in a single stroke, or because more astute counsel prevailed, the Communists avoided the appearance of an overt seizure of power. Those who were aware of the fraud in the elections were, of course, stunned. But as no politician could safely stand up and publicly denounce the elections for what they were—Pfeiffer was to try, and to pay, for it—the masses were unaware of the vast extent of the fraud.

The Communists continued the comedy of the coalition, modestly nominating a Smallholder puppet as Prime Minister. For themselves, in the Cabinet, they added only the Foreign Ministry. The real power in the Foreign Ministry became the Communist Director of Political Affairs, György Heltai, an educated, cultivated, and intelligent man. (Imprisoned later as a "Titoist," Heltai escaped during the 1956 Revolution and now directs the "Imre Nagy Institute" in Brussels, a study and research center for "national communism.")[1] These changes in the Foreign Ministry were most welcome from the point of view of my network, since Sara, the agent recruited by George before his departure, was a trusted employee in the Political Department.

Meetings with Sara were difficult. She didn't dare use the telephone, and to have been seen together would have been fatal. Furthermore, she was wary of long or unusual absences from her normal routine. We therefore met by prearrangement at various street addresses and always after dark. These addresses were reasonably close to her normal route from work to home, or from home to evening lectures she would have to attend. Having ascertained that I was not followed, I would drive early to a point near the rendezvous, watching her arrival to see that she was not being followed. If all was clear, we would both get in the car, and while driving to a point near her next stop, she would give me oral reports. We never had more than fifteen minutes, but they were well worth it. On one occasion she had full information on the use being made by the Communists of the Hungarian Legation in Bern for espionage purposes, supplemented by the interesting information that the Soviets in Switzerland were using the Hungarian couriers for transmission of their own material. This information I sent to both Washington and to Peter in Switzerland; as the Hungarian couriers passed through the American Zone of Austria en route from Bern to Budapest, the information turned out to be of great practical value.

On the political scene, the seeming Communist moderation had the effect of lulling some of the opposition politicians into the belief that they would survive. Such hopes once again operated to prevent the kind of unity which alone offered any hope of saving the situation. The Communists could therefore continue their tactics of destroying the opposition piecemeal. For his temerity in questioning the elections, Pfeiffer and his Independence Party were the first targets for liquidation.

On September 20 Edmund reported to me that the AVO had received orders to visit all those persons who had signed the Independence Party's election petitions in the various districts. This involved thousands of persons, but it was done by the end of September. Under AVO threats, 70 per cent of the signers of the petitions withdrew their signatures. The Communists convoked a Parliamentary Committee, and the procedure was begun to declare all votes for the Independence Party null and void, and dissolve the party.

What was needed now was an authoritative voice to speak out honestly on the subject of the elections. Zoltan Tildy, the President of the Republic, was obliged by the Communists to make a public statement expressing his satisfaction with the conduct of the elections and their results. Any lesser voice could be calumniated and silenced, so, on hearing Tildy's statement, I concluded that was that. Or so I thought.

Two days later Mark, with ill-concealed glee, asked me to see Dr. Viktor Csornoky, the President's son-in-law. Csornoky had a not too savory reputation as a black-marketeer and general profiteer from his father-in-law's high position. He came to my apartment, quite openly, and notwithstanding his reputation I found him likable. He was of an ebullient nature and obviously enjoying his vicarious importance. He got to the point quickly. "The President," he said, "wishes to escape the country. Once safely in the West, he will make a statement finishing with these ridiculous elections once and for all. What can you do for us?" I was flabbergasted—but I felt an instant excitement. Tildy's role in the past two years could not easily be forgiven or forgotten, but the fact was that he was the President of Hungary. This single gesture, if it could be pulled off successfully, would compensate for at least some of his errors; its international effect would be tremendous.

"Why has the President already endorsed the elections?" I inquired. Csornoky shrugged. "He was forced to by threats," he said. "You know as well as I do that he is not a completely free agent." This was an understatement, and I refrained from mentioning that the chief hold on Tildy was the AVO's dossiers on the financial doings of both his son and son-in-law. "It is not an easy operation," I said. "Are you absolutely sure the President is firmly decided on this course?"

"Absolutely," said Csornoky. He then handed me a list of eleven names, including the President's. "These persons must accompany the President," he said. The list included what appeared to me to be all conceivable family connections of the President and his wife. "How much time can you give me?" I asked Csornoky. "Whatever you need to insure success," he answered. "But the President is extremely anxious that it should be done as soon as possible. He wishes to serve the country in this, and the sooner he can speak out in the West, the greater will be the international political impact." He then gave me some ideas of his own on technique, including his thought that the operation would be much more practicable from the President's country residence at Lake Balaton—a very long but narrow body of water—rather than from the city of Budapest. It occurred to me that if he thought so, probably the President's AVO Division Fifteen "bodyguards" thought so too. "Give me two weeks," I said. "And ask the President to spend several days at

Lake Balaton during the last ten days of that period." Csornoky
agreed and said he would call on me again in exactly two weeks.

That night I dropped in to see Helen to tell her that I must see
Guy the next day. The prospects of this operation both frightened
and exhilarated me. Guy's initial reaction was one of disgust. "I
wouldn't lift a finger to save any of them, and particularly not
Tildy," he answered sourly after I told him of Csornoky's request.
"It's not a question of saving Tildy," I reminded him. "The problem is to put the President of Hungary in a safe place where he can
render the only valuable service to the nation left to him." Guy
thought for a while. From the slow change of expression on his
face I could see him being captured by the challenge of the thing.
"Let's do it," he said. "It'll really be a good one." He decided to
spend the next few days examining the possibilities of running the
operation from Budapest, give me his conclusions from that, and
then go to Lake Balaton for ten days. "I need a holiday," he said.

For once my Headquarters reacted with something approaching
enthusiasm and displayed atypical restraint in not demanding full
details of my scheme for the President's escape. As if to compensate for this, however, they sent a message insisting that the situation for Paul had become too dangerous and that I send him out of
the country immediately. I sent this message to Paul through Jane,
who promptly brought back the terse reply that he was holding to
our agreement that he would tell me when he felt it necessary to
leave. Jane left no doubt in my mind that Paul found the message
offensive, and considered himself a better judge of his situation
than Washington, with which I was inclined to agree. My reply,
conveying this idea, produced a prompt rejoinder. "Failure to insure Paul's safety will be on your personal responsibility," the message kindly read. It was a comforting thought.

In a few days Guy brought the results of his survey of the Presidential Palace in Budapest. "It's out of the question," he said.
"He's in there like a cigar in its wrapper. We'd never get him out,
let alone more than three blocks away before the entire AVO would
be on us. If we had him go to dinner out in Buda it would be even
worse. That brigade of bodyguards he travels with surround him
even more out than in." He then went off to Lake Balaton, about
which he was more optimistic.

Two days later I was having a drink at my apartment with a
correspondent of one of America's best-known publications, when
suddenly Csornoky appeared at my door, unannounced and cheer-

ful as ever. I motioned that I had someone with me, at which he nonetheless entered, introduced himself, and was immediately in lively conversation. Csornoky was no conspirator, for which he would ultimately pay dearly. To my consternation, in the midst of general conversation—I can only assume he felt reassured that my other guest was an American and felt this to be security enough—Csornoky handed me another list. "These three names must be added to those I gave you," he said. "They are people who have served my father-in-law well, and we cannot leave them behind." I tried to appear to attach small importance to the matter, but Csornoky went on. "As you asked, my father-in-law will spend the next four days at the lake. I will be there too, to look over the matter. I still believe it must be done from there." I agreed perfunctorily. After some further conversation, in which Csornoky let no opportunity go by to stress to my guest that his father-in-law was the President, he left.

My correspondent friend turned to me laughing. "So the President's taking it on the lam. What a nice story that is." This man had been an intelligence officer of no small accomplishments during the war; I decided that some frankness was the best policy. Giving him no details, I told him that he had stumbled on something about the importance of which he could have no doubt, and that he was under no circumstances to use this information in any way. I warned him that lives were involved, and United States Government interest as well. He assured me categorically that he would behave as though he had heard nothing. He left for the West the next day. It was not good, but it seemed the best possible in the circumstances, and certainly superior to a denial on my part followed by the correspondent's snooping about after a possible story.

At this point, the departure of the Navy's scientists, which had been bubbling along for two months, suddenly came to a boil. At their repeated requests, I had gradually disbursed the entire $5,000 to them. Some of this had been used for bribes to obtain passports, and they had assured me they would be ready to leave early in the week during which Guy was at Lake Balaton. Since they were leaving legally, I had arranged passage for them on the American military airplane which flew regularly between Vienna and Budapest, Bucharest, and Sofia. The day before their scheduled departure, two of the scientists came to see me. The AVO had categorically refused a passport for one of the wives.

The dilemma they posed was an unhappy one. The husband

refused to leave without his wife. The work of the entire group could not go forward with one member missing. And those with passports were certain they would be revoked or discovered to be invalid if they delayed their departure any longer. Guy was at Lake Balaton and would not be back for a week. Strictly speaking, I should not personally become involved in any operation while the President's escape was still pending. Nevertheless, for all I knew, the failure of these scientists to leave Soviet-controlled territory might ultimately be an even greater blow to Western security.

I told the husband that his wife must come to my apartment immediately after dark, but without having been seen either leaving her own home or en route to me. He was to spend his last night at home, and throughout the evening he was to talk as much as possible, giving his neighbors the impression that he was not alone. In the morning he was to have a tearful farewell at the door of his apartment, taking care that no one was to see that he was crying to an empty foyer. Meanwhile, his wife would have to spend the night in a box—but the box would be on the airplane with them in the morning. To my surprise the husband seemed delighted at the prospect of his forthcoming dramatic performance, and even promised a passable imitation of his wife's voice.

I watched the wife's arrival that evening on the Var—she had walked the entire distance and was not followed. I could only take her word that no one had seen her leave her home. Fortunately, she turned out to be petite. From my collection of crates I chose one that gave her room to turn from side to side, but not long enough to stretch to her full length. She was due for a rough fifteen hours, but she seemed to find that preferable to the prospect of years before her without her husband. I padded the crate with blankets and pillows to muffle the sounds of her moving and to make it slightly more comfortable. The joints of the crate were not quite flush, so she would have some air. I hammered down the top, stenciled "Fragile" and "U.S. Government Property" all over the crate, and addressed it to "The American Legation, Vienna." A muffled voice from inside said "Eet ees quite comfor-table." Fifteen minutes later a truck from the Motor Pool drove up, as I had ordered, and two GIs loaded the case aboard. I noted it was fragile and said, "Don't kick that around too much in the garage to-night."

"Nah," one of them answered. "It'll stay on the truck. The rest of this stuff is going on the same plane." That was something at least. It was going to be a long night for both husband and wife, but to have had the truck pick the crate up in the morning and go straight to the airport would have been too revealing, and any movement of such a crate later in the night would have aroused the suspicions of the Hungarian guards who stood by the Military Garage. Some American soldiers in Bucharest had pulled the same trick only a month before with three Rumanians; it had worked, but one week later the Soviet Command had requested by name the return of the three Rumanians who had left illegally on the American aircraft. I hoped the Soviets would assume we wouldn't be so stupid as to try the same trick again so soon.

The next morning, after the plane's departure, I dropped in to see Mark. I knew he had been out at the airport, and he knew that I had arranged the departures of the scientists. He gave me a very fishy look.

"Plane get off all right?" I queried him.

"It did," he said. "Took off right over my jangled nerves."

I looked at him.

"The military don't send cases marked 'Fragile' to the American Legation in Vienna. They send them to the military. But fortunately the Hungarian guards at the airport don't know that and the Russians can't read." He sighed.

"I thought it was more diplomatic that way," I said.

"Well, we will now hope and pray," he rejoined.

We never heard a word about it from either Soviets or Hungarians. But I heard from the Navy. Several weeks later when I was in Vienna Hugh introduced me to probably the most worried-looking Lieutenant-Commander I had ever seen. "Look," he said. "We appreciate all you did, and all that, but that $5,000 was supposed to get those people all the way to the *United States!* You blew all that money just getting them to Vienna. I can never face the Bureau of Accounts." I signed an affidavit certifying that the money had been properly and necessarily disbursed in Budapest and that, without that having been done, there would have been no scientists for the Navy. But I was far from pleased with myself. The operation had been sloppy, risky, and amateurish. Such methods could not be permitted with the President.

Guy returned the following week from Lake Balaton. "This is going to be very tough," he said, "but it can be done." He outlined his plan. It was complex and required split-second timing, but it was feasible. The only limitation was that with the very best of luck it could work for no more than eight people. It was quite impossible to approach the Presidential villa from the land side. The property had a considerable shoreline, however, and the only possible access was thus from the lake. This would involve crossing in boats, taking aboard the family at separate points along the property's lakefront, recrossing the lake to rendezvous points, and probably even traveling in separate groups to the frontier. This meant automobiles, boats, safe houses, and, most importantly, men. Guy was sure of only a sufficient number of all four to permit taking care of eight persons. To involve more men would risk a leak; to utilize more cars and boats would make the operation physically too conspicuous and unwieldy. Besides, eight people would take care of the immediate family.

I passed this information to Csornoky. His reaction was to express serious doubt that his father-in-law would be able to go with any lesser number than the fourteen he had already specified. Personally I felt him to be rather petulant about the matter. I explained the physical difficulties; and then I emphasized the national interest which was at stake. Csornoky promised only to consult the President and let me know as soon as possible. I spoke again with Guy about it. He was adamant and refused categorically to risk the enterprise with more than eight persons. His point was certainly valid: it was simply that with any larger number some people were certain to be caught; in the confusion he would not be able to guarantee that the President himself would not be among the unlucky ones. I began to worry. Tildy was not a man in whom I had had much faith up to now; if he ran true to form he would make the wrong decision again. But there was always the fact that in crisis men often rise above their usual form.

The next blow fell from an unexpected quarter. My correspondent friend's publication came out in America with a report that the President of Hungary was making plans to escape, in order to denounce the Communist frauds in the August elections. It wasn't even one of those "it is rumored" stories; it was all stated as fact, thereby showing how omniscient this particular journal was and giving the reader, safe at home, the sensation, cheap but so flattering, of being "on the inside."[2] In this case I was sure that no matter how cheap the sensation, the cost would be high. (My bitterness at this development is not necessarily at odds with my conclusions in Part I about the necessity to hide operations from the press as well as the public and the opposition. This correspondent was the recipient of a clearly labeled official confidence which he had given his word not to violate.)

The word spread quickly and was noted in Parliament. I briefly had the odd impression that I could sense the feelings of the entire country: the great majority of the population quietly—and hopefully—watching to see if it would be true; the Communists maneuvering quickly but silently to insure that it would not come true.

I did not expect to see Csornoky again. To my surprise he came to see me about a week later. His father-in-law was due to speak to the nation by radio that evening, and Csornoky arrived just as the President started to speak. "What is he saying?" I asked him. Csornoky laughed. "He's saying that reports that he is planning to leave the country are hostile fabrications against Hungarian democracy; that the elections were honest and reassuring for the future of the country, and he stands proudly at his post to guide the nation to even greater democratic achievements," he replied. Then, as the President still orated on, Csornoky said, "Now you will understand that my father-in-law is more than ever anxious to leave—and quickly."

I understood nothing of the kind; here the danger had quintupled, but that seemed to make no difference. Csornoky continued, "However, he cannot abandon those near to him and loyal to him to the fate that would surely come to them if left behind. Therefore, I must insist that we go as fourteen persons." This made no sense at all to me. I told Csornoky that the danger was now infinitely greater, and he should be talking about fewer persons rather than more. The danger and practical risks seemed to count not at all with him, nor was he really in the least disturbed by the American publication of Tildy's intentions. It was plain that he was living in some kind of dream world and felt no pressing need to adapt to reality; it was as though he felt himself in command of events. "I am sorry," I said. "Eight will be difficult enough, but I cannot take the responsibility for any more." Csornoky did not appear overly disturbed; he simply remained firm. "We are a very close family," he said. "It must be fourteen or not at all." With that he left. He had little more than a year to live.

(President Tildy stayed in Hungary. Some months later Csornoky was appointed Minister to Egypt. While there, ignoring his surveillance by his own staff, he made blatant attempts to get in touch with Western intelligence organizations. Summoned to return to Budapest for consultation, Csornoky returned, was arrested, tried, and hanged. Tildy was obliged to resign the Presidency, which went to the Socialist Szakasits, who had merged his party with the Communists. During the Revolution in 1956, Tildy, his father-in-law killed by the Nazis and his son-in-law by the Communists, emerged as a Minister of State in the Imre Nagy Government. He is reported to have behaved courageously throughout, refusing to leave the Parliament building during the Soviet attack on the night of November 4 until all other members of the Government and its loyal employees had gotten away. There followed arrest, imprisonment, and limited detention until his death in 1961.)

1. Heltai came to the United States in the mid-1960's, initially to Columbia University, where he began by teaching history (and was somewhat taken aback by the educational attainments of American university students—twenty years before this became a matter of national concern and debate in the United States). He nevertheless followed an academic career, becoming Professor of History at Charleston College, Charleston, South Carolina.
2. *Time.*

CHAPTER VII

Escape

Except for Guy's ten-day absence at Lake Balaton, the escape chain had been operating smoothly. With members of Parliament the matter was fairly simple: as the Communists sliced away at the opposition, they would ask for waiving of the Parliamentary immunity of the various legislators under attack; between the request and the Immunities Committee's action—always as requested—

there was usually a lapse of two or three days. During this period the menaced deputy had to be moved out. At first this was not so difficult, but as more and more escapes occurred during this delay, the AVO began surveillance of their intended victims, even before the orders for arrest had been issued. The situation was further complicated by the understandable desire of deputies who planned to escape to make a final fiery speech in Parliament. As this was too obvious a signal of what was afoot, I was forced to insist that many such deputies whom we were moving out either make their "swan song" unrecognizable as such or forgo altogether their chance to have the last word.

The attack against the Independence Party was successful in early October, and then began the process of lifting the immunity of the various Independence deputies. On October 14 Pfeiffer himself, with his wife and five-year-old daughter, had to flee. He was being closely watched, but we managed successfully. Hugh told me later that Pfeiffer's escape was even complicated in Vienna, thanks to the Americans themselves. Pfeiffer arrived in Vienna in the middle of the night; the next morning, before Hugh had been able to move him on to the American Zone of Austria, the Vienna German-language newspaper published by the American Occupation authorities printed a large photograph of Pfeiffer on the front page, saying he was rumored to be in Vienna. Hugh thereupon had to alter his plans to have Pfeiffer and his family driven to the American military airport at Tulln, an enclave in the Soviet Zone, and instead have him flown out in a small plane from a landing strip in the American sector of Vienna.

With persons other than deputies, we had to rely on either their own knowledge of their danger or such information as Edmund was able to pass out from the AVO itself. I had informed the members of the network that they would be taken out whenever they felt the moment necessary or opportune. Henry, who had been inactive for some time, had already taken advantage of the offer. But these were not the only sources of our "clients."

In October Mark sent an American businessman, the representative of one of the important American interests in Hungary, to see me. I saw this man often; he was normally a cheerful, pleasant type of executive whose chief worry was, he thought, dickering with the Soviet representative of the confiscated German minority interests in the same company. This day, however, he was all nerves. Hesitantly, almost embarrassedly, he disclosed the fact that he had received word from his colleague in Bucharest that fourteen Rumanians would arrive two days hence, in illegal flight from Rumania. These were key employees of various British and American enterprises in Rumania, and the companies had decided to try to save them. My caller's task was to arrange their escape from Hungary, and he was worried sick at the thought. Fourteen in one group was something more than we were equipped to handle, so leaving him to cope with his nerves for forty-eight hours, I told him only to come back on the morning of the second day.

Guy was taken aback at the prospect of fourteen persons, but then the challenge interested him. As a result of his trip to Balaton, he had arranged additional safe house facilities there, so he decided to try it. He gave me three different rendezvous points in Budapest for the Rumanians for the day of their arrival. I gave these instructions to my American friend, and he gratefully resumed his normal coloration. The next night I checked with Helen, who said only—speaking for Guy—that "The lake has now become a very popular Rumanian resort."

Some days later I was lunching with Mark, and his telephone rang. He listened briefly, then looked at me and said, "I'll call you back in a few minutes." Sitting down, he said, "Now what are you up to? The Ministry of the Interior, strange to say, has just called the Legation to say that the Police in Győr are holding an American couple who were arrested near the border and who have neither money nor documents. They claim they were just touring Hungary and were supposed to go by train to Vienna tonight, but were robbed. The Ministry wants to know if we know anything about them. A Mr. and Mrs. Tompkins from Detroit. Do you know anything about them?"

I certainly didn't; an American couple "touring Hungary" at this epoch was too fantastic to be believable, and Mark knew as well as I that no such phenomenon existed. But obviously some unknowns were in trouble; whoever they were they merited a helping hand. I suggested to Mark that he tell the Ministry that he knew all about Mr. and Mrs. Tompkins, that they were distinguished American citizens, that it was an outrage to hold them under arrest after they had suffered the additional indignity of being robbed, and that he insist that the Police put them on the next train for Vienna.

Mark did so, and to our surprise the Ministry called back some hours later to report that they had released "Mr. and Mrs. Tompkins" and put them on the Vienna train.

I had to wait a week to see Guy to get the answer to this puzzle. It seemed that he had been moving the Rumanians from the lake to his farm in groups of two and four. His instructions were specific: no one was to carry either personal documents or any foreign money, and if apprehended they were to avoid disclosing, if possible, their true nationality, since Guy feared this would arouse too acute an AVO interest. "Mr. and Mrs. Tompkins" had been part of a group of four who were apprehended—fortunately not by the Border Guards, but by the Police in a routine check—in a village not far from the farm. The driver said he had merely been hired by his passengers in Györ to show them the countryside; he had been released. "Mr. and Mrs. Tompkins," having obeyed Guy's instructions, gave their story, speaking only English, and said that their companions were merely fellow travelers they had joined in Györ whom they did not know otherwise. Their companions, two Rumanian men, had unfortunately not followed Guy's instructions; they had both Rumanian documents and money and were accordingly taken to Budapest to prison. (Some months later they were expelled to Czechoslovakia and from there eventually reached the West.) "Mr. and Mrs. Tompkins," however, had put on such a good show of outraged indignation that the Police had finally telephoned to Budapest for instructions. Mark's response was so effective that the Police not only put "Mr. and Mrs. Tompkins" on the train to Vienna, but paid their fare and helped to clear them through the Austrian side of the border as well. It was a worthy and satisfying bureaucratic short circuit.

For most of the time that I had been in Budapest I had known and occasionally saw Lila, a cousin of Eugene. Herself an aristocrat, Lila was embroiled in an emotional vendetta against aristocracy which had its origins in the loss during the war of someone she loved, killed by the Germans. The tendency of many of the Hungarian aristocrats either to favor or at least not to fight the Germans had as a consequence appeared to her in an intensely personal light. She was not a Communist, but she had no objection to the Communist surgery on Hungarian society so long as it represented for her the destruction of the aristocracy. We often argued politics, in a very friendly way, for notwithstanding the force of her feelings, she was keenly intelligent and recognized the influence on her political views of her own emotional history.

During one such discussion, in October, I found her torn by contradictory feelings. She still supported the Communist program, but by now its execution had become distasteful to her. She lamented not at all the gradual destruction of the opposition parties, but she could not stomach the violence being wreaked on so many, most particularly on exactly those who had most courageously fought the Germans. I gave it as my view that this was a deliberate policy and an integral part of the system she favored, since it was aimed, not at remedying injustice in Hungary, but at rendering Hungary totally subservient to the Soviet Union. She reflected on this, obviously loath to concede the point. Nor did she. But after a considerable silence she said, "You know, I see Rajk once or twice every week." I knew she was friendly with the Minister of the Interior, but I did not know to what extent. "Yes," she went on, "I see him, and we talk, usually for an hour or so. He often tells me their plans for various people. I don't know why, but he does. So I often know who is in danger." She thought for a while longer. Then she smiled quickly. "So I will tell you when good people are in danger. Maybe you can discreetly do something about them."

I didn't press the point. I merely said, "Let me know."

This was an unexpected source of help, and as it turned out, most timely and welcome. By the end of October the campaign against the Independence Party had very nearly run its course. Paul and one or two others were still in Parliament, but the Communist aim had been achieved, and Paul's time was approaching. Meanwhile, Edmund was informed by a source in Division One of the AVO that the next on the list marked for destruction were the Socialists. The aim here was to achieve the merger of the Socialist and Communist Parties. To this end, the AVO planned to start a campaign against the Right-wing Socialists which would accuse them of conspiracy and then drag in any Left-wing Socialists who still held out against merger. Sam and Edmund, taking stock of their positions as Right-wing Socialists, Edmund's post in the AVO, and the risks of their connection with me, felt themselves seriously endangered. Lila, following her first talk with Rajk after our conversation, told me the same general story. Much as I regretted it, I told Guy we had two very valuable passengers with whom there could be no slip-ups. This was a nervous wait: the incident with the Rumanians had made us somewhat jittery, but at the end of a week Guy reported another successful operation.

In the disaster which was engulfing Hungary it was incomprehensible still to see those who felt they would succeed where others were failing. An American oil executive took me to task at this stage: "You Government people are too alarmist about this Communist thing. It's just a problem of working along with them. They need what we have so we'll be all right." Six months later, with two of his American colleagues beaten in prison and his company's properties taken over by the Hungarian Government, he hastily left the country. Some months before, an American newspaperman had expressed the view to me that American policy in Eastern Europe was "reactionary." He now returned to Hungary somewhat chastened, to replace his American predecessor who had been arrested and expelled, to find a substitute for his Hungarian stringer—who, having originally put me in touch with the Socialists, came to me for help and was taken out by Guy—and to try to arrange the release from prison of his own secretary whom he well knew to be innocent.

On November 7 I went to the Soviet reception marking the thirtieth anniversary of the Revolution. In one year so much had transpired that the Russians didn't even make an effort to be polite, but more or less ignored their American guests. I talked for a while with Istvan Barankovics, leader of the Democratic People's Party. I found him ridiculously confident and annoyingly condescending. He was now the leader of the largest opposition party and the second largest party in the nation. Far from being uneasy at such prominence, he parroted the same sure optimism which had animated the Jesuits. He even spoke of the gains he would make in the next elections. I had to laugh, but not from amusement. I do not pretend to be a prophet, but I was sure of what I said to Barankovics: "Within one year, most of us here who are neither Russian nor Communist will have fled the country, be in prison, or be dead." Barankovics laughed at my little fantasy. Less than eleven months later he was in flight to the West, his party smashed and his Cardinal facing trial.

I turned away to speak with Jozsef Kövago, the young and popular Smallholder Mayor of Budapest. He was, in contrast to Barankovics, utterly dejected; the mounting attack on the Socialists was, he knew, the signal that the end was close at hand. I told him of Barankovics's optimism. "Ridiculous," said Kövago. "Can't he see he's next?" Kövago seemed so certain of his own fate that I said to him, "If you wish to leave, I shall arrange it." He thought at length, and then he thanked me, warmly. "No," he said. "Someone has to stay." It was to be almost ten years before I saw him again. Then he had behind him eight years in prison and two weeks as Mayor of Budapest again during the 1956 Revolution. With the final Soviet attack on November 4 he this time chose exile.

Before their departure Sam and Edmund had told me that their leadership had decided to send Karoly Peyer as their representative to the West. The Communist press had by now mounted a full-scale attack on the Right-wing Socialists, and suddenly the State Prosecutor asked for the lifting of Peyer's Parliamentary immunity so that he could be arrested for plotting against the state. On November 15 his immunity was waived, but the day before—after considerable difficulty on my part in persuading the old man not to make the most fiery speech of his long career—Guy had spirited him out to Austria. The Communist press howled at Peyer's disappearance, and then reported it as officially known that Peyer was still in the country, in hiding.

Guy had been sufficiently interested in the case to accompany Peyer to the frontier himself. He had returned immediately to Budapest, and was so bemused by the Communist claims as to Peyer's whereabouts that he had gone to see his former chief Rajk, on the pretext of a friendly call. It was completely in character for Guy, and he told me of his interview with the Interior Minister with high glee. He had teased Rajk, saying that if he, Guy, were still in the Police, all these wanted persons would not be escaping so freely. Guy recounted how Rajk had leaped to his feet saying, 'We know where Peyer is. And we will have him in our hands within four days." Going to a map of Hungary, he showed Guy an area to the north blocked off in red marks. Stabbing with his forefinger, Rajk said, "He is hiding somewhere in here. But he won't escape us." Guy noted silently and comfortably that the marked area was nowhere near his farm.

I recalled Guy's coup two years later when Peyer arrived in the United States and was not permitted to land in New York. He was taken into custody and transferred immediately to Ellis Island. Apparently neither his fight nor his flight had had much effect on the American "anti-Socialist prejudice."

But another vignette of the period also showed the weakness of dogmatic judgments. During a reception at the Hungarian Parliament for some visiting American Senators and Representatives, I watched Congressman John Davis Lodge of Connecticut engage in a rather showy harangue against the Communist President of the National Assembly, Imre Nagy. No one could foresee that ten years later the Congressman's brother, as U.S. Ambassador to the United Nations, would indict the Hungarian Government before world opinion for the death of this same Imre Nagy.

Ten days after Peyer's escape Paul sent word through Jane that he was already under surveillance and that he would have to leave within three days at the maximum. I went to see Helen, to leave word that I wanted to see Guy urgently, and found that she had the same word for me from Guy. I went to Guy's apartment, where I found him with serious news. "We cannot function for at least two weeks," he said. "Perhaps even longer." I said he had to be joking, but it was perfectly clear he was not. Guy explained that three days before the AVO had arrested a British agent, a woman. She had talked, and the result was the arrest of some one hundred persons. Even simple smugglers were lying low; no one knew how much wider the AVO would drag their net. In addition, since the escape of Peyer, maximum security precautions were being taken along the entire frontier. Guy's men had passed him word they would be unable to move anyone for an indefinite period; it was his own guess that it would take about two weeks for the dust to settle.

I didn't have two weeks to risk with Paul, and I did have the responsibility for his safety fixed firmly and inescapably on me. The timing couldn't have been worse, but there was nothing to be done about that. I told Guy to keep me informed of any new developments, and went home to figure what to do. With relatively inconspicuous people it was sometimes possible, provided they had a passport, to have them openly buy a railroad ticket to Vienna and then buy a ticket to Prague under another name. While the police checked for them at the Austrian border, they could sometimes cross the Czechoslovak border without difficulty. Once in Prague, they could fly to Zurich, thereby evading the Soviet controls at the border of the American Zone of Austria. But Paul was too conspicuous, and he would be actively sought by the police for arrest the moment his Parliamentary immunity was lifted. The problem was complicated by his already being under surveillance, no doubt precisely to prevent his escape before Parliament acted on his case. I was not prepared to risk the airplane again, and in any event it was not due soon enough. There was only one solution. I would have to drive Paul myself to Austria or to Czechoslovakia.

I settled on Vienna; as Paul had no passport, his fate once in Czechoslovakia was too uncertain, and the audacity of the more dangerous route to Vienna was in its favor.

The operation could be done only under cover of my official position, undesirable as that was. I could certainly not disguise myself as a Hungarian, and in any event to have done so would have instantly closed the border to me. Any other nationality was also out of the question: I had by now a fair collection of Soviet gray passes, which was the only thing which interested the Soviet sentries along the road, and I could forge the names on them easily, but the Hungarian Border Guards would insist on my passport, and a passport was not so quickly or easily forged.

I thought at first to take Paul and his wife in the trunk of my car, a small prewar German Mercedes, but then I realized that to leave Jane behind, known as a friend of Paul's and privy to the escape arrangements, would be fatal. When I told her she would have to come as well, she agreed, but asked that Simon, his wife and baby also accompany us. As I had by now decided on a Chevrolet delivery truck belonging to the Military Mission, I agreed. With Paul's wife we were now six adults and a three-year old infant.

At this point I had a stroke of luck. I was loath to travel the road to Vienna in full daylight, but to travel at night—even though there were fewer patrols, the border posts were more negligent, and the contents of my truck invisible—would have aroused suspicion since American trucks always made the run in the daytime. However, at almost the last minute an agreement was reached with the Hungarians over an American correspondent who had been arrested: he would be released, provided he was over the border by the following midnight. As he was being driven out in the late afternoon, I let it be known that I would personally drive a truck containing his and his family's belongings, as a way of insuring that the Hungarians kept to their agreement. It was improvised cover, but it was cover nonetheless. And it meant moving Paul a day earlier than he had planned—but that was an advantage as well.

The afternoon of the day of departure, I dropped in to see Mark and left a sealed letter with him. It contained my resignation from the Military Mission, in case something went wrong and it became necessary to disown me. I didn't tell Mark its contents, but told him only to open it if he did not hear from me in three days. I then gave him a coded message for my Headquarters, telling them what I was doing. I was certain they would receive it too late to stop me even if they wished.

As soon as it was dark I went to the garage and picked up the truck. I drove to my apartment. There, hidden behind a pile of rubble, I loaded four large cases into the truck, threw in blankets and pillows, two large tarpaulins, and rope. It was a bitterly cold night, so I put on an Army parka, in one pocket of which I carried a Walther automatic and three clips of ammunition. I had no such dramatic intention as shooting my way through a roadblock; but the AVO was capable of methods other than an overt arrest, and drunken Russian troops were not to be confused with sentries on duty.

Jane was waiting for me at the Coronation Church. We drove to a quiet street in Buda where Simon, his wife and baby waited. Then instead of continuing on out the Vienna road, I turned up a high hill just to the north of Buda. A great forested knob, the unpronounceable Harmashatarhegy—Three Border Mountain—looked out over the entire city of Budapest, to the east to the Great Hungarian Plain, and to the north as far as Slovakia. A wild expanse, it was a favorite summer picnic spot, but in late autumn and winter no one went near it. Nine years from this night it was to be the last hideout of the Revolutionary Freedom Fighters of Budapest. It was there we would meet Paul and his wife—if they had evaded surveillance. If they had not, the rendezvous might include some uninvited guests.

I arrived at the appointed spot and made a wide U-turn, with my lights full on. They caught only Paul and his wife, behind a tree. It was 8:30, as fixed, and they had made it successfully—with no baggage. It was a long and steep walk up the mountain, and it had been preceded by crossing almost the entire city on foot. Nevertheless, the precautions were worth it. Paul had lost his "shadow" while still in Pest, and his wife, leaving their house in the morning, had not been followed. In the still night ours had been the only vehicle they had heard moving on the mountain.

By the light of a flashlight the five adults and the child slipped into the crates. Paul and his wife were in one, Simon's wife and the baby, who had been drugged, were in another, and Simon and Jane in a third. I then maneuvered the crates around so that the open ends all faced in toward the center of the truck. The fourth crate I put next to the rear door, blocking the access to the others. I then covered all the crates with the tarpaulins and arranged the rope to look as though the crates were all bound and lashed down. I locked the door, got behind the wheel, started the motor, and swung back down the hill and onto the Vienna road. There were six people only a few inches from me, but I felt very, very lonely.

From Budapest to the border I drove steadily. None of the road-blocks was manned—one advantage of traveling during the dinner hour—and we scarcely saw another car on the road. I had told my passengers that when I knocked three times they could talk among themselves softly; when I knocked twice they were to maintain absolute silence. As we entered towns I would knock twice—instantly there was not a sound. Safely out in the country, where a sudden stop was no longer likely, I would give three knocks, and the voices would resume their murmur and even, occasionally, there would be a laugh. In the talking periods, even though I was not in the conversation, my queasiness would disappear and I would become calm; but in the silences I became tense and worried.

At the border point near Hegyeshalom, I knocked twice and pulled up in front of the Customs. Here again luck. The Czecho-slovaks had just taken over five Hungarian villages on the south bank of the Danube opposite Bratislava—granted them by the Peace Treaty. In so doing they had cut the main Budapest-Vienna road and taken over the old Hungarian border station. This one was a mere temporary shack, with no lights in front and no facili-ties for examining the cars. I left the truck in the dark and went into the building. In a few minutes my papers were cleared, with barely a word, and I was back in the truck. The guards didn't even look out as I drove off.

I had no sooner knocked three times and settled down to driving than I had to quickly knock twice and pull up before the Czecho-slovak occupants of the former Hungarian border station. They were very put out that I had wandered into Czechoslovakia. I blamed it all on the Hungarians. They had not yet built a new road to avoid Czechoslovak territory, and they were so lazy that the necessity for a detour from the former main road wasn't even marked. The Czechoslovaks were mollified and, berating and abus-ing the Hungarians, permitted me to continue on.

I explained to my "cargo" what had happened and then knocked for silence. A few miles farther on, the Austrian guards checked me through politely. I wanted to ask where the Soviet roadblocks were on this night, but, on the assumption that the Austrian border guards in the Soviet Zone were handpicked by the Soviets, refrained from showing any such interest.

Between the Austrian border and Vienna there were usually three or four roadblocks operating, but one never knew where they would be, except for the final one at Schwechat, just outside Vienna. Some five miles from the border I finally saw the first one, but there were no sentries on duty. I knocked three times and drove on.

Just when I was beginning to congratulate myself on having chosen a good night, a dim light showed ahead. I quickly knocked twice and slowed to a stop as my headlights shone on a barrier and a Russian tommy-gunner.

I rolled down my window, and he came and leaned against the side of the truck, his gun slung over his shoulder. "Zdrastye." "Zdrastye." By a flashlight he studied my pass and then handed it back to me. He flashed the light over my shoulder into the back of the truck.

"What are you carrying?"

"I don't know."

"How is that—you don't know?"

"Listen, I'm just a courier," I answered him. "They tell me to drive a load to Vienna, I do what I'm told. They don't explain it to me."

He laughed. "But what is it?"

I shrugged. "How would I know? Diplomatic papers, some general's furniture, more papers. I don't know."

He walked around the truck shining his flashlight inside. I prayed for not a move from anyone and thought instantly of someone sneezing. Then I hastily obliterated the thought, for fear my six passengers might get the idea telepathically.

The sentry came back to the front of the truck. "Come on, let's look at it anyway," he said. I felt my gun. I couldn't tell how many more sentries, if any, were in the nearby hut, but it was a ridiculous thought. I'd never make it that way.

"Open it up," he repeated. But he was not very forceful about it, and he hadn't yet unslung his gun. I didn't move. Instead I sighed.

"Can't do it," I said.

"Why not?" he asked and leaned against the window.

I reached for my cigarettes and brought out a pack. I took one first myself. Russians can be bribed, but the worst mistake is to offer a Russian a bribe. For him a bribe must be either something he took by violence or a gift of pure friendliness. I saw him eye the cigarettes.

"For one thing, they don't allow me to, so I'll get in trouble," I said. While talking, I extended the pack to him. He took two cigarettes. As I kept on talking, I shook more cigarettes to the front of the pack, paying no attention to his lifting of cigarettes out two by two. "For another thing," I continued, "it's a lot of trouble. I get out on a cold night, unlock the door, then have to wrestle with all those lashings and tarpaulins. I've still got a way to go, and it's not early." He had now taken ten cigarettes. I still held the pack there, while ignoring it. He took two more and then stood back.

He grinned. "Spasibo," he thanked me. "You can go." He raised the barrier.

I smiled back at him and drove off—not too fast. I was so shaken I even forgot to let my passengers talk. My mind was totally taken up with the luck I had just had, and worry about the next checkpoint. Between the two thoughts I kept up a constant dialogue with Soviet sentries in my head, until finally I came under the glaring lights of the Schwechat roadblock. This would be the last one. The barrier was up, but a sentry with a tommy gun was in the roadway, motioning me to go on.

Never had the cobblestones of Vienna felt so good, never had the grimy buildings seemed so welcoming. As we drove into the Ring, I banged three times on the crates and shouted, "Becs!" Even the Hungarian name for Vienna sounded good. A muffled but rousing cheer came from the back, and then excited talk, in which I could hear the relief. I stopped at a hotel in the American Zone, called Hugh, and then drove to the address he gave me. In addition to providing lodgings Hugh thoughtfully brought along a bottle of French cognac. We had a small party—at which I regret to say I left very little cognac for the others.

The following day I exchanged my truck for the car which had brought the American correspondent to Vienna. I had no desire to promote any further public associations between myself and trucks, particularly when the AVO would be suspicious over Paul's departure. Then I telephoned Mark in Budapest and made irrelevant conversation about books; he had now heard from me and had no need to open the letter I had left with him. Also I had a plan, and might not make it back to Budapest before the three days were up.

I had heard from both Edmund and Guy that the Soviets maintained one road between Hungary and Austria for their sole use. According to what they told me, no Hungarian or Austrian checkpoints were maintained on this road, and there was only one Soviet checkpoint, at the frontier itself. Most importantly, they had heard that if traveling at night, it was only necessary to give a signal with the headlights—three flashes—and the barrier was raised without even the necessity to stop and show documents. I may have been a bit lightheaded from Paul's successful escape, but it seemed a timely moment to find this road.

Hugh knew of the road, but only that it was supposed to be slightly to the south of the main Vienna-Budapest road, and he did not know the signals. Studying the map, I realized that the Schwechat checkpoint's main purpose was to prevent unauthorized travelers—meaning everyone but Austrian citizens and the Soviet military—from reaching that road, since at Schwechat another road forked to the south, from which other crossings could be reached. By taking the main road and turning off to the south after the Schwechat checkpoint, one could reach the south road by country lanes—provided they were not blocked.

I started about 9 in the evening, fortified by a lively Viennese cocktail party. Rolling out of Vienna to the east, I paused at the Schwechat checkpoint and was again in luck. No sentry. I turned off to the south, and at a distance I could only guess as approximating the location of the road I had picked as most likely, I took the first turn to the east. The land began to be slightly hilly, which meant I was running too far to the south, out of the Danube Valley, so at the nearest crossing I turned to the northeast.

Passing through a village—every shutter closed and not a light showing anywhere—I remarked that the village seemed to go on for an exceptionally long time. Then I began to see shadowy figures moving about, outside the range of my lights. By now I was completely lost within the village, so I stopped and dimmed my lights.

I stepped out of the car. The houses in the darkness had strange profiles—high, thin, slanting chimneys rose black against the star-lit sky. All around me was the deep hum of voices—speaking Russian. Of all places to be, I was in the middle of a Red Army tank park. The "chimneys" were the elevated guns of the tanks, and hundreds of Soviet soldiers were lounging and walking about in the dark after their dinner. My presence was, at best, subject to misinterpretation.

My first instinct was to get in the car, turn around, and get out as quickly as possible. I then realized that would look undesirably mysterious. Instead I approached a group of Russians. Nothing was visible in the dark except the vague forms of their greatcoats, and I knew I was only a dark shape to them.

There is a way of speaking in Russian which, when translated into English, is rudely offensive to Americans; to the Russian it most often signifies authority. Gruffly, impatiently, without greeting, I said, "Where is the road to Hungary?" A pleasant, respectful voice answered almost immediately. "You took the wrong turn. Go back to the second corner, turn left, and then keep straight on. Five kilometers."

Five kilometers to the east I made out the dim light of a sentry post and then the red-and-white striped barrier. I did not slow at all; one—two—three, I flashed my headlights. A small figure ran up to the barrier. Just in time the bar rose, and I swept past under it. The figure in the dark looked for the brief instant I glanced at him like an Austrian, not a Soviet guard, but it didn't matter. The road did exist, and the signal was three flashes. It was useful to know.

By now my own situation was precarious. The Peace Treaty had come into effect. The Military Mission was winding up its affairs prior to departure. I saw no prospect of arranging another cover for myself, and the possibilities of cover for a successor were no better. In this much of my mission I had failed. My failure was the opposite side of the coin of the Soviet success in winning their race against the time limit of the Peace Treaty. Even if a suitable cover could be found for another agent to follow me, he would not have much to work with. My network was now exactly half of what it had been. Furthermore, fear had now reached such proportions that it was highly doubtful that reliable new agents could be recruited for some time to come, and least of all those in key positions. The possibility of a "sleeper" network, such as Sam and Edmund had in mind, was always to be considered, although the recruiting involved grave risks in the atmosphere of terror which reigned.

All this I reported to my Headquarters, though with no immediate response. I did not report to them that I myself was becoming increasingly nervous. Several weeks after my return from Vienna Guy still maintained that it was too risky to operate. I felt an air of impending danger; I wondered whether in the last few months I had not exposed myself in some way of which I was not aware. I went over in my memory all of my conversations, their circumstances, my meetings, the various escapes. No single detail seemed wrong, but the whole added up to a pattern of excessive activity. I took to sleeping with my gun by my bed; although I had no illusions about its possible usefulness, it was reassuring.

In early December my premonitions took on a concrete form. Lila told me of her latest conversation with Rajk. In continuation of their pressure on the Socialists for a merger, the AVO was planning a show trial of various arrested Right-wing Socialists. The charge was conspiracy, but it was necessary that the victims be shown to have been in touch not merely with the West, but specifically with the Americans. The reasoning was simple but effective. This trial was addressed to those Socialists, not necessarily Right-wing, who still opposed merger with the Communist Party. To show the Socialist "conspirators" as being in touch with the British, with a Labor Government in power in England, would possibly have led only to further argument. To make the point unmistakably clear, involvement with the Americans was desired, since this would show the Right-wing Socialists as "traitors to the working class." To this end, the AVO was considering the possibility of arresting an American victim. Besides, Rajk had further confided to Lila, the AVO was certain that the Americans had been playing a large role in the numerous recent escapes of wanted persons, and he had hinted that they had a quite good idea of which American was responsible.

Lila was extremely agitated about this news, although not for exactly the same reason that produced a similar effect on me. Lila was devoted to her cousin Eugene, and she feared that, because of his associations with American companies and Americans, he was likely to be one of the victims. She had tried to persuade him to leave the country, but he had refused. She wanted me, as a friend of Eugene, to persuade him to leave. This I readily agreed to do, for plural reasons, of which only my friendship for Eugene was, of course, known to Lila. I also sent off a message to my Headquarters, reporting this latest information, but without comment. Rajk, I conjectured, could be as close to the identity of the American who was "responsible" as he had been to capturing Peyer.

Persuading Eugene to leave took a long night. Neither the wine nor gypsies playing lugubriously in the back room of a small café helped, but when we had alternated tears with laughter, and deep melancholy with surging optimism, in the exact proportions which Magyar custom demands for such evenings, Eugene finally agreed that he would not be of much use to anyone if he was rotting in prison and that this time no neutral intervention would save him as it had from the Germans. He had made a business trip to the West earlier in the year and still had his valid passport. I had the Military Mission buy a railroad ticket to Prague and wired Peter to buy an air ticket Prague-Zurich and mail it to Eugene at a hotel in Prague. Just before he left, I saw Eugene and told him to reserve me a hotel room in Zurich.

My Headquarters had become as jittery as I was. I had received a reply to my last message. It was simultaneously contradictory and explicit: "LEAVE HUNGARY WITHOUT CONSPICUOUS HASTE BUT IN NO CASE LATER THAN FOUR DAYS."[1]

I hastily consulted Guy. He considered the operation to be finished and planned to use his farm now for its original purpose—his own escape. He agreed, however, to take with him anyone I wished to send him, provided they did not exceed four persons. I had, in fact, five persons remaining from the network for Guy to take. I approached them all, hoping I could persuade Guy at the last minute to accept the extra person.

Lila was not a member of the network, strictly speaking, but she had certainly contributed to saving some lives, and I had come to trust her in her oddly correct role. She thanked me, but she was not interested; she believed the terror was a temporary phase, and after that would come the Hungary she wanted to see. At the time of Rajk's arrest as a "Fascist, American spy, and Titoist agent" in 1949, Lila was fortunately out of the country on Government business. She never returned.

Anna stayed for similar reasons of optimism and duty. Her optimism unfortunately was based on even flimsier foundations than Lila's. She was arrested when the final campaign against the Church got under way in 1948 and spent seven years in prison.

Helen made the same decision. Arrested in 1949, she also spent seven years in prison.

Louis had been elected to Parliament in one of the splinter parties. So long as his party was not under attack he did not feel entitled to leave. But he gave me his melancholy smile; "I shall join you before long," he said. Six months later his party was destroyed, and happily he did make good his escape to the West.

Sara well knew that she had but one place to go from the Foreign Office, namely prison. She also had her fiancé already out of the country. She accepted Guy's good offices with pleasure.

I made up my accounts in preparation for leaving, to be dispatched by Mark in the usual manner. It had been what one might call a bargain operation. The eighteen months had cost the American taxpayer, including my salary—well below half the total—some $20,000.

In reporting my expenses I was, of course, confronted with my insubordination. I had, by a considerable margin, disobeyed my orders and exceeded my authority. In doing so I had deliberately accepted the fact. Now I was obliged openly to state it. Headquarters had authorized me to remove twenty-five persons from the country. On one line of my accounts, including funds I had advanced to Guy for the escape of himself, his mistress, and Sara—which took place successfully two weeks later—but excluding both a scientist's wife and the cost of gasoline for one trip to Vienna accompanied by Paul and five others, I wrote a single comprehensive entry: "Expenses for escape of 67 endangered persons, at average $100 per person—$6,700." A total of 74 persons. I wish it had been more. But I was never reproached that it was not less.[2]

On a December night, cold and clear, I drove down from the Var for the last time. I gave a long last look to the Danube, which knew no politics—and all politics. I was deeply sad, with an ache I well knew would not quit me for years, if ever. On the way out of Buda I stopped at two cafés. But each delay was an empty tribute to those who could not go free; each glass, each effort to live again in these walls among these people was vainglorious; I finally realized that I had to accept my own frustration and live with my own sadness, respecting the suffering of those whose part was and would be greater.

As I rolled through the towns and villages and along the deserted highway to the West, I certainly found no solace in the knowledge of defeat. But in the frozen, waiting countryside I at least avoided bitterness; there was the minor compensation of having at least tried.

Two weeks later, the young and popular King of Rumania, ordered bluntly by Vishinsky to abdicate, would pass along the rails by the side of this same road into exile, signaling another final conquest. Two months later Czechoslovakia, just across the river which I glimpsed from time to time, would be swallowed into the Soviet Empire, under the threats of Zorin to call in the Red Army. We still pay for the pride which brought about these falls.

Beyond Győr, but before the border at Hegyeshalom, I turned off the main road to the south. Watching my mileage carefully, I turned again at a familiar crossing, this time to the West. Again I saw before me the red-and-white striped barrier and the dim light of the sentry hut. One-two-three, I flashed my headlights. I couldn't be sure, and my nerves were far from being as controlled as the first time. But I didn't slow down. Again it worked. The still undistinguishable little figure raised the bar in perfect but illegal co-ordination.

This time bypassing the Red Army tank park, I turned north on small country roads until I came out again on the Vienna-Budapest highway. Five miles later I halted at the Schwechat checkpoint. A sleepy and surly Soviet sentry looked at my documents—a valid gray pass and one that had the name and date forged. He looked only at the seals.

Rudely, he told me to go on. But I was not the least offended. As the buildings of Vienna swallowed me up, I knew that I was tired and that I was beginning a letdown which would last for months.

Nevertheless, my feelings were not undiluted. For myself, there had really been no need to take this surreptitious way out of Hungary. But I had not done it for myself. The Frenchwoman, my intended bride, was an invention for my chief in Washington. Common sense and my heart demanded that I bring with me, on my last trip, the Hungarian lady. Both were satisfied by the seventy-fifth passenger.

1. Cf. *Foreign Relations of the United States, 1947,* Vol. IV, Washington, Government Printing Office, 1972, p. 400.

2. On the other hand, as of forty years later, neither has any part of the United States Government proferred thanks of any sort. The Department of State has been steadfast in its refusal to consider the matter—or even to discuss its 1948 suppression of documentation amounting to such thanks. The final episode came in 1987 when the Honor Awards Committee of the Department of State, responding at last to a 1985 suggestion by an Administration official that some recognition be accorded these services, asserted, "[We are] not able to mobilize our procedures today to deal with a situation that far away." A curious reaction for a department which, almost more

than any other I can think of in the Government, is beholden to the historical sense. The State Department Committee's refusal to even consider this
matter came in the same week in which the press announced the Department of Defense's award of a Purple Heart to a veteran of the First World
War.

NEW YORK 1962

*The operation described in the preceding chapters contains a num-
ber of illustrations of the reality of secret operations. For one thing, it
shows the complexity of these operations and their close interrela-
tionships. What started as a straight secret intelligence operation
became, under the pressure of events, a political operation, and then
concluded as an escape chain. Similarly, it shows the intricate but
unbreakable web of human relationships in the secret war: the real
and vital impact on the lives of persons in a distant land of an
official statement in Washington, the effect on the people and future
of an entire nation of the arrest of a single man, the chain of events
by which an argument in a political party can lead to the final
disruption of an intelligence network.*

*For another thing, it demonstrates the constant compromise with
the ideal which is an unavoidable characteristic of secret operations
in practice. Bargaining with Guy, improvising in the escape of the
scientist's wife or of Paul—all involved necessary compromises with
the classical principles and ideals of secret operations.*

*The reader may also have noted that this particular operation was
characterized by a certain undesirable rashness. To cite a few instances: I twice exposed Mark to considerable risk. It was he, for
example, who passed the money to Majoros without my having
checked as to whether the man was in fact Majoros or merely an*

agent provocateur. *Again, I urged him to assure the Interior Ministry that he knew the identity of "Mr. and Mrs. Tompkins, of Detroit," without considering the possibility that this might be a trap set by the AVO. The escapes of both the scientist's wife and of Paul certainly involved grave risk, the clandestine elements far outweighing the improvised covert elements. Lila also represented a considerable danger; I was banking—correctly, as it turned out—on her innate decency, but she could have been an attempted AVO penetration. And, with the advantage of hindsight, I could, let us face it, have refused Csornoky admittance into my apartment when the American correspondent was present.*

It is quite true that in each of these individual instances the operation was successful or at least unharmed. (In the case of the American correspondent, it was the President's decision more than the correspondent's violation of his word which obstructed the operation.) Nevertheless, taking all these instances together, they form a pattern of rashness which is just the sort of thing bound ultimately to bring about the downfall of an agent. In emergency circumstances—which I believe these were—it may be necessary to entertain such risks; but neither the agent nor his case officer should be under any illusion, because of individual successes, that he is pursuing anything but a dangerous course.

In the intervening years I have sometimes reflected on the possibility that the 75 escapes, or a considerable number of them, may have represented a condonation, a tacit concurrence, by the Soviets and Hungarian Communists. For this to be so, however, it is necessary to assume that the Communists desired to avoid the opprobrium of the arrest and prosecution of these various persons. Nothing in their reactions at the time nor in their subsequent behavior toward those who did not escape even remotely suggests that this was the case. Furthermore, they would have had to have achieved a successful penetration of the operation, and nothing has ever come to light indicating that this occurred. (I still come across traces of the operation: twelve years after the fact I found myself at a dinner in Mexico City seated next to a delightful lady whose conversation disclosed her to be none other than "Mrs. Tompkins, of Detroit." It was only then that I also learned that a man I had known in Europe for some five years was one of her arrested traveling companions.)

As for my having exceeded my instructions, I can only repeat what I said at the beginning of this book: the secret agent's objectives are to him, necessarily, of paramount and highly personal impor-

tance. In this case, the rapidly deteriorating circumstances—and the absence of any subsequent reprimand—can only be presumed to indicate that the case officer, on due reflection, decided the agent's actions accorded with his own objectives—a happy outcome which is definitely the exception and not the rule.

It is quite possible that this book has posed more questions than it has answered. If that is the case, the reader may wish to pursue the subject at his leisure in the daily newspapers. In so doing, it is my hope that he will be aided in his understanding by the various criticisms—particularly of American practice—which have appeared herein. At the same time, these criticisms cannot be a source of comfort to any possible Soviet reader. In spite of their early advantages in the field of political operations, the Soviets are laboring under a severe handicap in the secret war. It is simply that their basic policy and objectives are false. The human condition does not support a single nation's rule of the world. No single set of ideas, no single catechism of beliefs, no single doctrine or purpose or scale of values can uniformly animate all men everywhere. Man's unity lies in his diversity.

Ironically, as through all of human history, we shall have to continue to fight for the right of diversity. That is what the secret war— international or individual—is about.

AFTERWORD
REMINISCENCES

THE SEARCH FOR TRUTH CERTAIN

The known facts are simple. Raoul Wallenberg was born in 1912 to a prominent and wealthy Swedish family with important industrial interests. He studied at the University of Michigan and received a B.A. in architecture from that institution. He subsequently worked for a Central European trading company. In 1944 he was sent by the Swedish Foreign Ministry to the Swedish Legation in Budapest. As a diplomat of a country neutral in World War II, Wallenberg was able, by the issuance of Swedish documents and the creation of safe houses, to save thousands—some say 20,000—Hungarian Jews from extermination by the Nazis and Hungarian Arrow Cross. In mid-January 1945, during the Soviet siege of Budapest, Wallenberg, picked up by the Soviets, spent a night at Red Army headquarters in the city. On January 17 he left for Debrecen, in the east of Hungary, apparently to apply to the Soviet High Command for food and medicine for the Jewish survivors.

Wallenberg never reached Debrecen—at least not as a free man. Seized by the Soviets en route, his fate was a mystery for the rest of the century. During those years Wallenberg was honored in the Avenue of the Righteous in Yad Vashem in Israel, and was the fourth person—the first being the Marquis de Lafayette—to be granted honorary U.S. citizenship by the U.S. House of Representatives.

In December 1993, as a slightly roundabout result of a mention of my service in Hungary in a magazine, I received a letter from Dr. Jean Kloos-Fishman, secretary of The Raoul Wallenberg Association in Beer Sheva, Israel.

"I have been involved for the past ten years in efforts on behalf of Raoul Wallenberg," Dr. Kloos-Fishman wrote, "and in collecting data relating to his rescue work and disappearance.

"A recent news report which received media attention stated that the CIA had disclosed that Raoul Wallenberg had worked for American intelligence whilst a diplomat in the Swedish Legation in Budapest (July 1944–January 1945). Herschel Johnson, who was U.S. minister in Stockholm at the time, is quoted as a source of the information. I would mention that Iver C. Olsen, who had contact with Wallenberg and was a special attaché to the War Refugee Board that initiated Wallenberg's mission, is reputed to have been an American intelligence agent.

"I am writing in the hope that you may have some knowledge of Raoul Wallenberg's activities or whereabouts. I should greatly appreciate any information or suggestions from you on the subject."

I was dilatory in replying to Dr. Kloos-Fishman's request. I explained it when I finally wrote to her on May 15, 1994:

"At the time of receipt of your letter, during the year-end holidays, I would have been able to reply to you with a minimum of information, i.e., I arrived in Budapest, assigned to the American Legation, in April 1946, a year after Raoul Wallenberg was seized by the Soviets. I learned of that event from Hungarians, who also informed me of Wallenberg's actions to save Jews during the German occupation. The American Legation in Budapest had no official information on Wallenberg's wartime actions or on his disappearance, though the staff knew from Budapest gossip of both. As Political Officer at the American Legation in Budapest, I was never approached officially by anyone concerning Wallenberg, nor did I ever receive any inquiries or instructions regarding him from my superiors in Washington, nor from our Embassy in Moscow. Wallenberg's disappearance happened, of course, before either the American diplomatic or military missions arrived in Budapest from their entry point into Hungary at Debrecen—not that that would have altered the outcome."

But I thought a recent inquiry about Wallenberg would be of interest:

"I do not personally have any information additional to the preceding," I cautioned, "but on February 4 of this year I was interviewed concerning Wallenberg by Bert Vos, Dutch Television Channel 2 producer. . . . The interview was filmed for the Dutch Evangelische Omroep TV program, which I understand runs from Monday to Sunday on Channel 2 from 1800 to 1900 hours. (Dutch friends have already written me that they saw the program in the first half of March.) The interview was arranged by John P. Elliott, Washington Correspondent of EO Dutch Television and Radio. . . . This interview raised some questions that may be pertinent to your inquiry.

"I was pressed very strongly—though always courteously—by Mr. Vos as to why the American Government had done nothing, at least while I was in Budapest, about obtaining Wallenberg's release by the Soviets. My efforts to explain the situation prevailing in 1946–1947 were not what I would call successful. Finally, I was obliged to respond that the question should properly be addressed to the Swedish Government rather than the American.[1]

"Prior to that, however, I endeavored to explain to Mr. Vos—and thus to the Dutch TV audience—that those of us representing the American Government in Hungary in 1946–1947 had no knowledge of Wallenberg's activities in Hungary other than what we were told by the Hungarian populace. In the absence of any information to the contrary, I can only assume that the American Embassy in Moscow at the time was similarly devoid of official inquiries or instructions. I pointed out that the statement that Wallenberg while in Hungary 'was working for the United States War Refugee Board' was of recent vintage, and I had never heard of it until its recent publication in the press.

"I may add for your information that at a recent dinner where all the guests were, like myself, individuals who had been in American Government service connected with foreign affairs throughout the Second World War and later, I raised the question of the 'War Refugee Board.' Not a person, including myself, had ever heard of its existence.[2] (Though I was not during the war years entirely unacquainted with Jewish escapes from Occupied Europe. While stationed briefly in the Dominican Republic in 1944, one of my duties was oversight of the Jewish settlement at Sosua, primarily funded by American Jewish organizations, and established as a result of Trujillo's ostentatious offer—but much

appreciated by those who escaped as a result—at the prewar
Evian Conference to give refuge to European Jews).

"But to return to the 'War Refugee Board:' as I pointed out to
Mr. Vos, well more than eleven million Americans were in Government service of one kind or another during the Second World
War, and the U.S. Government was honeycombed with hundreds
of organizations and offices that sprang up under various auspices for the duration and thereafter expired. Presumably the
'War Refugee Board,' even—and perhaps particularly—if it was
a personal inspiration of the President, was one of these.

"I may also add that your letter refers to one Iver C. Olsen, 'a
special attaché to the War Refugee Board . . . reputed to have
been an American intelligence agent.' I believe it was Mr. Elliott
who, when I mentioned this name to him, replied, 'Oh, yes, he
was the O.S.S. man in the American Embassy in Stockholm.'
This may well have been the case, although I must point out that
being the O.S.S. man in our Stockholm Embassy and 'a special
attaché to the War Refugee Board' are not necessarily the same
thing. Similarly, I am an Honorary Life Member of the Veterans
of the O.S.S., and our list of members contains one 'Olsen,' but
not 'Iver C. Olsen'—which is not to say that Iver Olsen either
never became a member of the Veterans of the O.S.S., or that he
may [not] have died long since.[3]

"I endeavored—I fear without success—to convey to Mr. Vos
the circumstances that prevailed in Hungary in 1946 and 1947.
Without in the least diminishing the Wallenberg tragedy, I
pointed out that thousands upon thousands of people in Hungary
had been seized by the Soviets in Hungary in 1944–1946 (and
were still being carried away in 1947, e.g., Bela Kovacs, Secretary-General of the majority Smallholders Party). There were
numerous nationalities involved, but of course the great majority
were Hungarians—including, among countless cases of particular distinction, the former Prime Minister, Istvan Bethlen.
(Whose fate Stalin personally dangled in front of Hungarian
envoys in Moscow: 'Would you like to have Bethlen back?' 'Oh,
no, sir. No, sir.') For those of us representing American interests
in Hungary, and *unaware* of an American connection to Wallenberg, these thousands weighed more heavily in our then-current
considerations. (I repeat, this was so without in any way dimin-

ishing our respect for Wallenberg's exploits, as we heard of them locally, or our sympathy with his plight.) It should be remembered that, regrettable as it may be, the fact is that Wallenberg's fate only became a *cause célèbre* some years later.

"In response to Mr. Vos's question as to why I thought Wallenberg was seized by the Soviets, I replied that the Soviets seized people for one of two reasons: (1) the person seized was a specific target; or (2) as were the vast majority of cases, random seizures (and in Hungary, more common than in Austria or Czechoslovakia, for example—but not Poland—as what, despite the Armistice of 1944, had been an enemy country). In this connection, I said that if Wallenberg had an American connection, and the Soviets were aware of that connection—which, if he did have, they very likely might know it, particularly if the connection was one established in Stockholm—that alone would be fully sufficient to cause his seizure as a specific target.

"The Soviet efforts to rid all of Eastern Europe of persons actively linked to Western governments began with the arrival of the Red Army and went on for years, as we all know. In Hungary, I may add from personal experience, the Soviets also made specific targets—for hostile pressure, seizure, abduction, or incarceration—of those who had actively resisted the Nazis and survived.

"This exchange with Mr. Vos led to his next question, i.e., what if Wallenberg was in reality a Soviet agent? Mr. Elliott had mentioned this possibility in earlier conversation, sketching some of the features of Wallenberg's background which raised this as a hypothesis. I answered that I had never heard of or considered this possibility. But, I added, if it were the case, it would make Wallenberg an even more specific target for seizure by the Soviets. Stalin, with his paranoid suspicion, had already, during the war, had some of his own best people in the West murdered, e.g., Ignacz Riess and Willy Muenzenberg. After the war Stalin was intent on bringing back to the Soviet Union all those who had worked as his agents outside the Soviet Union. Some were seized and returned. Some willingly obeyed his order to come to the Soviet Union. All were promptly imprisoned—cf. Leopold Trepper.

"Mr. Vos's final question asked my own belief as to Wallenberg's fate. My answer—and I have given it in a few talks I have given—is that the final Soviet reply, i.e., that he died in prison in 1947 . . . was most probably the truth. The death rate among those in the Gulags during and immediately after the war was very high indeed. Bethlen himself was, I believe, dead by 1947. If Wallenberg was an American agent (or merely suspected as such), or a Soviet agent, or a double agent, his demise could have come quickly. If his was a random seizure, there is the chance he could have lasted longer; Hungarians, seized civilians and war prisoners both, did return to Hungary alive for years after the war."

The "final Soviet reply" to which I referred was, as I recall, one of several statements by the Soviet Government over the years, usually in response to successive Swedish inquiries. At the outset, that is, say, 1945–1948, while Wallenberg was in fact being held by them, the Soviets' answer was that they knew of no such person. From about 1957 on—the first such reply being given by Andrei Gromyko, then Foreign Minister of the USSR—the answer was that Wallenberg had died of a heart attack in 1947.

Dr. Kloos-Fishman replied to my letter much more promptly than I had to hers. On June 19, 1994 she wrote thanking me, and added some comment:

"Regarding the War Refugee Board, the subject had been well documented in 5 volumes of a series edited by David S. Wyman (Garland, 1989–1991). According to these books Iver C. Olsen was the WRB representative in Sweden. Incidentally, journalist Elenore Lester in her book, *Wallenberg, The Man in the Iron Web*, states on page twenty, 'Iver C. Olsen, who represented the War Refugee Board in Stockholm, but also had connections with the Office of Strategic Studies . . . '—the book was published in 1982." After recounting a meeting of her own with the Dutch Evangelische Omroep TV, she continued, "It is true that Raoul Wallenberg's fate became an international cause in later years, but his remarkable rescue work was recognized by 1947 when he was nominated for the Nobel Prize."

She concluded, "The possibility that Raoul Wallenberg is still alive may be remote, but I believe that there is a moral obligation to try to clarify his fate. The Swedish Government does not accept the Russian claim that Wallenberg died in 1947."

When she wrote to me, Dr. Kloos-Fishman apparently did not have access to the memoirs of one Yelisey Tikhonovich Sinitsyn, a Russian KGB general, who had retired in 1982 at age seventy-three. Following his retirement, Sinitsyn (who died in 1995) wrote his memoirs. Although there is no indication how widely they were circulated, Sinitsyn's memoirs were known to the Swedish Government by April 1995 (and thus, presumably, to Wallenberg's family). Sinitsyn had had considerable experience in Scandinavia. He had in fact been posted in Stockholm in 1944, where he played a supporting role to Alexandra Kollontai, the Soviet Ambassador to Sweden (one of the few Old Bolsheviks *not* liquidated by Stalin), in her successful efforts to bring about an armistice between Finland and the Soviet Union. With that armistice Sinitsyn went on to Finland, leaving Stockholm before Wallenberg's enlistment in the Hungarian enterprise.

The last of four versions of Sinitsyn's memoirs contains a lengthy and dramatic account of his learning in December 1945 from a friend in *Narkomindel*, the Soviet Foreign Office, of the arrest of Wallenberg in Hungary in January of that year, of Wallenberg's presence in Moscow, and of his refusal to confess to espionage for the Americans and for "the Zionists." Sinitsyn's story was that Wallenberg was in the hands of Viktor Semyonov-ich Abakumov, then heading SMERSH—*Smyert' Shpionam,* "Death to Spies and Diversionists," the Soviet military counter-intelligence service. Abakumov, who appears briefly in Aleksandr Solzhenitsyn's *The First Circle*, was closely tied to Lavrenty Beria, Stalin's chief executioner. Sinitsyn expresses indignation at the arrest of Wallenberg, a Swedish diplomat, since Sweden represented Soviet wartime interests in Finland—and presumably elsewhere as the Red Army moved west. There is clear irritation that Abakumov was keeping the Wallenberg case secret from Sinitsyn's own *NKVD*. He asserts that the Assistant Commissar for Foreign Affairs, Pavel Dekanozov (Ambassador to Germany at the outbreak of war) had replied to a Swedish Government inquiry about Wallenberg during 1945 that he "had been found, and that measures had been taken for his safety," but without mention of his being held in Moscow.

Sinitsyn's memoirs[4]: "Thinking over Wallenberg's fate, I could imagine only one way for him to get out of prison alive: to get him to collaborate with the Soviet intelligence service [*NKVD*], his only task being to get a most-favored position for the Soviet Union in an economic collaboration with the Wallenberg industrial empire. He would certainly agree to such a condition, because he would realize that it is the only way he can be free."

Sinitsyn's problem was to get Abakumov to agree to turn Wallenberg over to the intelligence service (*NKVD*). Sinitsyn approached his chief, Pavel Mikhailovich Fitin, with the suggestion that Fitin go to the Commissar for Internal Affairs, Beria, and get Beria to order Abakumov to turn Wallenberg over to Fitin's service. This did not appeal to Fitin. Sinitsyn took another tack. He said, "Abakumov must absolutely be made to understand that Wallenberg, not even mistreated and tortured, would talk against himself, because he would know that path would lead to death. Abakumov must be made to understand that killing Wallenberg would lead to honor neither for him nor for the Soviet Union." Sinitsyn then suggested to Fitin that Abakumov be asked to investigate the possibility of getting Wallenberg to collaborate with the Soviet intelligence service. "Abakumov may regard it as a victory of his own," Sinitsyn said. "For us it is important that Wallenberg leave the prison alive."

Accordingly, Fitin and Sinitsyn met with Abakumov. The meeting did not go well, according to Sinitsyn. After an initial rebuff by Abakumov, Fitin said, "We propose that you terminate the investigation of Wallenberg, and that together we try to persuade him to collaborate with the Soviet intelligence service. The Wallenberg case may continue to be handled by the military counterintelligence, but your investigators would be helped by our experienced recruiter-intelligence staff. Consequently, the case is solved when Wallenberg agrees to work for the Soviet Union."

Replying that his office had "many competent recruiters," Abakumov said that his investigators intended "to get Wallenberg to admit that he has collaborated with the American intelligence service and international Zionist Center." Sinitsyn answered with an interesting paean of praise for the Wallenbergs: "I said the diplomat Wallenberg had been in Budapest for the Swedish Government to protect the interests of the Soviet Union and to protect Hungarian Jews from the cruelty of the Germans and local fascists. The Wallenberg family has billions in Sweden, and they have never been against the Soviet Union. On the contrary, during the war the Wallenberg factories conscientiously delivered ball bearings and machine tools to the Soviet Union. Without them our machines would still have been in the fields. Almost daily, our planes flew by night across the Finnish lines, landed in Sweden, and got ball bearings there for our aircraft factories. In 1944 one of the Wallenbergs traveled to Finland at the request of our ambassador in Stockholm, Alexandra Kollontai, to try to convince the Finns to start negotiations for an armistice with the Soviet Union. We then needed troops from the Finnish front for the decisive attack on Berlin. You will only get Wallenberg to admit to espionage against the Soviet Union by torture, and even with that, the executioners are not always successful. . . . I think you will not get such an admission from him even with torture. In that case, what is the final result for Wallenberg?"

Angered, Abakumov retorted, "We are not executioners! We are only the punishing sword of the Soviet Union,[5] and we will soon get an admission out of Wallenberg that will show he has been spying against the Soviet Union." Further denunciations of Wallenberg by Abakumov followed, ending with his statement: "The investigations are approaching the point at which Wallenberg will start to tell the truth about his criminal activity. As for the recruitment of Wallenberg for the Soviet intelligence service, that will only become possible after he has admitted his enemy activity against the Soviet Union. The recruiters of *SMERSH* are trying to recruit him. We will ask for help from the intelligence services only if our own resources are insufficient. I cannot give you any other answer. As to your claim that Wallenberg has been arrested and kept in prison illegally, you are wrong! He did not come from the German zone to the region liberated by Soviet troops only to take a walk. He had enemy intentions, but was arrested in time."

"After the meeting with Abakumov," wrote Sinitsyn, "we got occasional reports that Wallenberg was interrogated daily, so that he was exhausted, but stubbornly continued to deny all the accusations against him." In March 1946 Commissars in the Soviet Government were transformed into Ministers. The People's Commissariat for Internal Affairs was split into the Ministry for Internal Affairs (*MVD*) and the Ministry of State Security (*MGB*). Abakumov, ever the protegé of Beria, became Minister of State Security, an appointment, wrote Sinitsyn, "that made Wallenberg's situation decidedly more difficult."

According to Sinitsyn, in mid-June 1946, Staffan Söderblom, the Swedish Ambassador to Moscow, meeting with Stalin, asked for his assistance in locating Wallenberg. Sinitsyn was taken aback. "I reflected that the Swedes had asked for Stalin's help unnecessarily," he wrote. "That was their fateful mistake. The Ambassador ought to have gone to the Foreign Ministry to ask personally for help from Viacheslav Molotov, who, in my opinion, would have handled the case according to international law. He would not have started by making a fool of himself in the eyes of world opinion, as happened.

"Only a month after Ambassador Söderblom met Stalin, Assistant Foreign Minister Andrei Vyshinsky—clearly with Stalin's permission—reported on the search for Raoul Wallenberg: 'I have made a search of the organs in question. As a result of a careful scrutiny it has been found that Wallenberg is not in the Soviet Union and that he is unknown to us.' . . . In my opinion, before Söderblom's visit, Stalin asked Abakumov for a report on the Wallenberg case. Abakumov was, of course, obliged to tell Stalin that Wallenberg denied any contacts with the American intelligence service and the International Zionist Center, and that he did not give the information the interrogators needed. It was clearly on the basis of this discussion that they decided not to release Wallenberg, to kill him secretly, and to tell the Swedes that Wallenberg was not in the USSR and was 'unknown to us.'

"In the autumn of 1947 Pavel Mikhailovich Fitin came to Moscow on duty. He told me that Raoul Wallenberg had been shot in the Lubyanka, but that the man's relatives had been told that he died by an infarction of the heart. . . .

"I have not been able to find the exact date when the Swedish diplomat was killed. Not even the operational staff of the Third Administration (previously *SMERSH*) at the Ministry of State Security knew when he was shot or poisoned. It is at least certain that Wallenberg was killed before July 7, 1947. The Foreign Ministry of the Soviet Union gave July 7, 1947 as the date of Wallen-

berg's death from inflammation of the heart in its communication
to his relatives, but only after strong pressure from public opinion
in Sweden and from the relatives. At the present time [i.e., some
time well prior to 1995] it is very difficult to determine the date
of Wallenberg's death. Many of those who took direct part in the
killing, and their witnesses, are dead, either of old age, or as victims of punishment, such as Abakumov. The organizer of, and
the one responsible for, Wallenberg's death, Minister Viktor
Abakumov and part of his investigating group were shot in 1954
as enemies of the Soviet Union. The executor got his punishment
for his many crimes."

I cannot assess Sinitsyn's veracity. Much of what he wrote
about the Wallenberg case is plausible. Assuming that he was
writing in the mid- or late 1980s, it had already been Soviet
orthodoxy for years to denounce the countless murders of Stalin's reign as the work of "Beria and Abakumov." This is applicable even if Sinitsyn's account was *KGB* disinformation—
though the questions arise, why and what for? Other parts of
Sinitsyn's story—e.g., his indignation at Wallenberg's arrest and
interrogation as a violation of international law—don't quite fit a
KGB general who began his service in the *NKVD* in 1938, and in
1956 was attached to the Hungarian Ministry of Security, where
he worked closely with Yuri V. Andropov, then Soviet ambassador in Budapest. (Andropov later headed the *KGB*; in November
1982, at Brezhnev's death, he became General Secretary of the
Party, and leader of the Soviet Union. He died in 1984, having
provided the precedent for current Russian President Vladimir
Putin's rise from head of the Russian security service to the
nation's highest position.)

Still, Sinitsyn's account offers more detail than any other
source about Wallenberg's fate.

In 1991, the Soviet Union having disappeared, a joint Russian-
Swedish commission on Wallenberg was established—due to
make their reports in January 2001. In 1991 President Yeltsin
named a Russian Presidential Commission to look into the
Wallenberg affair. It was headed by Aleksandr Yakovlev.[6] In
November 2000, Yakovlev announced that Wallenberg had been
shot in 1947 in the Lubyanka. Yakovlev said that Vladimir Kry-
uchkov, former head of the *KGB* (and one of the conspirators in

the 1990 attempted coup d'etat against Gorbachev), had acknowledged the execution in a private conversation. The Russians continue to insist that all documentation relative to Wallenberg have been destroyed.

However, in May 1996 *U.S. News & World Report* published a lengthy article detailing assertions by various witnesses of post-1947 sightings of Wallenberg. There are three independent consultants to the joint Russian-Swedish commission on Wallenberg. Arne Ruth, former editor-in-chief of *Dagens Nyheter*, whose article in the January 7, 2000 issue of *The Washington Post* is cited in note 1 above, stated in the same article that he is familiar with those consultants' reports, and that all three, for different reasons, are of the view that Wallenberg survived beyond 1947.

On December 22, 2000 a verdict signed by the Russian Procurator General was published. It stated that Wallenberg and his driver were wrongly arrested on charges of espionage in 1945, were imprisoned as "socially dangerous," and were held for two-and-a-half years until they died. "The real causes of their arrest and imprisonment, the true circumstances of their deaths . . . have not been found," the announcement said.

A Swedish Foreign Office spokesman dismissed that claim as "one more version" in the series of Soviet and Russian accounts of Wallenberg's fate. The family demanded a full account.

On January 12, 2001 the Russian-Swedish commission reported it had reached no agreement on Wallenberg's fate. Both sides referred to reports from other Soviet prisoners of sighting Wallenberg after 1947. But this time the Russians reverted to Gromyko's 1957 statement that Wallenberg had died in a Soviet prison in 1957 from a heart attack. The Swedes doubted that this was so. Promising further efforts, the Swedish Prime Minister commented, "It cannot be said that Raoul Wallenberg is dead."

The long search continues.

THE BETROTHED

In the spring of 1948 a historically unusual event occurred. Much attention was directed at the time to Josip Broz Tito's defiance of Josef Dzhugashvili—what came to be called the Tito-

Cominform break. To be sure, Tito's challenge to Stalin was unusual, but not historically so. Others had defied Stalin in the past. Some had even survived (Jay Lovestone, longtime head of International Affairs at the AFL-CIO, comes to mind).

The Albanian Communist leader, Enver Hoxha, quickly chose to side with the Soviets against the Yugoslavs. The result of the rupture between the Yugoslavs and the Soviets was the geographical isolation from the Soviet Union of a Soviet dependency, Albania. It was this isolation of Albania that was historically unusual. To the best of my knowledge, there had not been, in the three centuries of expansion of the Russian Empire, another occasion where a place already in Russian hands had been, without war, cut off from Russian or Russian-dominated territory.

In 1948, Albania—isolated from the Soviet Union—stood out, vulnerable. It was both detached from Soviet support and, for the moment, immune to direct Soviet attack. Between Albania and the nearest Russian forces lay Yugoslavia. Across the Adriatic from Albania was Italy, about to become a founding member of NATO. South of Albania, Greece was embroiled in civil war, as Soviet-supported Greek Communists fought Western-supported government forces.

The Soviets were quick to take advantage of their sea connection to Albania. Their base on the Albanian island of Sazan, across from Italy at the Straits of Otranto, threatened Western naval access to the Adriatic.

Even before these developments, the British were concerned about Albania. Their missions in Albania during the war had been harassed and finally expelled, at war's end, by Hoxha and by the Albanian Communists. The Albanians had then, without notification, mined the Straits of Corfu. Two British warships were severely damaged, with loss of life. There was thus considerable pressure among the British for action against Albania. Chief among the proponents were Julian Amery and others who had served in Albania during the war, and who felt not only hostility to Hoxha and company, but also some debt to those Albanians who had been their allies there, and were now either in exile or in great trouble.[7]

The year 1948 also saw the Communist coup in Czechoslovakia, the Berlin Blockade, and the initiative from the U.K. for a

North Atlantic Treaty. In the turmoil, the U.S. National Security Council passed NSC 10/2, a decision authorizing covert action. The Office of Policy Coordination (OPC) was created for that purpose. Headed by Frank G. Wisner, it was lodged in the CIA for *housekeeping and logistics only.* OPC took its guidance from the Policy Planning Staff of the State Department and, when necessary, from the Joint Chiefs of Staff.

Among the early actions undertaken by OPC was an operation against Albania. This was the result of the country's exposed position, of proposals from the British for a joint operation, and of the difficulty at the time of mounting such an operation from other-than-British territory.

We began with the political preparations—the formation of an Albanian Committee as a rallying point and as a source both of information and personnel. Our initial operational chief in the field was Robert Low. Low had been the OSS agent whose 1942 expulsion from Turkey is described, but not identified, on page 73 of this book. In 1947 he had been the East European correspondent of *Time-Life,* and is mentioned, but not identified, in that connection on page 239 above. Low was succeeded as operational chief in the field in 1950 by Michael Burke, also former OSS.[8]

Early in 1949, Low was sent to Rome—the center of the Albanian emigration—to bring about the formation of a leading Committee. Low spent several months, seated Turkish-fashion in the Borghese Gardens, urging a number of Albanian elders toward agreement. Eventually, it came about and, with the agreement of the French services, the Albanian National Committee announced its formation in Paris that same year.

Before that occurred, however, it was necessary to clear matters with Zog, the Albanian king, then residing in Egypt. A landowner and chieftain from the north of Albania, Ahmed Zogu had proclaimed himself president in 1925, and in 1928 declared himself king. He and his queen, Geraldine,[9] and their infant son fled to Greece in 1940, narrowly escaping invading Italian forces. Zog's goodwill was necessary to the enterprise because his supporters in the emigration, led by Abas Kupi (with whom the British had worked closely in Albania during the Second World War), were numerous and politically important.[10] Low and Julian

Amery duly waited on Zog, whose initial reaction was negative. The next day, however, they extracted from him an agreement not to oppose the committee or the actions to be taken in its name. (As it happened, by 1952 the operation was entirely American—and closely tied to Zog.)

Many authors (a number of whom, such as Peter Grose, were serious and highly capable analysts of intelligence matters, including, unfortunately, Michael Burke) have written to the effect that this was an operation to overthrow the Albanian Communist Government. It was not— *at least not in its early versions*. As Franklin Lindsay, who was Wisner's chief of operations for Eastern Europe (and my immediate chief), has often tried to explain, "It was a probe." The ground rules were to ascertain whether there was sufficient opposition to Hoxha inside Albania for an effort to overthrow him to have a reasonable chance of success—without leading to larger hostilities, of course. It was not an operation to overthrow Hoxha.

In the late summer of 1949 preparations were begun for the first landings of agents in Albania. This was to be done by ship, from Malta. At this point, steps were taken to reflect the fact that this was a joint Anglo-American operation.

Which brings us to Harold Adrian Russell Philby.

Much has been written about Philby.[11] Sent to represent the British SIS in Washington in 1949, he was recalled to London in 1951 when General Walter Bedell Smith, then Director of the CIA, informed the British that there would be no contact between the CIA and SIS so long as Philby was in the British service. This decision was precipitated by the flight from London to the Soviet Union in 1951 of Guy Burgess and Donald Maclean, who, as time would eventually tell, were tipped off by Philby of their scheduled arrest. Ousted from the British Service, Philby ended up in the Middle East as a correspondent—with a tenuous connection to the SIS as the British searched for confirmation of Philby's Soviet service. With his exposure by the British as a longtime Soviet agent imminent in 1963, Philby fled to the Soviet Union from Beirut.

Philby was generally, and ultimately widely, known as "Kim."

Even his book, *My Silent War*, written in Moscow and published in the West in 1967, gave the author as "Kim Philby."

Kim: The influence of Rudyard Kipling is more widespread than one would think. I have a childhood friend who was fascinated by a Kipling character, and I am in the seventh decade of calling him Gunga Din.

Apparently, Franklin Delano Roosevelt was similarly fascinated. During FDR's second term Louis Johnson, who later became Truman's Secretary of Defense, conceived a great longing to be Secretary of War. Active in Democratic politics in Washington, a contributor of time, money, and influence, Johnson had some claim to recognition. But in 1940 the President appointed Henry Stimson as Secretary of War. Johnson, disappointed, retired to his law practice in West Virginia.

A couple of years later, the telephone rang in Johnson's home. The operator said the White House was calling. The President wished to speak with Mr. Johnson. One can only imagine the thoughts that rushed through Johnson's mind while he waited for the connection to be made. FDR came on the line. "Louis," he said. "I want your help. As you know, I favor the independence of India after this war. Meanwhile, I do not want to have to rely on the British for information about the progress of this important development. I want you to go to India, and to be my eyes and ears with the leaders of the Indian independence movement."

Johnson, stunned, finally managed to blurt out, "But Mr. President, I know nothing about India." FDR's answer was quick. "Come, come, Louis," he said. "You've read *Kim*."[12]

As the Albanian operation, duly authorized, was for the first few years a joint Anglo-American operation, Philby and I, when together, constituted the command of the operation. I saw a great deal of him. At the time, even taking into account the professional basis of our association, I considered him a friend.

Kim, when I knew him, was devoid of pretension. He was witty, courteous, and not lacking in engaging warmth. His smile, suggestive of complicity in a private joke, conveyed an unspoken understanding of the underlying ironies of our work. He was capable. Behind the modest, slightly rumpled exterior, there was no mistaking a quick mind and a tenacious will.

He spoke with a marked stammer (which, together with his "Oxbridge" accent, must have made his later Russian difficult indeed for his listener to comprehend).[13]

Not too long ago I was told a story of Philby in his Moscow years. An Englishman who knew Philby, encountering him in Moscow, told Philby that a film was being made about him. Philby asked who was playing him. "Michael Caine," was the answer. Philby reportedly recoiled, "But he's not a gentleman!" I don't deny the possibility of this side to Philby, but I myself never encountered it.

One English author some years ago wrote of Philby's "large house, servants, and his lavish entertaining. It is surprising that his affluence did not arouse the suspicions of his superiors." This is pure embroidery. I spent a number of evenings at Philby's. They were very wet indeed; in their farther reaches they were sometimes even uproarious. Lavish they definitely were not. No doubt there was a servant (Embassy First Secretaries in Washington still have them), but I never saw one. The house was not unduly large for a family with four children and a fifth on the way. Aileen, Kim's second wife,[14] was not beyond worrying about how they could manage to raise all five. The furnishings were sparse: Kim exhibited a noteworthy disregard for décor. Luxury, *chez* Philby, was a full martini pitcher and several bottles of whisky. It mattered not a whit who served them, or from what one drank.

Why was Philby so successful? For one thing, he came to us with a very high reputation. Americans are admirers of "Young Turks." (Whether this was actually the case with respect to the original "Young Turks," at the end of the last century, is another question.) And Philby was, of course, a certified "Young Turk," having been the ringleader of a sort of revolt of younger officers in MI-6, who then showed his mettle by consigning to oblivion the man who had given him his chance in that organization. For another, the CIA generally, having worked closely with the British during the Second World War, was devoid of the anti-British sentiment afflicting some parts of the American government and population—if there is any doubt as to the importance of those sentiments, see Isaiah Berlin's *Washington Despatches 1941–1945*. The British SIS was held in high regard by those who had had close wartime connections with it. And there was Philby's undeniable charm.[15]

In the days when Philby and I worked together, our communications were often sparse, slow, and erratic, whereas the British worldwide communications network was one of two invaluable assets that the British War Cabinet had retained at all costs during the wartime liquidation of British overseas holdings. (The other was the British reinsurance business.)

On three successive occasions Kim came into my office with urgent reports that I had not yet received through our channels. The third time, when I again had to confess ignorance, Philby, with an air of anxious helpfulness, asked, "Well, look, in these circumstances, wouldn't you like us to handle your communications for you?" I had no idea, of course, that this poisoned apple was doubly poisoned. In declining it, I laughed. Philby's charm was that he laughed, too.

As H. R. Trevor-Roper (Lord Dacre), Regius Professor of History at Oxford, so accurately put it, "We were all wrong." I am not exempt: until Philby's 1963 disappearance from Beirut I had him on a list of people to receive complimentary copies of this book.

Earlier, about 1952, I think, when I was in Paris, I had the use of a flat in London and frequently spent time there. One day I ran into James Angleton, CIA chief of counterintelligence, in Paris's Crillon Hotel. Knowing nothing of the facts, my feeling at that time was that Philby had been railroaded from the British Service by American pressure. I therefore told Jim that unless he thought it undesirable for any reason, my intention was to invite Philby for drinks the next time I was in London. Jim said he thought it was a very good idea. "I still feel," he said, "that Philby some day will head the British Service."

Philby came for drinks. He was looking somewhat seedy, and was subdued. But he said he was going to write his history of the Spanish Civil War, and all would be all right. I told him to keep in touch. I am pleased that he did not.

But even after he fled to Moscow, Philby could be mischievous—and worse. It is well known that one of Philby's first jobs in Moscow was to write the memoirs of the Soviet agent Konon Trofimovich Molody, a.k.a. Gordon Lonsdale. Before the book appeared in England, *The Observer* in London had already published a front-page piece on Philby that I had written under the name of Felix. Philby in Moscow almost certainly had seen it. When the book came out, Philby's riposte was in the frontispiece. In the photo Lonsdale was pictured seated and laughing uproariously at an open book before him. The title was clearly visible.

It was the English edition of this book.

The May 26, 1968 issue of *The New York Times Book Review* carried a lengthy review of four Philby books, including his own *My Silent War*, again done under my name of Felix.

This time Philby's riposte—if riposte it was—took somewhat longer. With the passage of time there was little mystery about the identity of "Christopher Felix;" in the late 1960s it apparently took no more than two telephone calls in London to get both my name and address (see Introduction to the Second Edition). Also, on October 30, 1984 BBC-TV broadcast a film about the Albanian operation entitled "The Cost of Treachery," which one must assume Philby's Soviet friends recorded for him. Along with a number of others, I figured, and was identified, in the film.

About 1985 a friend in London told me that Philip Knightley, the British writer who had worked for some time on a book about Philby, and had seen him once in Moscow, had asked Philby—in a kind of joint exercise in condescension—"Who can one really talk to among the Americans?" Philby's answer (reported to me but not by Knightley) was, "Jim McCargar. He's intelligent and has a social conscience."

Under the ostensible compliment was, of course, the kiss of death. Praise from Philby was *not* what I, or any American officer, needed.

There was a curious substratum to this dart from afar.

In one of his "autobiographical reminiscences" written during his Moscow years, and finally published in 2000 (see Note 11), Philby wrote that in the summer of 1933 he applied for the Civil Service, giving as a reference (Sir) Dennis Robertson, the economist, who had been his tutor at Trinity College, Cambridge.[16]

Robertson wrote Philby that he had received an inquiry from the Civil Service, but, as Philby put it years later in Moscow, "Robertson told me that . . . he was afflicted by doubt. Would I really be happy in the Indian service? Would I really be able to come to terms with a system, many features of which would be repellent to me? . . . He urged me to think it over. If I persisted, he said, he would be happy to recommend me in respect of character and ability, but would also feel impelled to mention my 'strong sense of social justice.'" This letter, wrote Philby, put an end to his ideas of the Civil Service.[17]

Did my "social conscience" equal his "sense of social justice"—with the consequences that the latter, in Philby's version, had for him?

All writers about Philby accept, most without demur, the contention—slyly advanced by Philby himself in his *My Silent War*—that the information he passed to the Soviets resulted in the prompt Albanian capture of infiltrators sent into Albania as part of the Anglo-American operation. I have always disputed that he did so in the detail generally ascribed to him. Once assigned to Washington, it goes without saying that he informed the Soviets that this Anglo-American operation was under way. (Philby in his previous assignment, in Turkey, would not have been informed of the earlier consideration of an Albanian operation; in fact, as noted above, his transfer to Washington was part of the arrangements to begin the operation.) He was also certainly able to give the Soviets ex-post-facto information concerning operations into Albania. But not the kind of advance information of operations that would result in the immediate capture of infiltrators by the *Sigurimi*.

This view is based on two facts. First, my successor on the American side of the operation (I left in May 1950), who was in charge after the boat operations from Malta were abandoned, told me repeatedly that he never gave operational information to Philby. (He said that in my presence to Nicholas Bethell, one of the authors who credit Philby with more than his due, whom it apparently failed to impress.) Second, after Philby's removal from Washington in 1951 and shortly thereafter from MI6, the seizure by the Albanian authorities of infiltrators, practically on arrival, continued for some two years.

A former colleague, who knew Philby, rang me after reading Peter Grose's *Operation Rollback*. When we touched on the Albanian operation, he snorted, "It was Angleton who gave the operation to the Italians." Jim Angleton, of course, had participated in establishing the postwar Italian service, and was highly influential with the Italians. (So that his account to me, a few days after it happened, of the first voyage from Malta to the Albanian coast with infiltrators aboard was a report to him from the Italian service. This is recounted briefly on page 124 of this book.)

So far as the security of the Albanian operation was concerned, my feeling was that the interests and ambitions of Albania's neighbors posed the major problem. The Italian interest, with Albania just across the Straits of Otranto, and a large Albanian population resident in Italy, was evident. The Albanian community in Italy, from which the great majority of Albanian volunteers came, was deeply penetrated both by the Italian service and by the Italian Communist Party (and the attached Soviet agents alongside). The Yugoslavs, desirous of Western support against the Soviets, did nothing against the operation, but disapproved and watched it closely. The Greeks, even though heavily occupied by their own civil war, insisted all along that much of neighboring Albania was really the Greek province of Northern Epirus. In fact, it was my theory that one of the rare leaks about the operation was due to the Greeks. This episode is told, without identification, on pages 92–93 of this book.[18]

However exaggerated the assumptions and claims of Philby's contributions to the failures of the Albanian operation, there is no doubt about the magnitude of his services over the years to the Soviets. In 1991, four years after Philby's death, the Russians issued a commemorative Philby postage stamp. Joseph Brodsky, 1987 Nobel Prize for Literature laureate, was incensed. *The New Republic* published a lengthy cry of pain by Brodsky in its April 20, 1992 issue. He rightly interpreted this act as a deliberate slap of Western faces by those who issued the stamp.

Among Brodsky's denunciations of Philby's various sins was the interesting suggestion that Philby was not the ideological convert that he and his Soviet masters claimed. Once Philby performed his first service for the Russians, wrote Brodsky, they had him. His alternatives were ruin and prison, or continued services for them. The foundation of Philby's career was not loyalty, suggested Brodsky, but blackmail, the threat of exposure. This is worth examining.

In another of his "autobiographical reminiscences" written in Moscow, Philby took up the question of his religious beliefs:

"In respect to religion, I have never wavered in my rejection. I must have been nearly six when I scandalized my grandmother by informing her that there was no God. She was a Christian in the sense that she professed belief . . . But she never took me [to church] with her or spoke to me of such matters. Therefore, as religion never obtruded itself . . . my skepticism must be referred to the kindergarten, where the miraculous element was stressed in a manner supposedly attractive to small children. In my case the result was the opposite to that intended. I reacted in frank disbelief, repelled in particular by the wide gap between the powers attributed to Christ and the trivial use to which he put them. Why cure one leper? Why not all lepers? And so on. No argument I have since heard or read has dented my unbelief, nor can I remember the slightest twinge of religious experience. From earliest childhood to the present day, I have found the evidence of the senses far more 'miraculous' than any flight of faith."

Philby's own writings, his depictions of himself, claim an adult life that was, to the end, the embodiment of faith. It was neither a Christian nor a Moslem faith; it was not faith in a religion, but it was no less religious. His was the Marxist faith, the belief in the Communist dream—to which, through countless trials and even periods of doubt, he asserted, he remained faithful. Hayden Peake, in his Philby chronology (see Note 11), states that in the spring of 1933 Philby won a prize of fourteen pounds at Trinity College, Cambridge, and spent it all on the works of Marx. That autumn he was in Vienna and active in the Communist underground. The next spring he applied to join the British Communist Party.

Oleg Kalugin, at forty the youngest *KGB* general, and head of the First Directorate, who worked closely with Philby in the 1970s and became his friend, bears witness in his memoirs to

Philby's faith.[19] Describing his first meeting, in 1972, with the then-demoralized Philby, Kalugin wrote, "The famed spy, who had risked his life to serve what he believed was a noble Communist cause, had been driven half-mad by the paranoia and idiocy of the *KGB*. No doubt he was also driven to despair as he saw the cause to which he had devoted his life transformed into the shabby reality of modern-day Soviet life. Philby was as disillusioned as any of us, perhaps more so." The dark of night, when faith is challenged, and wavers.

"During the 1980s," Kalugin continued, "Kim still lived well and in relative freedom, but he never again enjoyed the support that I and my underlings had given him. . . . He and Rufa [Philby's Russian wife] complained about the callousness of their new *KGB* handlers. He also became more vocal in his criticism of the Soviet Union, though, like me, he wanted to continue believing in the Communist dream that had inspired him since his youth." Did he? Had it?

Kalugin quotes Philby, declining Kalugin's offer of a larger Moscow apartment, as saying, "I'm a conservative at heart, though I'm not one of those people who would like your country to go back to Stalin's times." It was, of course, exactly during "Stalin's times" that Philby proclaimed his Soviet faith.

An accomplished liar (the judgment is professional, not moral), Philby's deception had few, if any, limits.[20] Philby's third wife, Eleanor (who, until her affair with Philby, had been the wife of the Middle East correspondent of *The New York Times*), having been replaced in Philby's affections in Moscow by the wife of Donald Maclean, wrote a memoir of her time with Philby. (It was published in England as *The Spy I Loved*, but in America as *The Spy I Married*.) "He was," she wrote, "the most lovely and devoted husband." But she portrayed, strikingly if unconsciously, a man whose expressions of sentimental ardor were as intense (if not exaggerated) on the penultimate day of the relationship as on the second. What Eleanor Philby showed was a sentimental facade, resistible by few women, that is one day transferred—intact and seemingly without any intervening reconstruction—to another site.

The implication was that Philby's sentimental energy existed independently of any specific female stimulus—and that its expressions were reactions to some subterranean need of his own, rather than to the person on which they were lavished. However subconscious, this too is a form of deception. We are all, perhaps, given to this form in one degree or another. But the degree is important. At a point, subconscious deception merges into cruelty.

E. H. Cookridge, writing about Philby in 1968, referred to Aileen, Philby's second wife: "It seems that before Aileen was afflicted with a nervous disease, they were very much in love, and Kim always showed her great affection and tenderness, particularly during her illness." Kim did indeed show Aileen "great affection and tenderness" at the time I knew them. And Aileen was already ill—but the illness did not become "nervous" until after Philby's dismissal in 1951 from the SIS. Thereafter, in her last years, when Aileen took to intimating that Kim was a Russian agent, he went to great pains to explain to their friends that she had become mentally ill, and dangerously so. I was told that Philby reinforced those explanations by ostentatiously sleeping in a tent in their garden, the physical danger at Aileen's hands inside the house being too great to risk.

This kind of cruelty was cousin to another side of Philby's "faith." Oleg Kalugin wrote of George Blake, another of the British defectors living in Moscow: "He told me several times that Soviet Intelligence promised him that none of the people he identified as agents in the USSR had been shot. He clung naively to that belief; I didn't have the heart to tell him that his work led directly to the deaths of dozens of agents behind the Iron Curtain. . . . Blake . . . did tell NBC News in 1991 that he realized he had made a mistake. But, said Blake, at the time he began spying for the *KGB* he strongly believed in the Communist cause."

Philby, on the other hand, died in 1988 without ever betraying any remorse for the many men whose deaths he arranged. When mentioned in his own book, they appear as fools or robots. Kalugin noticed his complete equanimity on this subject: "Philby knew that his spying and tips to the *KGB* had doomed many men, and it didn't seem to haunt him; he wrote off the victims as casualties of the Cold War."

Here lies the significance of Joseph Brodsky's suggestion that once Philby had performed his first service for the Soviets, they had him. Once he had performed that service—particularly if he erred, as he later did by bringing Burgess into his house in Washington—he could no longer pose in time as a disillusioned intellectual hanger-on. Stephen Spender, Ignazio Silone, André Gide, Richard Wright, Arthur Koestler—they and great numbers of others all found Communism attractive in the 1930s. And they abandoned the cause in due course. But they were not *NKVD*, or *KGB*, operatives. Philby could discern the distinction. He was bright and perceptive enough to know that if he attempted to break with the Soviets, it was not just ruin or prison in Britain that awaited him, but—as with Krivitsky, Reiss, Muenzenberg, and countless other former servants of "the Center"—the menace of death at the hands of the Soviets, anywhere at anytime.

The betrothal had not led Philby to a union. He was not a bridegroom. He was "Agent Tom," the *KGB*'s name for him, believing only in himself, and always under suspicion by his hosts. He was simply a survivor. Of his mother Philby in Moscow wrote, "She never tired of telling me that life was a desperate struggle for survival, and that only unremitting work and fearsome drive would pull me through. Sometimes during adolescence, she would induce panicky thoughts of early death from starvation and exposure."

A determined survivor.

TRIUMPHS

In War

In 1944 I was commissioned in Naval Intelligence. My aim was to be assigned to one of the OSS missions to Eastern Europe. With its notoriously high regard for OSS, ONI had other ideas. Having supported my views by commenting to the Navy captain in charge of Intelligence assignments, "Captain, you can't do this to me," I was shot out of a gun to the Aleutian Islands. There I did penance at a freezing, windswept coaling station for Soviet merchant ships for a while, and then became Foreign Liaison Officer for the Unalaska Sector, based at Dutch Harbor.

There I thought I had, at last, a great intelligence triumph. In early August 1945 a Soviet ship's captain confided to me that, ordered by radio to open sealed instructions given him, he found they said, "The Soviet Union is at war with Japan. Head for the nearest friendly port." Not to alert the captain to my anticipated triumph, I pretended this was no surprise, and in due course headed for our radio shack. There I sent off a message reporting the information and the source to ONI.

I confess to a certain pride. I realized that, of course, the Chief of Naval Operations, the Joint Chiefs, the White House, would have known secretly if anything was afoot. But Naval Intelligence, with its far-flung network, would have penetrated the veil of secrecy before any others.

Six hours later the captain, in a state of great agitation—obviously he had been talking with his *politruk* (his "political instructor;" we used to call them commissars, but that was to denigrate a very high rank indeed)—summoned me to the ship. He nervously, but flatly, denied his previous information.

I went back ashore, reporting to ONI that the captain had retracted his earlier report, and went back to bed. And awoke to Radio Moscow's announcements that the Soviet Union was at war with Japan.

In Peace

I spent many years in France. Reading *Le Monde*, I usually found pretty tough sledding. *Le Figaro* was lighter, more agreeable. It also had the great advantage of a regular column, more accurately, a commentary, by Raymond Aron. The French system—as has been remarked often enough—is different. There one does not become a commentator by starting out in journalism and then working up over time to a regular column, as in America. In France, one becomes someone first. Then people want to know what you think, so you can publish comment. Where the American columnist tends to pontificate, the French commentator prefers analysis, through which opinion seeps.

Raymond Aron had been with de Gaulle during the Second World War (he was only nine when the First War broke out), editing the resistance paper, *La France Libre*. But that did not make him a journalist. He was a philosopher. He was professor of sociology at the Sorbonne, and then professor at the Collège de

France, a distinction indeed (shared by such notables as Lévi-Strauss, founder of structuralism). Aron had been one of the leading participants in the Congress for Cultural Freedom. His books were many, among them *L'Opium des Intellectuels, La Tragédie algerienne, La République impériale*, and a remarkable study of Clausewitz. His *Mémoires* appeared in 1983, the year of his death.

In 1980, "secret wars" and their complications behind me, I was a Special Assistant for International Affairs to the Chairman of the National Endowment for the Humanities. (In keeping with the academic world of which this government agency is a part, my correct title was "Special Assistant for Comparative Cultures.") The chairman, Joseph Duffey, quite without my input, decided to invite Raymond Aron to Washington as a guest of the Endowment. I thought it was a great idea, particularly as I—an admirer, even a fan, of Aron—was charged with issuing the invitation.

There was a possibility that Aron would not accept. In 1967 he had shown his dissatisfaction when it came out that the Congress for Cultural Freedom was funded by the CIA. Once in Paris, I enlisted the help of the American Cultural Attaché, Richard Arndt, who was on good terms with Aron. Arndt arranged the appointment, and we repaired to Aron's office in the Boulevard Raspail.

I said to Aron that I had a proposal to make to him, and that I did not want his answer that day. I said, which was true, that I was leaving Paris the next day, but would return in two weeks, and asked him to give me his answer only then. I then suggested his visit to Washington, and explained to him that the centerpiece of his visit was to be a conference and luncheon with a number of leading American journalists—which was also true. Arndt then rallied in support, pointing out to Aron that differences of opinion among American journalists, particularly between liberal and conservative, were such that they no longer even spoke to each other. We felt, said Arndt, that his prestige was such that he could help to induce less antagonistic relations among them.

Aron appeared impressed by Arndt's point. We left without his decision, but when I returned in two weeks, he accepted Duffey's invitation.

At Duffey's instruction the first event planned for the visit was a dinner in Aron's honor at the Carlton Hotel, where he was residing. It was a dinner of fifteen or sixteen people: Katherine Graham, Zbigniew Brzezinski, Congressman Sidney Yates (who chaired the House Committee that determined the Endowment's budget), and other dignitaries.

But before dinner Duffey and his wife, Anne Wexler, arrived early. When Aron appeared, I introduced him to his host and hostess. They all promptly sat in a friendly little circle. After the usual pleasantries Aron, affable and stimulated, opened the conversation. He understood, he said, that relations among American journalists were now so stressed that those of opposing schools of thought were not even on speaking terms.

Duffey shook his head. "No," he said. "No, I wouldn't say that."

The dinner went off very well except that the wine steward was reeling drunk. Numerous events followed. The centerpiece, the conference and luncheon with journalists, was a success. Those present ran a gamut: Anthony Lewis, George Will (who insisted that his friend Alexander Haig, who was getting a haircut down the hall from the conference, be invited to drop by, which he was and did), James Chace, Charlayne Hunter-Gault, Suzanne Garment, and more. (James Reston, who accepted my call only on my third try, stated that he would not attend as he would be "travelling with the President.")

Word of Aron's visit circulated and I received a call from the political adviser to the Commander-in-Chief, NATO Atlantic, in Norfolk, Virginia. There was to be a NATO conference at Annapolis. Would Professor Aron join them? NATO would pick him up in Washington and would bring him to Dulles Airport in time for his return flight to Paris. Aron accepted cheerfully.

On the day of his departure I went to Dulles Airport to meet him, to bid him farewell, and to put him on his plane for Paris. In due course Aron arrived, escorted by two U.S. Navy officers, who had flown him in from Annapolis. Aron, encumbered by papers and small packages, appeared a bit tired. I was solicitous. The visit had gone off well, I thought, and I had had the privilege of several days with someone I admired.

The Navy officers departed. Aron, silent, and I sat for a few moments before his flight was called. He looked at me and finally spoke. "What is the real reason," he asked, "that I was invited here?"

It was a knife to the heart.

In *academe*

In the autumn of 1996, the fortieth anniversary of the Hungarian Revolution, a number of Hungarian, American, and Canadian scholarly institutions convened a conference in Budapest. The subject was "Hungary and the World, 1956, the New Archival Evidence." I was invited to attend, to submit a paper, and to participate in a panel on the Free Europe Committee. I had assisted in the founding of the committee in 1949, and had been director of the committee's political operations in Western Europe at the time of the Revolution.

The figure that loomed over Hungary during the Revolution was the Communist Prime Minister, Imre Nagy, seized afterward by the Soviets and executed. One of the features of the collapse of Soviet domination of Hungary was the disinterment and reburial of Nagy, with full honors, in Budapest.

In the years 1946 and 1947, described in Part 2 of this book, I had met Imre Nagy, but I did not know him. He was certainly more personable than Gerö, or Rakosi, whom I knew slightly more. But as Nagy's star began to rise after 1953, Aladár Szegedy-Maszák, who had been the Hungarian Minister to the United States, and was by then working at the Voice of America, explained to me Imre Nagy's appeal to the Hungarian people (leaving aside his policies). "Imre Nagy," said Aladár, referring to Nagy's looks and manner, "is every Hungarian's grandfather." He was widely addressed as "Imre Bacsi," meaning "Uncle Imre," but Aladár insisted he looked like the classic grandfather, not uncle.

This characterization was particularly interesting in view of Nagy Imre's paternity. The story is standard late nineteenth century, "*K und K*." (Some may recall the assertion of some Hungarian historians, more whispered than advertised, that the father of Thomas Masaryk, founder of Czechoslovakia, was indeed a coachman, but a Magyar coachman working on the Slovak [Hungarian] side of the border next to the estate on the Moravian [Austrian] side, where Masaryk's mother worked.)

Let us go back to 1944. In October of that year a Hungarian delegation went, ostensibly on a hunting trip, to Eastern Slovakia, where Russian officers met them and conducted them to Moscow. The rest of the plot, as we know all too sadly, failed when the planned Hungarian troop movement to Budapest was obstructed, and the Germans and Szalasi took over. Nevertheless, the Hungarian Armistice was signed in Moscow. One of the signers, a member of the "hunting trip," was Geza Teleki,[21] only son of the prime minister, Pal Teleki, who had committed suicide in protest of the German passage through Hungary to invade Yugoslavia in 1941.[22]

The Armistice Delegation returned to Hungary—to Debrecen—on the same train with a number of the returning Hungarian Communists who had taken refuge in the Soviet Union (and survived, as not all of them did; Bela Kun, who headed the 1919 Communist regime in Hungary, had been executed on Stalin's orders). The trip was long, and Geza Teleki shared a compartment day after day with Imre Nagy. They were on good terms. One day, the moment being appropriate, Teleki asked Nagy, "Do you know who your father was?" Geza, who *did* know, said that Nagy looked at him for some time, without resentment, and without speaking, and then simply nodded.

According to Geza Teleki, it was the classic story: small-town girl of very modest circumstances becomes pregnant. The putative father is a scion of a distinguished family. A transaction takes place. The child is born. Both the distinguished family and the child go on, separately, to other things. The child became not only Prime Minister, but a national hero, an avatar of what it is to be Magyar.

The family was the Counts Somssich.

It would be difficult to find a Hungarian family that could trace its ancestry further back into the misty origins of the Hungarian aristocracy. Or to find one more Magyar.

It seemed to me a pertinent and interesting historical point. I therefore planned to cite it in my remarks to the conference. I had, in fact, included the story in the paper I submitted, but had deliberately left out the Somssich name, to be revealed only at the conference itself. This would be *my* contribution to scholarship, to history.

The conference took place in the Hungarian Academy of Sciences, a truly magnificent building. In the Great Hall, where plenary sessions were held, I had some difficulty in keeping my attention on the speakers, so alluring were the caryatids that every couple of yards lined the sides of the two-storied room. Those on the Acropolis or among the Elgin Marbles were, in my estimation, inferior.

The night before the Free Europe Committee panel was to speak, I attended a conference at the Central European University. Among the speakers was Miklos Vasahelyi, Imre Nagy's secretary during the revolution. His account of those days was fascinating. He did not mention Radio Free Europe (RFE). But some other speakers did. (I did not, limiting myself to a brief account of how the United States, by customary fumbling, managed not to have a Minister in Hungary in the autumn of 1956.) The subject of Radio Free Europe stirred the audience, and strong views about Americans were expressed.

The next morning I sought to warn my American colleagues on the Free Europe Committee panel that we were facing a hostile audience. They were not impressed. Figuring myself immune to the hostility, as I had not worked at Radio Free Europe, I shrugged. The moderator was Professor Istvan Deak, of Columbia University. "Fifteen minutes," for each speaker, he stipulated. As each spoke, dwelling on one or the other aspect of Radio Free Europe, the noise in the hall grew.

I was the last speaker. By then, what had been a murmur had grown to loud comments. I said nothing about Radio Free Europe, but kept to details of the period of the revolution that I had picked up at the time. Although I abbreviated my remarks, I had tried to include too much. As the end of my fifteen minutes approached, I hastily shifted to the story of Imre Nagy's paternity. The noise in the hall approached an uproar. As I reached the climax of my story, Deak gavelled me down. "Time's up," he ordered.

I retired from the lectern. All over the hall members of the audience were on their feet, arms raised, shouting for attention to their questions and comments about Radio Free Europe.

At the end, we filed down the majestic staircase and out onto the esplanade on the banks of the Danube. I saw a friend who had been in the hall, fairly near the lectern, during my talk. "Tell me," I asked him. "The name Somssich. Mean anything to you?"

"No," he said. "I heard something about Somssich back up there, but the noise was so great I have no idea what it was about."

—CHRISTOPHER FELIX
(JAMES McCARGAR)
Washington, D.C.

July 2001

1. In an article about Wallenberg that appeared in *The Washington Post* on January 7, 2001, Arne Ruth, former editor-in-chief of the Swedish daily, *Dagens Nyheter*, stated, "Sweden never vigorously pursued [Wallenberg's] release from Soviet custody in the early period after his arrest."

2. This statement was correct when it was written. I did not learn of the existence of the War Refugee Board until late 1995 or early 1996. The material that I received at that time, of course, also confirmed the existence at Stockholm, representing the OSS and the War Refugee Board, of Iver Olsen.

3. See Note 2.

4. I have not seen published versions of Sinitsyn's memoirs. These quotations are of passages having to do with Wallenberg excerpted from those memoirs, and privately provided to me in 1995, after my correspondence with Dr. Kloos-Fishman. They have gone through at least three, and if you include my efforts to put them into readable English, probably four translations. To quote them is not to give them full faith and credit.

5. A cant phrase referring to the emblem of the *NKVD* (created in succession to the *OGPU* in 1934), which depicted a serpent struck down by a sword, thereby implying both the legitimacy and the nobility of the secret police function.

6. Yakovlev retains some prestige as the close associate of Mikhail Gorbachev noted for his support of *glasnost*. He was present at the November 1985 meeting in Reykjavik, Iceland between President Ronald Reagan and Gorbachev. While the two leaders met in a room on the ground floor of a schoolhouse, their entourages were in a room above. Arthur Hartman, the American Ambassador to Moscow, approached

Yakovlev as the author of a book about Soviet-American relations that made no mention, for example, of Soviet missiles in Cuba or other well-known aggressive Soviet moves during those years. Hartman pointed out to Yakovlev a succession of such omissions in his book. Yakovlev listened carefully, and finally commented, "But you have read the book!" Hartman answered that he had. Yakovlev said, "Maybe I should, too."

7. Julian Amery's account of his wartime service in Albania, *Sons of the Eagle*, published shortly after the war, became our Bible on Albania and Albanian ways.

8. Both these men were *sui generis*, but over the years Low often reminded me of Hemingway, and Burke of John Huston—the latter including the retreat to Ireland. Among his talents Low included a lively sense of humor. When Low was in retirement, Greek shipping magnate Stavros Niarchos, with whom he was once associated, took Low on a cruise on his yacht. Among the guests was a very attractive young Austrian woman, whose preference seemed to be for Low, rather than for Niarchos. The two men talking later on deck, Niarchos, miffed, asked Low why he thought the young Austrian preferred Low to him. Low, who lived comfortably but modestly, answered, "It must be my money, Stavros." Burke's memoirs, *Outrageous Good Fortune* (Boston: Little, Brown, 1984), tell of his OSS wartime exploits, though nothing significant about the Albanian operation, and in absorbing detail of his later associations with the Ringling Bros. Barnum & Bailey Circus, the New York Yankeees, and Madison Square Garden—and of his impulse to retirement in Ireland.

9. Zog was more cosmopolitan than press accounts depicted him in the 1920s and 1930s. He—like Tito and so many others—had served in the Austro-Hungarian Army. In Vienna he had absorbed the local reputation for the beauty and charm of Hungarian countesses. As king he therefore summoned a number of young Hungarian aristocratic ladies to Tirana that he might choose his queen. One candidate remarked in confidence that, once wed, she would take over the country. She was overheard and dismissed. Zog's final choice was Countess Geraldine Apponyi, granddaughter of a prominent Hungarian statesman. Her mother was American.

10. Kupi, with his hawk-like countenance, was a true mountain chieftain. In 1956 I was charged with reorganizing the Albanian Committee. I did not sit in the Borghese Gardens, as Low had done, but the various elders came to an apartment that I had rented for the purpose. Kupi arrived on a hot, stifling day. I invited him to take off his jacket. With some embarrassment he did so, revealing that he was armed with a silver-handled Colt revolver. "Given to me by Colonel Low," he explained. Indeed, seven years before I had broken various laws to buy the silver-handled Colt, and to ship it hastily under diplomatic cover to Rome.

11. The best guide through the mass of Philby material is the critical bibliography by Hayden Peake contained in *The Private Life of Kim Philby, The Moscow Years*, by Rufina Philby, Mikhail Lyubimov, and Hayden Peake, Fromm International, New York, 2000, 295–429. The book also contains four "autobiographical reminiscences" written by Philby in Moscow over the years, and annotated by Peake, as well as a detailed and useful chronology of Philby's life, also by Peake.

12. It appears, however, that Philby himself was not so fascinated. The moniker "Kim" was apparently bestowed on him as an infant by his parents, then in India. In later life, in Moscow, Philby wrote: "Many publicists have recently jumped at the coincidence of the two Kims. But I am deliberately tentative about it because, although I heard much of Kipling in my youth, it was not until the war that I actually sat down and read *Kim*."

13. In one of his "autobiographical reminiscences" (see Note 11) Philby gives an odd explanation of the origin of his stammer (odd, considering that it stayed with him his whole life): "The one important event of the passage [by ship with his mother from India to England, when Philby was about four] was an acquaintance I struck up with a boy named Guy Sells, who was a full year older than myself. He was the grandest thing I had ever seen, and the grandest thing about him was his stammer. By the end of the voyage I had caught it, good and proper. It has since cost me some embarrassment and fatigue, but it may also have served me well. It is easier to talk out of turn without a stammer, than with one."

14. It was not until after Philby's flight to Moscow that I learned of his first wife, Litzi Friedman, whom he had met in Vienna in 1933.

15. Although his charm was denied by some. In a 1994 panel discussion of Philby at Georgetown University, I referred to Philby's "charm." The next speaker was Robert Lamphere, who had been the FBI's chief liaison with Philby 1949–1951. His first remarks were a vehement denial of any Philby "charm." In his memoirs Lamphere wrote, "I'd never liked Philby."

16. Robertson was a friend of Philby's father, St. John Philby. According to Hayden Peake's chronology (see Note 11) it was Robertson who introduced Philby to Guy Burgess at Cambridge in 1932.

17. Hayden Peake, in his Philby chronology (see Note 11) uses different wording, saying that Robertson in summer 1933 "says he can't recommend Philby, 'unfit . . . too far left.'"

18. The correspondent was Cyrus Sulzberger, and the paper *The New York Times*. Sulzberger wrote the story from Greece.

19. Oleg Kalugin, *The First Directorate*, St. Martin's Press, New York, 1994, 121–47. Kalugin broke with the KGB in the summer of 1990, and ran for a seat in the Congress of People's Deputies from the Krasnodar region. He won the election. He was in the Moscow White

House during the tense days of the attempted coup of August 1991. He now lives in the United States.

20. According to Hayden Peake's chronology (see Note 11) when Nicholas Elliott confronted Philby in Beirut with his service to the Soviets, Philby wrote a four-page confession—saying he stopped serving the Soviets in 1949—and gave it to Elliott, in response to Elliott's offer of immunity. Philby did not tell his KGB contact in Beirut of his confession, but spoke of more interrogations to come, with the result that the Soviets decided to bring Philby to the Soviet Union.

21. When packing for the "hunting trip," Geza carefully included his striped trousers and cutaway, the diplomatic uniform of the day. When the Hungarian delegation presented itself at the Kremlin, Teleki was in his diplomatic attire. The other members of the delegation, observing that they were in the capital of the "workers' state," showed up in jackets and open shirts. After the signing of the armistice, Molotov took Teleki aside and told him, "You have honored us in your way, and we are grateful. We shall not forget." Not only did Geza Teleki become Minister of Education in the Provisional Government, but when the time came for him and his family to leave Hungary, the Russians posed no obstacles (though we had to resort to some extracurricular means to get his very valuable library out of the country).

22. I was appalled when visiting Hungary in 1991, my first return since leaving in December 1947, at the remark of a guide who took us to see the Holy Right Hand of St. Stephen. As we left the chapel, the guide took me by the arm and led me to a pew marked "Grof Teleki Pal," with a date. "Here," said the guide, "is where the Prime Minister spent the last day of his life." I was moved, and murmured, "Before committing suicide." "Oh, no!" the guide said. "The Germans killed him." When I told some members of the family, they merely shrugged, and said they knew the Communists had spread this story to deny the Prime Minister the nobility of his act—and to keep people aroused against the Germans. The story has a sad ending. As Geza Teleki, living in Washington, D.C., aged, both he and his wife fell ill. In the end, both were bedridden. Geza first shot his wife, then killed himself—with the same pistol that his father had used to end his life.